# VOCABULARY

## for the High School Student

### FOURTH EDITION

# Vocabulary books by the authors

A Scholarship Vocabulary Program, Books I–III

Vocabulary and Composition Through Pleasurable Reading, Books I–V

Vocabulary for Enjoyment, Books I–III

Vocabulary for the High School Student, Books A, B

Vocabulary for the High School Student

Vocabulary for the College-Bound Student

The Joy of Vocabulary

# VOCABULARY
## *for the High School Student*

FOURTH EDITION

**HAROLD LEVINE**

*Chairman Emeritus of English,*
*Benjamin Cardozo High School, New York*

**NORMAN LEVINE**

*Associate Professor of English,*
*City College of the City University of New York*

**ROBERT T. LEVINE**

*Professor of English,*
*North Carolina A & T State University*

AMSCO

**Amsco School Publications, Inc.**
315 Hudson Street, New York, N.Y. 10013

Text and Cover Design: One Dot Inc.
Composition: Brad Walrod/High Text Graphics, Inc.


Please visit our Web site at: *www.amscopub.com*


When ordering this book, please specify:
*Either* **R 788 P** *or*
VOCABULARY FOR THE HIGH SCHOOL STUDENT

ISBN: 1-56765-127-5
NYC Item 56765-127-4
Copyright © 2005 by Amsco School Publications, Inc.

Printed in the United States of America

1 2 3 4 5 6 7 8 9 10     11 10 09 08 07 06 05

# Preface

The principal aim of this updated and enlarged edition is to help high school students build a superior vocabulary and learn the skills of critical thinking, close reading, and concise writing. The exercises in this edition have been written expressly to teach these and other desirable skills at the same time as vocabulary.

Like its predecessors, this edition involves students in a variety of vocabulary-enriching activities in chapter after chapter.

**Learning New Words From the Context** (Chapter 1) presents one hundred sixty short passages in which unfamiliar words can be defined with the help of clues in the context. By teaching students how to interpret such clues, this chapter provides them with an indispensable tool for vocabulary growth and, at the same time, *makes them better readers.*

**Enlarging Vocabulary Through Central Ideas** (Chapter 2) teaches twenty groups of related words. In the EATING group, students learn *condiment, glutton, palatable, succulent, voracious,* and other *eating* words. Each word studied in such a group helps students learn other words in the group.

**Enlarging Vocabulary Through Anglo-Saxon Prefixes** (Chapter 3) teaches words beginning with eight Anglo-Saxon prefixes, like FORE-, meaning "before," "beforehand," or "front." Knowing FORE-, students can more readily understand *forearm, forebear, foreboding, foreshadow, foreword,* etc.

**Enlarging Vocabulary Through Latin Prefixes** (Chapter 4) does the same with twenty-four Latin prefixes. It is easier for students to understand *discontent, discredit, disintegrate, dispassionate,* and *disrepair* when they know that the prefix DIS- means "opposite of."

**Enlarging Vocabulary Through Latin Roots** (Chapter 5) teaches words derived from twenty Latin roots. If students, for example, know that the root HERE- means "stick," they can better understand *adhere* ("stick to"), *cohere* ("stick together"), *incoherent* ("not sticking together"; "disconnected"), etc.

**Enlarging Vocabulary Through Greek Word Elements** (Chapter 6) teaches derivatives from twenty Greek elements, like AUTO-, meaning "self." Among the ten AUTO- words taught in this chapter are *autocrat* (ruler exercising self-derived power), *automation* (technique for making a process self-operating), and *autonomy* (self-government).

**Expanding Vocabulary Through Derivatives** (Chapter 7) teaches students how to convert one newly learned word into several—for example, *literate* into *illiterate, semiliterate, literacy, illiteracy,* etc. The chapter also provides an incidental review of some basic spelling rules.

**Understanding Word Relationships and Word Analogies** (Chapter 8) supplements the numerous explanations and hints given throughout the book on dealing with analogy questions. This chapter is principally for students who are unfamiliar with analogy questions, or are having difficulty with them.

**Dictionary of Words Taught in This Text** is intended as a tool of reference and review.

Whenever something is learned, it is likely soon to be forgotten unless it is used. Therefore, students must be encouraged to use—in their writing and class discussions—the words and skills they are learning in this book. If a wordy paragraph can be made more concise or if undesirable repetition can be avoided by use of a synonym—they should be expected to do so because they have been using these very same skills hundreds of times in the exercises of this book. When a strange word can be understood from a knowledge of its root or prefix—or from clues in the context—they should be challenged to define it and to verify their definition in the dictionary. Above all, they should be encouraged to own a good dictionary and to develop the dictionary habit.

—The Authors

# Contents

## *Chapter 2* Enlarging Vocabulary Through Central Ideas   79

# Chapter 6 Enlarging Vocabulary Through Greek Word Elements   276

*Chapter*

# Learning New Words From the Context

## What is the context?

The context is the part of a passage in which a particular word is used and which helps to explain that word. Suppose you were asked for the meaning of *bear*. Could you give a definite answer? Obviously not, for *bear*, as presented to you, has no context.

But if you were asked to define *bear* in the phrase "polar bear," you would immediately know it refers to an animal. Or, if someone were to say, "Please stop that whistling—I can't bear it," you would know that in this context *bear* means "endure" or "stand."

## Why is the context important?

An important point for those of us who want to enlarge our vocabularies is this: the context can give us the meaning not only of familiar words like *bear*, but also of unfamiliar words.

Suppose, for example, you were asked for the meaning of *valiant*. You might not know it, unless, of course, you already had a fine vocabulary. But if you were to meet *valiant* in the following context, you would have a very good chance of discovering its meaning:

> "Cowards die many times before their deaths; The valiant never taste of death but once."
>
> —WILLIAM SHAKESPEARE

From the above context, you can tell that the author is contrasting two ideas—"cowards" and "the valiant." Therefore, "the valiant" means the opposite of "cowards," namely "brave people." *Valiant* means "brave."

## *In what ways will this chapter benefit you?*

This chapter will show you how to get the meaning of unfamiliar words from the context. Once you learn this skill, it will serve you for the rest of your life in two important ways: (1) it will keep enlarging your vocabulary, and (2) it will keep making you a better and better reader.

*Part*

**1**

# Contexts With Contrasting Words

## *Pretest 1*

Each passage below contains a word in italics. If you read the passage carefully, you will find a clue to the meaning of this word in an opposite word (antonym) or a contrasting idea.

For each passage, write on your paper (a) the clue that led you to the meaning and (b) the meaning itself. The answers to the first two passages have been inserted as examples.

1. It is the responsibility of every driver to be entirely *sober* at all times. Drunk drivers pose a danger to themselves, to their passengers, and to everyone else on the road.

    *a.* CLUE:      ***sober* is the opposite of "drunk"**

    *a.* MEANING: ***sober* means "not drunk"**

2. One sandwich for lunch usually *suffices* for you, but for me it is not enough.

   *a.* CLUE:    *suffices* **is in contrast with "is not enough"**

   *b.* MEANING  *suffices* **means "is enough"**

3. Plastic dishes last a long time because they are unbreakable. Ordinary china is very *fragile.*

4. Our tennis coach will neither *confirm* nor deny the rumor that she is going to be the basketball coach next year.

5. Don't *digress.* Stick to the topic.

6. Your account of the fight *concurs* with Joanne's but differs from the accounts given by the other witnesses.

7. "I greatly fear your presence would rather increase than *mitigate* his unhappy fortunes."
   —JAMES FENIMORE COOPER

8. Roses in bloom are a common sight in summer, but a *rarity* in late November.

9. The tables in the restaurant were all occupied, and we waited more than ten minutes for one to become *vacant.*

10. There are few theaters here, but on Broadway there are theaters *galore.*

11. "I do not *shrink* from this responsibility; I welcome it."
    —JOHN FITZGERALD KENNEDY

12. Ruth is an experienced driver, but Harry is a *novice*; he began taking lessons just last month.

13. A bank teller can usually tell the difference between genuine $100 bills and *counterfeit* ones.

14. When I ask Theresa to help me with a *complicated* assignment, she makes it seem so easy.

15. On the wall of my room I have a copy of Rembrandt's "The Night Watch"; the *original* is in the Rijks Museum in Amsterdam.

16. "Friends, Romans, countrymen, lend me your ears;/I come to bury Caesar, not to praise him./The evil that men do lives after them;/The good is oft *interred* with their bones;/So let it be with Caesar."—WILLIAM SHAKESPEARE

17. In some offices, work comes to a halt at noon and does not *resume* until 1 P.M.

18. When we got to the beach, my sister and I were *impatient* to get into the water, but Dad was not in a hurry.

19. Off duty, a police officer may wear the same clothes as a *civilian.*

20. The candidate spoke for less than 20 minutes. At first, the audience appeared friendly and supportive, nodding and occasionally applauding. Before long, however, listeners turned *hostile,* voicing their disapproval with shouts and boos.

## *Study Your Lesson Words,* **Group 1**

| WORD | MEANING AND TYPICAL USE |
|---|---|
| **civilian** (*n.*)<br>sə-'vil-yən | person who is not a member of the military, or police, or firefighting forces<br>    Eight of the passengers were soldiers and one was a marine; the rest were *civilians.* |
| **complicated** (*adj.*)<br>'käm-plə-,kā-təd | hard to understand; elaborate; complex; intricate<br>    If some of the requirements for graduation seem *complicated,* ask your guidance counselor to explain them to you. |
| **concur** (*v.*)<br>kən-'kər | agree; coincide; be of the same opinion<br>    The rules of the game require you to accept the umpire's decision, even if you do not *concur* with it. |
| **confirm** (*v.*)<br>kən-'fərm | state or prove the truth of; substantiate; verify<br>    My physician thought I had broken my wrist, and an X-ray later *confirmed* his opinion. |
| **confirmation** (*n.*) | proof; evidence; verification |
| **digress** (*v.*)<br>dī-'gres | turn aside; get off the main topic; deviate<br>    At one point, the speaker *digressed* to tell of an incident in her childhood, but then she got right back to the topic. |

**fragile** (*adj.*) √
'fra-jəl

easily broken; breakable; weak; frail
    The handle is *fragile*; it will easily break if you use too much pressure.

**galore** (*adj.*)
gə-'lȯr

aplenty; in abundance; plentiful; abundant
(galore always follows the word it modifies)
    There were no cabs on the side streets, but on the main street there were cabs *galore.*

**genuine** (*adj.*)
'jen-yə-wən

actually being what it is claimed or seems to be; true; real; authentic
    The oil painting looked *genuine,* but it proved to be a copy of the original.

**hostile** (*adj.*)
'häs-təl

of or relating to an enemy or enemies; unfriendly; inimical
    In the heat of battle, allies are sometimes mistaken for *hostile* forces.

**impatient** (*adj.*)
im-'pā-shənt

not patient; not willing to bear delay; fretful; anxious
    Five minutes can seem like five hours when you are *impatient.*

**inter** (*v.*)
in-'tər

put into the earth; bury; entomb
    Many American heroes are *interred* in Arlington National Cemetery.

**interment** (*n.*)

burial; entombment; sepulture

**mitigate** (*v.*)
'mi-tə-,gāt

make less severe; lessen; alleviate; soften; relieve
    With the help of novocaine, your dentist can greatly *mitigate* the pain of drilling.

**novice** (*n.*)
'nä-vəs

one who is new to a field or activity; beginner; apprentice; neophyte; tyro
    There are two slopes: one for experienced skiers and one for *novices.*

**original** (*n.*)
ə-'rij-ə-n°l

work created firsthand from which copies are made; prototype; archetype
    This is a copy of THANKSGIVING TURKEY by Grandma Moses. The *original* is in the Metropolitan Museum of Art.

**original** (*adj.*)

1. belonging to the beginning; first; earliest; initial; primary
    Miles Standish was one of the *original* colonists of Massachusetts; he came over on the "Mayflower."

2. inventive; creative

**originality** (*n.*)

freshness; novelty; inventiveness

**rarity** (*n.*)
'rar-ə-tē

something uncommon, infrequent, or rare
    Rain in the Sahara Desert is a *rarity.*

**resume** (*v.*)
ri-'züm

1. begin again
    School closes for the Christmas recess on December 24 and *resumes* on January 3.

2. retake; reoccupy
    Please *resume* your seats.

**shrink** (*v.*)
'shriŋk

1. draw back; recoil; wince
    Wendy *shrank* from the task of telling her parents about the car accident, but she finally got the courage and told them.

2. become smaller; contract
    Some garments *shrink* in washing.

**sober** (*adj.*)
'sō-bər

1. not drunk; not intoxicated
    Someone who has been drinking should not drive, even if he or she feels *sober.*

2. earnest; serious; free from excitement or exaggeration
    When he learned of his failure, George thought of quitting school. But after *sober* consideration, he realized that would be unwise.

**suffice** (*v.*)
sə-'fīs

be enough, adequate, or sufficient; serve; do
    I had thought that $60 would *suffice* for my school supplies. As it turned out, it was not enough.

**vacant** (*adj.*)
'vā-kənt

empty; unoccupied; tenantless; not being used
    I had to stand for the first half of the performance because I could not find a *vacant* seat.

**vacancy** (*n.*)

unfilled position; unoccupied apartment or room

## *Apply What You Have Learned*

 ### EXERCISE 1.1: SENTENCE COMPLETION

Write the required lesson word on your answer paper. *Resume* is the answer to question 1.

1. The showers have just stopped, but they may soon __?__.
2. Their directions were __?__; yours were easy to follow.
3. Why are you __?__ to me? Aren't we friends?
4. We hope to move in as soon as there is a(n) __?__ apartment.
5. Experts can tell the difference between a copy and the __?__.
6. How many more chairs do you need? Will five __?__?
7. Paul doesn't play tennis as well as Amy; he is a(n) __?__.
8. If you __?__, you will waste our time. Stick to the topic.
9. There is only one __?__ on the committee; the other members are all army officers.
10. It may be unpleasant, but we must not __?__ from doing our duty.
11. Jobs, then, were not plentiful; now, there are openings __?__.
12. Is there a way to __?__ the pain? It is very severe.
13. What evidence do you have to __?__ your claim?
14. These cups are __?__; handle them with care.
15. Cemetery workers were instructed to __?__ the deceased immediately after the service.

 ### EXERCISE 1.2: SYNONYMS

Eliminate repetition by replacing the boldfaced word or words with a **synonym** from your lesson words. The answers to the first two items are *original* and *sober*.

1. Who lived here first? Were you the **first** tenant?
2. He is not **drunk**; don't accuse him of drunkenness.
3. I wanted to wait a day, but they were **unwilling to wait**.
4. She has just begun to learn to swim, Are you a **beginner**, too?

5. Stick to the topic. Don't **get off the topic**.

6. A dozen is more than enough. Even six would **be enough**.

7. I tried to be friendly, though they seemed **unfriendly**.

8. You lack proof. There is no witness to **prove** your story.

9. All rooms are occupied; not a single one is **unoccupied**.

10. This is really a great buy. It's a **real** bargain.

 **EXERCISE 1.3:** ANTONYMS

On your answer paper, enter the lesson word most nearly the **opposite** of the boldfaced word or words. The first answer is *original*.

1. This **copy** is so good that it looks like the __?__.

2. Trees were once a **common sight** here; now they are a(n) __?__.

3. The carpenter is a **veteran**, but his helper is a(n) __?__.

4. Her __?__ attitude shows she is not **sympathetic** to our cause.

5. Is the auditorium **being used**, or is it __?__.

6. Our opinions now __?__; we no longer **disagree**.

7. I can neither __?__ your statement nor **deny** it.

8. Say nothing to **intensify** his fears; try to __?__ them.

9. Out of uniform, a **soldier** looks like an ordinary __?__.

10. When we are **excited**, we are not capable of __?__ judgment.

 **EXERCISE 1.4:** CONCISE WRITING

On your answer paper, express the thought of each sentence in **no more than four words**, as in 1, below.

1. The people living next door to us were unwilling to put up with delay.

   *Our neighbors were impatient.*

2. People who are new to a field or activity need a great deal of help.

3. Rita misplaced the document from which the copies were made.

4. Which is the apartment that no one is living in at the present time?

5. Jones is not a member of the military, or police, or firefighting forces.

**EXERCISE 1.5:** SYNONYM SUMMARY

Each line, when completed, should have three words similar in meaning. The parentheses indicate the number of missing letters. On your answer paper, write the *complete* words. Answers to the first line are **empty, tenantless,** and **vacant.**

1. em (1) ty           ten (1) ntless          v (1) cant

2. abund (1) nt        pl (2) t (1) ful         g (1) l (1) re

3. compl (1) x          intr (1) cate            com (2) ic (2) ed

4. pr (2) f            ev (1) dence              veri (2) at (1) on

5. b (1) ry            ent (2) b                 (3) er

6. neoph (1) te        t (1) ro                  no (2) ce

7. nov (1) lty         inv (1) ntiveness         o (2) gin (2) ity

8. ser (1) ous         (2) rnest                 sob (2)

9. an (1) ious         fr (1) tful               im (2) t (2) nt

10. br (2) kable        fr (2) l                  frag (2) e

11. unfr (2) ndly       inim (1) cal              hos (2) le

12. all (1) viate       rel (2) ve                mit (1) iate

13. ver (1) fy          substant (2) te           con (2) rm

14. r (2) l             (2) thentic               gen (2) ne

15. rec (2) l           w (1) nce                 sh (2) nk

16. proto (2) pe        arch (1) type             (1) riginal

17. agr (2)             coin (1) ide              con (2) r

18. anim (1) sity       u (1) fr (3) dliness      hosti (2) ty

19. entom (1) ment      sep (1) lture             int (2) ment

20. s (1) rve           d (1)                     su (2) ice

**EXERCISE 1.6:** ANALOGIES

Which lettered pair of words—*a, b, c, d,* or *e*—most nearly expresses the same relationship as the capitalized pair? Write the letter of your answer on separate paper. The first three analogy questions have been explained to guide you, and their answers are (b), (a), and (e).

1. CONFIRM : DENY

   *a.* concur : agree        *b.* succeed : fail

   *c.* greet : welcome       *d.* disinter : unearth

   *e.* recoil : shrink

   *Explanation:* To **confirm** is the opposite of to **deny**. To **succeed** is the opposite of to **fail**.

2. NEOPHYTE : EXPERIENCE

   *a.* fool : judgment       *b.* pedestrian : foot

   *c.* superstar : recognition   *d.* motorist : license

   *e.* expert : skill

   *Explanation:* A **neophyte** lacks **experience**. A **fool** lacks **judgment**.

3. COMPLEX : UNDERSTAND

   *a.* painless : endure     *b.* tasty : consume

   *c.* inexpensive : afford  *d.* available : obtain

   *e.* vivid : forget

   *Explanation:* Something that is **complex** is hard to **understand**. Something that is **vivid** is hard to **forget**.

4. SOBER : INTOXICATED

   *a.* weak : frail          *b.* fretful : restless

   *c.* rude : impolite       *d.* inimical : friendly

   *e.* weird : strange

5. IMPATIENT : WAIT

   *a.* gossipy : talk        *b.* undecided : do

   *c.* stubborn : compromise *d.* industrious : work

   *e.* obliging : assist

6. INTENSIFY : MITIGATE

    *a.* prohibit : permit               *b.* deviate : digress

    *c.* verify : substantiate         *d.* deny : contradict

    *e.* relieve : alleviate

7. FRAGILE : BREAK

    *a.* inflexible : bend            *b.* rubbery : chew

    *c.* rare : find                 *d.* uncomplicated : grasp

    *e.* cumbersome : carry

8. CREATIVE : ORIGINALITY

    *a.* hostile : rancor              *b.* selfish : generosity

    *c.* sympathetic : ill will       *d.* unappreciative : gratitude

    *e.* frail : stamina

9. INTRICATE : SIMPLE

    *a.* vacant : unoccupied       *b.* abundant : scarce

    *c.* authentic : genuine       *d.* pleasant : agreeable

    *e.* uncommon : rare

10. CIVILIAN : COMBAT

    *a.* runner : marathon       *b.* accomplice : guilt

    *c.* passenger : navigation    *d.* singer : chorus

    *e.* guest : celebration

 **EXERCISE 1.7:** COMPOSITION

Answer in a sentence or two.

1. Why should a person handling fragile objects always be sober?

2. When might you resume a friendship with someone who had been hostile to you?

3. How might the police confirm that someone had indeed been interred?

4. In what situation might you become impatient when someone begins to digress?

5. Would a novice mechanic suffice to work on a very complicated engine? Explain.

## *Pretest 2*

For each passage, write on your paper (a) the clue to the meaning of the italicized word and (b) the meaning itself.

21. "Then such a scramble as there is to get aboard, and to get ashore, and to take in freight and to *discharge* freight!"—MARK TWAIN

22. The owner is selling his gas station because the profit is too small. He hopes to go into a more *lucrative* business.

23. I tried reading Lou's notes but I found them *illegible*. However, yours were easy to read.

24. Debbie, who has come late to every meeting, surprised us today by being *punctual*.

25. As I hurried to the board, I *inadvertently* stepped on Alan's foot, but he thinks I did it on purpose.

26, 27. "When I was a boy, there was but one *permanent* ambition among my comrades in our village on the west bank of the Mississippi River. That was, to be a steamboatman. We had *transient* ambitions of other sorts.... When a circus came and went, it left us all burning to become clowns.... Now and then we had a hope that, if we lived and were good, God would permit us to be pirates. These ambitions faded out, each in its turn; but the ambition to be a steamboatman always remained."—MARK TWAIN

28. When you chair a discussion, it is unfair to call only on your friends. To be *equitable*, you should call on all who wish to speak, without favoritism.

29. The only *extemporaneous* talk was Jerry's; all the other candidates gave memorized speeches.

30. "What's up" may be a suitable greeting for a friendly note, but it is completely *inappropriate* for a business letter.

31. If you agree, write "yes"; if you *dissent*, write "no."

32.     "Mr. Hurst looked at her [Miss Bennet] with astonishment.
    "'Do you prefer reading to cards?' said he; 'that is rather singular [strange].'
    "'Miss Eliza Bennet,' said Miss Bingley, 'despises cards. She is a great reader, and has no pleasure in anything else.'
    "'I deserve neither such praise nor such *censure*,' cried Elizabeth; 'I am not a great reader, and I have pleasure in many things.'"
—JANE AUSTEN

33. A child trying to squeeze through the iron fence became stuck between two bars, but luckily she was able to *extricate* herself.

34. When you let me take your bishop, I thought it was unwise of you; later I saw you had made a very *astute* move.

35. At first I was blamed for damaging Dad's computer, but when my sister said she was responsible, I was *exonerated*.

36. "If you once *forfeit* the confidence of your fellow citizens, you can never regain their respect and esteem."—ABRAHAM LINCOLN

37. Parking on our side of the street is *prohibited* on weekdays between 4 P.M. and 7 P.M. but permitted at all other times.

38. The caretaker expected to be praised for his efforts to put out the fire. Instead, he was *rebuked* for his delay in notifying the fire department.

39. If we can begin the meeting on time, we should be able to complete our business and *adjourn* by 4:30 P.M.

40. Before the new hotel can be constructed, the two old buildings now on the site will have to be *demolished*.

## *Study Your Lesson Words,* **Group 2**

| WORD | MEANING AND TYPICAL USE |
|---|---|
| **adjourn** (*v.*)<br>ə-'jərn | close a meeting; suspend the business of a meeting; disband; recess<br>When we visited Washington, D.C., Congress was not in session; it had *adjourned* for the Thanksgiving weekend. |
| **astute** (*adj.*)<br>ə-'stüt | 1. shrewd; wise, perspicacious; sagacious<br>Marie was the only one to solve the riddle; she is a very *astute* thinker.<br><br>2. crafty; cunning; sly; wily<br>An *astute* Greek tricked the Trojans into opening the gates of Troy. |
| **censure** (*n.*)<br>'sen(t)-shər | act of blaming; expression of disapproval; hostile criticism; rebuke; reprimand<br>Ali was about to reach for a third slice of cake but was stopped by a look of *censure* in Mother's eyes. |

**demolish** (*v.*)
di-'mä-lish

tear down; destroy; raze; smash; wreck
It took several days for the wrecking crew to *demolish* the old building.

**demolition** (*n.*)

destruction

**discharge** (*v.*)
dis-'chärj

1. unload
After *discharging* its cargo, the ship will go into dry dock for repairs.

2. dismiss; fire
One employee was *discharged.*

**dissent** (*v.*)
di-'sent

differ in opinion; disagree; object
There was nearly complete agreement on Al's proposal. Enid and Alice were the only ones who *dissented.*

**dissension** (*n.*)

discord; conflict; strife

**equitable** (*adj.*)
'e-kwə-tə-bəl

fair to all concerned; just; impartial; objective; unbiased,
The only *equitable* way for the three to share the $600 profit is for each to receive $200.

**inequitable** (*n.*)

unfair; unjust

**exonerate** (*v.*)
ig-'zä-nə-rāt

free from blame; clear from accusation; acquit; absolve
The other driver *exonerated* Isabel of any responsibility for the accident.

**extemporaneous** (*adj.*)
,ek-,stem-pə-'rā-nē-əs

composed or spoken without preparation; offhand; impromptu; improvised
It was obvious that the speaker's talk was memorized, though she tried to make it seem *extemporaneous.*

**extricate** (*v.*)
'ek-strə-,kāt

free from difficulties; disentangle; disencumber; release
If you let your assignments pile up, you may get into a situation from which you will not be able to *extricate* yourself.

**forfeit** (*v.*)
'fȯr-fət

lose or have to give up as a penalty for some error, neglect, or fault; sacrifice
> One customer gave a $150 deposit on an order of slipcovers. When they were delivered, she decided she didn't want them. Of course, she *forfeited* her deposit.

**illegible** (*adj.*)
i-'lej-ə-bəl

not able to be read; very hard to read; not legible; undecipherable
> It is fortunate that Miguel uses a computer to do his reports because his handwriting is *illegible*.

**legible** (*adj.*)

easy to read; readable

**inadvertently** (*adv.*)
,i-nəd-'vər-t°nt-lē

not done on purpose; unintentionally; thoughtlessly; accidentally; carelessly
> I finally found my glasses on the windowsill. I must have left them there *inadvertently*.

**inappropriate** (*adj.*)
,i-nə-'prō-prē-ət

not fitting; unsuitable; unbecoming; not appropriate; improper
> Since I was the one who nominated Bruce, it would be *inappropriate* for me to vote for another candidate.

**appropriate** (*adj.*)

fitting; proper

**lucrative** (*adj.*)
'lü-krə-tiv

moneymaking; profitable; advantageous; remunerative
> This year's school dance was not so *lucrative*; we made only $150 compared to $375 last year.

**permanent** (*adj.*)
'pər-mə-nənt

lasting; enduring; intended to last; stable
> Write to me at my temporary address, the Gateway Hotel. As soon as I find an apartment, I shall notify you of my *permanent* address.

**prohibit** (*v.*)
prō-'hi-bət

forbid; ban; enjoin; interdict
> The library's regulations *prohibit* the borrowing of reference books.

**prohibition** (*n.*)

ban; taboo; interdiction

| | |
|---|---|
| **punctual** (*adj.*)<br>'pəŋk-chə-wəl | on time; prompt; timely<br>    Be *punctual*. If you are late, we shall have to depart without you. |
| **punctuality** (*n.*) | promptness |
| **rebuke** (*v.*)<br>ri-'byük | express disapproval of; criticize sharply; censure severely; reprimand; reprove<br>    Our coach *rebuked* the two players who were late for practice, but he praised the rest of the team for their punctuality. |
| **transient** (*adj.*)<br>'tran(t)-zh(ē)-ənt | not lasting; passing soon; fleeting; short-lived; momentary; ephemeral; transitory<br>    It rained all day upstate, but down here we had only a *transient* shower; it was over in minutes. |
| **transient** (*n.*) | guest staying for only a short time<br>    The hotel's customers are mainly *transients*; only a few are permanent guests. |

## Apply What You Have Learned

 **EXERCISE 1.8:** SENTENCE COMPLETION

Write the lesson word that best fits the meaning of the sentence. *Rebuke* and *censure* complete the first sentence.

1. It is wrong to __?__ Sam only, with not one word of __?__ for the three others who are equally blameworthy.
2. As it was getting late, Lucy made a motion to __?__ the meeting.
3. A boxer who deliberately uses tactics that the rules of the ring __?__ will almost surely __?__ the bout.
4. A letter with a(n) __?__ address is undeliverable.
5. The complex has eighty unfurnished apartments to lease to __?__ tenants and four furnished ones to accommodate __?__ families.
6. It is illegal for a company to __?__ toxic wastes into our state's rivers.
7. Those who __?__ say they will not support the proposed settlement unless it is made more __?__.
8. Her remarks were not __?__; they had been prepared in advance.

9. The corporation's _?_ new line of breakfast cereals should enable it to _?_ itself from its financial difficulties.

10. Martha dashed out, _?_ leaving her keys behind.

 **EXERCISE 1.9:** SYNONYMS

Eliminate repetition by replacing the boldfaced word or words with a **synonym** from your lesson words.

1. Should we **ban** imports from nations that ban our products?
2. Cyclones **wreck** buildings, trapping victims in the wreckage.
3. The report clears them of blame, but it does not **clear** us.
4. The firm has fired two employees and may soon **fire** some more.
5. You are rarely on time; they are usually **on time**.
6. Low profits are driving farmers into more **profitable** pursuits.
7. Wait for a suitable occasion; this one is **not suitable**.
8. The **lasting** peace we were supposed to have did not last long.
9. Pat's handwriting is hard to read; Anita's is more **readable**.
10. He is entangled in a web of lies and cannot **disentangle** himself.

 **EXERCISE 1.10:** ANTONYMS

On your answer paper, enter the lesson word that is most nearly the **opposite** of the boldfaced word.

1. It makes no sense to _?_ a structure we may soon need to **build** anew.
2. People insist on _?_ treatment. **Unfair** practices must cease.
3. **Temporary** officers serve only until _?_ ones are chosen.
4. Clothes **suitable** for leisure wear may be _?_ for the office.
5. Many public places that used to **permit** smoking now _?_ it.
6. **Commendation** is much more pleasing to our ears than _?_.
7. The new owner turned an **unprofitable** business into a(n) _?_ one.
8. I cannot **concur** with your conclusions. I must _?_.
9. A **permanent** resident pays a lower daily rate than a(n) _?_.
10. Our bus was **late** again today; it is seldom _?_.

**EXERCISE 1.11:** CONCISE WRITING

Express the thought of each sentence in **no more than four words**, as in 1, below.

1. Jim strayed from the main topic without really intending to do so.
   **Jim inadvertently digressed.**
2. When are we going to bring our meeting to a close?
3. The laws by which we are governed must be fair to all concerned.
4. The comments she made were spoken on the spur of the moment, without any advance preparation.
5. The notes that you took are very hard to read.

 **EXERCISE 1.12:** SYNONYM SUMMARY

Each line, when completed, should have three words similar in meaning. The parentheses indicate the number of missing letters. On your answer paper, write the *complete* words. Answers to the first line are **disagree**, **object**, and **dissent**.

| | | |
|---|---|---|
| 1. disagr (2) | (2) ject | (3) sent |
| 2. l (1) se | sacr (1) fice | forf (2) t |
| 3. shr (2) d | w (1) ly | (2) tute |
| 4. prom (2) | time (2) | pun (3) l |
| 5. (1) reck | de (3) ish | r (1) ze |
| 6. last (3) | (1) table | (3) man (3) |
| 7. b (1) n | (2) boo | pr (1) hi (2) tion |
| 8. accident (2) ly (2) | care (4) ly | in (2) vertent |
| 9. impart (3) | (2) bias (2) | (1) quit (2) le |
| 10. (3) charge | (3) miss | f (1) re |
| 11. (2) proper | (2) becoming | (2) appropriate |
| 12. (2) quit | (2) solve | (2) one (1) ate |

| 13. fit (4) | prop (2) | (2) prop (2) ate |
| 14. (2) cess | (3) band | (2) jour (1) |
| 15. moment (3) | fleet (3) | t (3) sit (3) |
| 16. (3) hand | (2) tempo (3) eous | (2) prompt (1) |
| 17. profit (1) ble | remuner (1) tive | (2) crat (2) e |
| 18. dis (2) tangle | rel (2) se | (2) tricat (1) |
| 19. unread (1) ble | undecipher (1) ble | (2) leg (4) |
| 20. (2) fair | (2) just | (2) eq (2) table |

 **EXERCISE 1.13**: ANALOGIES

Which lettered pair of words—*a, b, c, d,* or *e*—most nearly expresses the same relationship as the capitalized pair? Write the letter of your answer on your answer paper.

1. ADJOURN : DISBAND
   - *a.* win : lose
   - *b.* differ : agree
   - *c.* raise : lower
   - *d.* bury : inter
   - *e.* alleviate : intensify

2. DEMOLISH : BUILD
   - *a.* prohibit : interdict
   - *b.* discharge : hire
   - *c.* sacrifice : forfeit
   - *d.* rebuke : reprimand
   - *e.* absolve : exculpate

3. ILLEGIBLE : DECIPHER
   - *a.* audible : hear
   - *b.* rare : find
   - *c.* accessible : reach
   - *d.* fragile : break
   - *e.* visible : see

   *Hint:* Something **illegible** is hard to **decipher**.

4. FOOL : ASTUTE
   - *a.* coward : valiant
   - *b.* inventor : creative
   - *c.* imitator : unoriginal
   - *d.* neophyte : inexperienced
   - *e.* accomplice : blameworthy

5. LUCRATIVE : UNREMUNERATIVE
    *a.* barren : unproductive
    *b.* scarce : unavailable
    *c.* becoming : inappropriate
    *d.* unjust : inequitable
    *e.* extemporaneous : impromptu

6. EPHEMERAL : DURATION
    *a.* spacious : capacity
    *b.* priceless : value
    *c.* enormous : size
    *d.* lofty : height
    *e.* insignificant : importance
    *Hint:* Something **ephemeral** is of little **duration**.

7. LATECOMER : PUNCTUAL
    *a.* liar : untrustworthy
    *b.* invalid : frail
    *c.* dictator : domineering
    *d.* gossip : talkative
    *e.* ally : inimical

8. OBJECTIVE : BIAS
    *a.* dependent : domination
    *b.* vengeful : hate
    *c.* illiterate : ignorance
    *d.* healthy : disease
    *e.* hesitant : doubt
    *Hint:* An **objective** person is free of **bias**.

9. FLEETING : STAY
    *a.* boiling : evaporate
    *b.* stable : disappear
    *c.* complex : puzzle
    *d.* amusing : entertain
    *e.* mitigating : relieve
    *Hint:* Something **fleeting** does not **stay**.

10. DYNAMITE : DEMOLITION
    *a.* food : agriculture
    *b.* fog : atmosphere
    *c.* oil : heating
    *d.* lumber : forest
    *e.* temperature : refrigeration

**EXERCISE 1.14:** COMPOSITION

Answer in a sentence or two.

1. Should a teacher rebuke a student for illegible writing? Explain.
2. Why wouldn't a boss discharge a worker for being punctual?
3. Give an example of inappropriate behavior that resulted in censure.
4. If the government must demolish houses, how can it do it in an equitable way?
5. Would an astute businessperson forfeit a lucrative contract? Explain.

*Part*

**2**

# Contexts With Similar Words

This section will show you how you may discover the meaning of an unfamiliar word or expression from a similar word or expression in the context.

1. Do you know the meaning of *remuneration*? If not, you should be able to learn it from passage *a*:

   *a.* All school officials receive a salary except the members of the Board of Education, who serve without *remuneration*.

   Here, the meaning of *remuneration* is supplied by a similar word in the context, *salary*.

2. What is a *baker's dozen*? If you do not know, try to find out from passage *b*:

   *b.* "Mrs. Joe has been out a dozen times, looking for you, Pip. And she's out now, making it *a baker's dozen*."—CHARLES DICKENS

   A dozen plus one is the same as a *baker's dozen*. Therefore, a *baker's dozen* must mean "thirteen."

3. Let's try one more. Find the meaning of *comprehension* in passage *c*:

   *c.* I understand the first problem, but the second is beyond my *comprehension.*

   The clue here is *understand.* It suggests that *comprehension* must mean "understanding."

Note that you sometimes have to perform a small operation to get the meaning. In passage *c*, for example, you had to change the form of the clue word *understand* to *understanding.* In passage *b*, you had to do some adding: twelve plus one equals a *baker's dozen.* In passage *a*, however, you were able to use the clue word *salary*, without change, as the meaning of *remuneration.*

## Pretest 3

Write the meaning of the italicized word or expression. (*Hint:* Look for a *similar* word or expression in the context.)

1. "In the marketplace of Goderville was a great crowd, a mingled *multitude* of men and beasts."—GUY DE MAUPASSANT

2. When I invited you for a *stroll,* you said it was too hot to walk.

3. Jane's little brother has discovered the *cache* where she keeps her photographs. She'll have to find another hiding place.

4. The *spine,* or backbone, runs along the back of human beings.

5. "The king and his court were in their places, opposite the twin doors—those fateful *portals* so terrible in their similarity." —FRANK R. STOCKTON

6. Ellen tried her best to hold back her tears, but she could not *restrain* them.

7. Why are you so *timorous*? I tell you there is nothing to be afraid of.

8. Harriet's *version* of the quarrel differs from your account.

9. Our club's first president, who knew little about democratic procedures, ran the meetings in such a *despotic* way that we called him "the dictator."

10. "The 'Hispaniola' still lay where she had anchored, but, sure enough, there was the *Jolly Roger*—the black flag of piracy—flying from her peak."—ROBERT LOUIS STEVENSON

11. The Empire State Building is a remarkable *edifice*; it has more than a hundred stories.

12. Some children who are *reserved* with strangers are not at all uncommunicative with friends.

13. The problems of the period we are living through are different from those of any previous *era.*

14. Why should I *retract* my statement? It is a perfectly true remark, and I see no reason to withdraw it.

15. CELIA [urging Rosalind to say something]. Why, cousin! Why, Rosalind! ... Not a word?
    ROSALIND. Not one to throw at a dog.
    CELIA. No, thy words are too precious to be cast away upon *curs;* throw some of them at me.
    —WILLIAM SHAKESPEARE

16. Jerry thought he saw a ship in the distance. I looked carefully but could *perceive* nothing.

17. Nina claims that I started the quarrel, but I have witnesses to prove that she *initiated* it.

18. "He praised her taste, and she *commended* his understanding."
    —OLIVER GOLDSMITH

19. Students attending private schools pay *tuition.* In the public schools, however, there is no charge for instruction.

20. "His facts no one thought of *disputing;* and his opinions few of the sailors dared to oppose."—RICHARD HENRY DANA

## *Study Your Lesson Words,* **Group 3**

| WORD | MEANING AND TYPICAL USE |
|---|---|
| **cache** (*n.*)<br>'kash | hiding place to store something<br>After confessing, the robber led detectives to a *cache* of stolen gems in the basement. |
| **commend** (*v.*)<br>kə-'mend | praise; mention favorably; compliment<br>The volunteers were *commended* for their heroic efforts to save lives. |
| **commendable** (*adj.*) | praiseworthy; laudable |
| **cur** (*n.*)<br>'kər | worthless dog<br>Lassie is a kind and intelligent animal. Please don't refer to her as a *cur.* |

**despotic** *(adj.)*
des-'pä-tik

characteristic of a despot (a monarch having absolute power); domineering; dictatorial; tyrannical; autocratic
The American colonists revolted against the *despotic* rule of George III.

**despotism** *(n.)*

tyranny; dictatorship

**dispute** *(v.)*
di-'spyüt

argue about; debate; declare not true; call into question; oppose; challenge
Charley *disputed* my solution until I showed him definite proof that I was right.

**disputatious** *(adj.)*

argumentative; contentious

**edifice** *(n.)*
'e-də-fəs

building, especially a large or impressive building
The huge *edifice* under construction near the airport will be a hotel.

**era** *(n.)*
'ir-ə

historical period; period of time; age; epoch
The atomic *era* began with the dropping of the first atomic bomb in 1945.

**initiate** *(v.)*
i-'ni-shē-,āt

1. begin; introduce; originate; inaugurate
The Pilgrims *initiated* the custom of celebrating Thanksgiving Day.

2. put through the ceremony of becoming a member; admit; induct
Next Friday our club is going to *initiate* three new members.

**initiation** *(n.)*

induction; installation

**Jolly Roger** *(n.)*
'jä-lē-'rä-jər

pirates' flag; black flag with white skull and crossbones
The *Jolly Roger* flying from the mast of the approaching ship indicated that it was a pirate ship.

**multitude** *(n.)*
'məl-tə-,tüd

very large number of people or things; crowd; throng; horde; swarm
There was such a *multitude* outside the store waiting for the sale to begin that we decided to return later.

**multitudinous** *(adj.)*

many; numerous

**perceive** (*v.*)
pər-'sēv

become aware of through the senses; see; note; observe; behold; understand
When the lights went out, I couldn't see a thing, but gradually I was able to *perceive* the outlines of the larger pieces of furniture.

**perception** (*n.*)

idea; conception

**portal** (*n.*)
'pòr-t²l

(usually plural) door; entrance, especially, a grand or impressive one; gate
The original doors at the main entrance have been replaced by bronze *portals*.

**reserved** (*adj.*)
ri-'zərvd

1. restrained in speech or action; reticent; uncommunicative; tight-lipped; taciturn
Mark was *reserved* at first but became much more communicative when he got to know us better.

2. unsociable; aloof; withdrawn

**restrain** (*v.*)
ri-'strān

hold back; check; curb; repress; keep under control
Mildred could not *restrain* her impulse to open the package immediately, even though it read, "Do not open before Christmas!"

**retract** (*v.*)
ri-'trakt

draw back; withdraw; take back; unsay
You can depend on Frank. Once he has given his promise, he will not *retract* it.

**spine** (*n.*)
'spīn

chain of small bones down the middle of the back; backbone
The ribs are curved bones extending from the *spine* and enclosing the upper part of the body.

**spineless** (*adj.*)

having no backbone; weak; indecisive; cowardly

**stroll** (*n.*)
'strōl

idle and leisurely walk; ramble
It was a warm spring afternoon, and many people were out for a *stroll*.

**timorous** (*adj.*)
'ti-mə-rəs

full of fear; afraid; timid
I admit I was *timorous* when I began my speech, but as I went along, I felt less and less afraid.

**tuition** (*n.*)
tü-'i-shən

payment for instruction

When I go to college, I will probably work each summer to help pay the *tuition*.

**version** (*n.*)
'vər-zhən

1. account or description from one point of view; interpretation

Now that we have Vera's description of the accident, let us listen to your *version*.

2. translation

THE COUNT OF MONTE CRISTO was written in French, but you can read it in the English *version*.

## *Apply What You Have Learned*

### EXERCISE 1.15: SENTENCE COMPLETION

Write the lesson word that best fits the meaning of the sentence. *Multitude* and *portal* complete the first sentence.

1. A(n) _?_ of desperate depositors gathered outside the closed _?_s of the ailing bank.

2. If you prove me wrong, I will gladly _?_ my statement.

3. It is hoped that the settlement just reached will _?_ a new _?_ of cooperation between labor and management.

4. Most of us would be too _?_ to try sky-diving.

5. Since you _?_ my _?_ of what was said at today's meeting, I am eager to hear your interpretation.

6. Many college students hold part-time jobs to help pay their _?_.

7. In our _?_ down Broadway, we passed one magnificent _?_ after another.

8. Sit up straight. Slouching tends to deform the _?_.

9. It is hard to _?_ why any people would prefer to keep their savings in a(n) _?_ at home, instead of in an insured savings bank.

10. Why are you so _?_ today? Don't you have anything to say?

**EXERCISE 1.16:** SYNONYMS

Eliminate repetition by replacing the boldfaced word or words with a **synonym** from your lesson words.

1. Her account of the incident is more believable than your **account.**
2. If he withdraws his objection to the plan, I will **withdraw** mine.
3. The malls were crowded. I had never seen such **crowds** there.
4. Why are they afraid of our dog? There is no reason to be **afraid**.
5. That **large building** was built just a year ago.
6. Your cousins must love arguments; they **argue about** everything.
7. It is hard to communicate with you if you are **uncommunicative**.
8. I knew the **hiding place** where my brother hid his baseball cards.
9. Teachers often **praise** us when we do something praiseworthy.
10. **Curb** your appetite for snacks. If uncurbed, it may cause problems.

 **EXERCISE 1.17:** ANTONYMS

On your answer paper, enter the lesson word that is most nearly the **opposite** of the boldfaced word or words.

1. A **valuable poodle** like Muffin is certainly not a(n) _?_.
2. **Censure** them for their faults, but also _?_ them for their merits.
3. Trained investigators _?_ details that others may **fail to notice**.
4. Nonswimmers are _?_ in a rowboat; swimmers are generally **unafraid**.
5. A **democratic** organization will not tolerate a(n) _?_ president.
6. Be **sociable**. Mingle with the other guests. You are too _?_.
7. They received **few** complaints, but we got a(n) _?_ of them.
8. Please allow me to _?_ the regrettable statement I **made** earlier.
9. **Let go.** Do not _?_ me.
10. Nations that _?_ hostilities may find it difficult to **end** them.

**EXERCISE 1.18:** CONCISE WRITING

Express the thought of each sentence in **no more than four words**.

1. A number of very large and impressive buildings are not being used.
2. How much do you have to pay for the instruction that you are getting?
3. I question the truth of the interpretation that they have presented.
4. The supervisor that we worked for acted like an absolute monarch.
5. Avoid injury to the chain of small bones that runs down the middle of your back.

 **EXERCISE 1.19:** SYNONYM SUMMARY

Each line, when completed, should have three words similar in meaning. The parentheses indicate the number of missing letters. On your answer paper, write the *complete* words. Answers to the first line are **behold**, **observe**, and **perceive**.

| | | |
|---|---|---|
| 1. beh (1) ld | (2) serve | perc (2) ve |
| 2. q (2) stion | challen (2) | dis (4) |
| 3. c (1) rb | ch (1) ck | (2) strain |
| 4. cr (1) wd | h (1) rde | (3) titude |
| 5. pr (2) se | com (4) | compl (1) ment |
| 6. dictator (4) | (2) ranny | (3) potism |
| 7. orig (1) nate | intr (1) duce | init (2) te |
| 8. (1) ge | epo (2) | (2) a |
| 9. tac (1) turn | reti (1) ent | res (2) ved |
| 10. (2) roll | (1) amble | w (1) lk |
| 11. afr (2) d | (4) ful | (3) orous |
| 12. acc (2) nt | interpr (1) tation | vers (2) n |
| 13. (3) pot (2) | (2) tocratic | domin (2) ring |

**14.** (1) ate          entr (1) nce          (3) tal

**15.** (2) say          with (4)              (2) tract

**16.** (2) ea           concept (3)          per (1) e (2) i (2)

**17.** (2) duction      (2) stallation       in (1) t (2) tion

**18.** m (1) ny         mu (3) tudinous      num (5)

**19.** (6) worthy       laud (4)             (3) mend (1) ble

**20.** arg (1) mentative   conten (2) ous     (3) puta (2) ous

 # EXERCISE 1.20: ANALOGIES

Which lettered pair of words—*a, b, c, d,* or *e*—most nearly expresses the same relationship as the capitalized pair? Write the letter of your answer on your answer paper.

**1.** CUR : DOG

   *a.* calf : cow          *b.* lamb : sheep

   *c.* elk : deer            *d.* nag : horse

   *e.* tadpole : frog

**2.** TUITION : INSTRUCTION

   *a.* dues : organization      *b.* interest : bank

   *c.* rent : shelter          *d.* fine : penalty

   *e.* tip : meal

*Hint:* **tuition** is payment for **instruction.**

**3.** STROLL : WALK

   *a.* hum : sing           *b.* drawl : speak

   *c.* gulp : swallow       *d.* dash : move

   *e.* snore : sleep

*Hint:* To **stroll** is to walk **slowly.**

**4.** DISPUTATIOUS : ARGUMENT

   *a.* obstinate : compromise      *b.* sociable : company

   *c.* restless : delay         *d.* indolent : exercise

   *e.* sober : exaggeration

*Hint:* A **disputatious** person is fond of **argument.**

5. EDIFICE : BUILDING
   a. apron : garment
   b. closet : storage
   c. canoe : vessel
   d. glider : plane
   e. banquet : meal

6. CACHE : CONCEALMENT
   a. umbrella : rain
   b. barrier : communication
   c. oven : fuel
   d. showcase : privacy
   e. automobile : transportation

7. SPINELESS : WILLPOWER
   a. impartial : prejudice
   b. enthusiastic : zeal
   c. inquisitive : curiosity
   d. resentful : anger
   e. dauntless : courage

8. TACITURN : SAY
   a. disgruntled : complain
   b. proficient : accomplish
   c. timid : fear
   d. literate : know
   e. frank : conceal
   *Hint:* A **taciturn** person has **little** to say.

9. RESTRAINED : FREE
   a. enlightened : educated
   b. reserved : withdrawn
   c. exonerated : guiltless
   d. uninvited : welcome
   e. contented : satisfied

10. JOLLY ROGER : PIRACY
   a. green light : danger
   b. full moon : illumination
   c. white flag : truce
   d. red carpet : hostility
   e. yellow ribbon : cowardice

 **EXERCISE 1.21:** COMPOSITION

Answer in a sentence or two.

1. How might people of the future perceive our current era?
2. When is it wise to restrain timorous feelings?

3. Should citizens dispute the policies of a despotic leader? Why or why not?

4. What type of portal might suit a grand edifice?

5. Why wouldn't you show your cache to a multitude?

## Pretest 4

Write the meaning of the italicized word or expression. (Look for a *similar* word or expression in the context.)

21. "When all at once I saw a crowd,/A *host*, of golden daffodils."
—WILLIAM WORDSWORTH

22. Choosing a career is a matter that calls for *reflection*, but I haven't yet given it enough thought.

23. How can Alice *tolerate* your whistling while she is studying? I would never be able to bear it.

24. We can't meet in the music room tomorrow because another group has reserved it. We shall have to *convene* somewhere else.

25. Some of the students who arrive early gather near the main entrance, even though they are not supposed to *congregate* there.

26. "'Ah, so it is!' Edmond said, and, still keeping Mercédès' hand clasped in his, he held the other one out in all friendliness to the Catalan. Instead, however, of responding to this show of *cordiality*, Fernand remained mute and motionless as a statue."
—ALEXANDRE DUMAS

27. I can *dispense with* a midmorning snack, but I cannot do without lunch.

28. Up to now Diane has always started the disputes; this time Caroline is the *aggressor*.

29. Some pitchers try to *intimidate* batters by throwing fastballs very close to them, but they can't frighten a hitter like Joe.

30. "Rip now resumed his old walks and habits. He soon found many of his former *cronies*, though all rather the worse for the wear and tear of time; so Rip preferred making friends among the younger generation, with whom he soon grew into great favor."
—WASHINGTON IRVING

31. The English Office is at one end of the hall, and the library entrance is at the other *extremity*.

32.   "'Slow, lad, slow,' he said. 'They might round upon us in a twinkle of an eye, if we was seen to hurry.'
      "Very *deliberately,* then, did we advance across the sand...."
      —Robert Louis Stevenson

33. Two hours ago the weather bureau predicted rain for tomorrow; now it is *forecasting* rain mixed with snow.

34. The old edition had a *preface.* The new one has no introduction at all.

35. Patricia's dog ran off with our ball and would not *relinquish* it until she made him give it up.

36. By noon we had climbed to a height of more than 2000 feet. From that *altitude,* the housetops in the town below seemed tiny.

37. "He bade me observe it, and I should always find, that the *calamities* of life were shared among the upper and lower part of mankind; but that the middle station had the fewest disasters."—Daniel Defoe

38. Yesterday it looked doubtful that I could finish my report on time. Today, however, it seems less *dubious.*

39. People at the zoo usually draw back when the lion roars, but this time they did not *recoil.*

40. Bears and bats *hibernate* in caves; frogs and lizards spend the winter in the earth, below the frost line.

## *Study Your Lesson Words,* **Group 4**

| WORD | MEANING AND TYPICAL USE |
|---|---|
| **aggressor** (*n.*)<br>ə-'gre-sər | person or nation that initiates hostilities or makes an unprovoked attack; assailant; invader<br>    In World War II, Japan was the *aggressor;* its surprise attack on Pearl Harbor started the conflict in the Pacific. |
| **aggression** (*n.*) | unprovoked attack; assault; invasion |
| **altitude** (*n.*)<br>'al-tə-,tüd | height; elevation; high position; eminence<br>    Mount Washington, which rises to an *altitude* of 6,288 feet, is the highest peak in the White Mountains. |

**calamity** (*n.*)
kə-'la-mə-tē

great misfortune; catastrophe; disaster
   The assassinations of John F. Kennedy and
Martin Luther King, Jr. were national *calamities*.

**calamitous** (*adj.*)

disastrous; catastrophic

**congregate** (*v.*)
'käŋ-gri-,gāt

come together into a crowd; assemble; gather
   Some homeowners near the school do not like
students to *congregate* on their property.

**convene** (*v.*)
kən-'vēn

meet in a group for a specific purpose
   The board of directors will *convene* next
Tuesday to elect a new corporation president.

**convention** (*n.*)

treaty; agreement

**cordiality** (*n.*)
,kȯr-jē-'a-lə-tē

friendliness; warmth of regard; amiability
   Pam's parents greeted me with *cordiality* and
made me feel like an old friend of the family.

**cordial** (*adj.*)

warm and friendly; gracious; hearty

**crony** (*n.*)
'krō-nē

close companion; intimate friend; chum;
associate
   Some students socialize only with their *cronies*
and rarely try to make new friends.

**deliberately** (*adv.*)
di-'li-bə-rət-lē

1. in a carefully thought out manner; purposely;
intentionally
   We *deliberately* kept Glenda off the planning
committee because we didn't want her to know
that the party was to be in her honor.

2. in an unhurried manner; slowly
   The chef measured out the ingredients
*deliberately,* wanting the amounts to be precise.

**dispense** (*v.*)
di-'spen(t)s

1. deal out; distribute
   Some charitable organizations *dispense* food to
the needy.

2. (followed by the preposition *with*) do without;
get along without; forgo
   When our club has a guest speaker, we *dispense*
with the reading of the minutes to save time.

**dubious** (*adj.*)
'dü-bē-əs

doubtful; uncertain; questionable
There is no doubt about my feeling better, but it is *dubious* that I can be back at school by tomorrow.

**extremity** (*n.*)
ik-'stre-mə-tē

very end; utmost limit; border
Key West is at the southern *extremity* of Florida.

**forecast** (*v.*)
'for-,kast

predict; foretell; prophesy; prognosticate
The price of oranges has gone up again, as you *forecasted.*

**hibernate** (*v.*)
'hī-bər-,nāt

spend the winter in a dormant or inactive state, as some animals do
When animals *hibernate,* their heart rate drops sharply and their body temperature decreases.

**host** (*n.*)
'hōst

1. large number; multitude; throng; crowd; flock
The merchant had expected a *host* of customers, but only a few appeared.

2. person who receives or entertains a guest or guests at home or elsewhere (Note also: *hostess*— a woman who serves as a *host*)
Dad treats his guests with the utmost cordiality; he is an excellent *host.*

**intimidate** (*v.*)
in-'ti-mə-,dāt

frighten; influence by fear; cow; overawe; coerce
A few spectators were *intimidated* by the lion's roar, but most were not frightened.

**preface** (*n.*)
'pre-fəs

introduction (to a book or speech); foreword; prologue; preamble; exordium
Begin by reading the *preface*; it will help you to get the most out of the rest of the book.

**preface** (*v.*)

introduce or begin with a preface; usher in; precede
Usually, I get right into my speech, but this time I *prefaced* it with an amusing anecdote.

**recoil** (*v.*)
ri-'koi(ə)l

draw back because of fear or disgust; shrink; wince; flinch
Marie *recoiled* at the thought of singing in the amateur show, but she went through with it because she had promised to participate.

| | |
|---|---|
| **reflection** (*n.*) <br> ri-'flek-shən | 1. thought, especially careful thought; cogitation; deliberation <br>     When a question is complicated, don't give the first answer that comes to mind. Take time for *reflection*. <br><br> 2. blame; discredit; aspersion; slur <br>     Yesterday's defeat was no *reflection* on our players; they did their very best. |
| **relinquish** (*v.*) <br> ri-'liŋ-kwish | give up; abandon; let go; release; surrender; cede <br>     When an elderly man entered the crowded bus, one of the students *relinquished* her seat to him. |
| **tolerate** (*v.*) <br> 'tä-lə-,rāt | endure; bear; put up with; accept; permit <br>     Very young children will cry when rebuked; they cannot *tolerate* criticism. |
| **tolerable** (*adj.*) | bearable; endurable |

## Apply What You Have Learned

 ## EXERCISE 1.22: SENTENCE COMPLETION

Write the lesson word that best fits the meaning of the sentence.

1. Many a(n) _?_ has occurred in the Alps on the Matterhorn, an almost unscalable mountain that rises to a(n) _?_ of 14,700 feet.

2. My teammates are confident of victory, but I am inclined to be _?_.

3. We will _?_ no more delays because our patience has already been stretched to its _?_.

4. The author's _?_ precedes the table of contents.

5. The United Nations has always called upon _?_ s to _?_ the territories they have seized.

6. If you stop to feed one pigeon, a flock of them will soon _?_ around you.

7. The candidate used to be a(n) _?_ of mine, but since our dispute there has not been much _?_ between us.

8. The _?_ greeted each of his guests with a cordial handshake.

9. Since this matter is important, let us proceed __?__ rather than hastily, with ample time for discussion and __?__.

10. Lower winter air fares will probably encourage more Northerners to __?__ in the South this year.

 **EXERCISE 1.23:** SYNONYMS

Eliminate repetition by replacing the boldfaced word or words with a **synonym** from your lesson words.

1. They cannot **frighten** that reporter with threats; she is not easily frightened.

2. Cassandra was able to **predict** future events, but no one ever believed her predictions.

3. Will they **assemble** here or at some other place of assembly?

4. People have reluctantly put up with increases in taxes, but they refuse to **put up with** reductions in services.

5. The guest of honor was a **close friend** with whom she has been friendly since grade school.

6. Our neighbor speaks **in an unhurried way**; he is never in a hurry.

7. We do not question your facts, but we think your interpretation of them is **questionable**.

8. The two are supposed to be friends, but sometimes there is no **friendliness** between them.

9. That family has had great misfortunes, but never such a **great misfortune** as this one.

10. Many youngsters will gladly forgo vegetables but are most reluctant to **forgo** dessert.

 **EXERCISE 1.24:** ANTONYMS

On your answer paper, enter the lesson word that is most nearly the **opposite** of the boldfaced word or words.

1. When David saw others __?__ from the giant Goliath, he went out with his sling to **confront** him.

2. The crowds that __?__ at the scene of an accident are often slow to **disperse**.

3. Don't _?_ all your supplies; **keep** some for yourself.

4. I **inadvertently** neglected to say hello, but she thought I had done it _?_.

5. The first **guest** arrived with a small present for the _?_.

6. The _?_ is brief, but the **index** runs to more than six pages.

7. The **invaded nation** is fighting to repel the _?_.

8. Sometimes what appears to be a(n) _?_ turns out to be a **boon**.

9. Some animals that are **active in the summer** _?_ when the weather turns cold.

10. We are **certain** about the election returns that have been verified, but we are _?_ about some of the others.

 ## EXERCISE 1.25: CONCISE WRITING

Express the thought of each sentence in **no more than four words.**

1. I spoke without giving careful thought to what I was saying.

2. The one who had invited us to her home as guests was warm and friendly.

3. Has the individual who made the unprovoked attack offered an apology?

4. What is it that made you draw back in disgust?

5. Read the introduction to the book in an unhurried manner.

 ## EXERCISE 1.26: SYNONYM SUMMARY

Each line, when completed, should have three words similar in meaning. The parentheses indicate the number of missing letters. On your answer paper, write the *complete* words. Answers to the first line are **doubtful, questionable,** and **dubious.**

1. dou (1) tful          q (2) stionable          dub (4)

2. h (2) ght            el (1) vation            alt (2) ude

3. ab (2) don           c (1) d (1)              (2) linquish

4. pred (2) t           prophe (1) y             (4) cast

| | | |
|---|---|---|
| **5.** gath (2) | (2) semble | (3) gregate |
| **6.** b (2) rable | (2) durable | toler (4) |
| **7.** ch (1) m | as (2) ciate | (2) ony |
| **8.** (2) vasion | ass (2) lt | ag (1) r (2) sion |
| **9.** grac (4) | h (2) rty | cord (2) l |
| **10.** thr (2) g | (3) titude | h (2) t |
| **11.** dis (2) trous | (4) strophic | (2) lamit (3) |
| **12.** co (1) rce | (1) ow | (2) timid (3) |
| **13.** ac (1) ept | en (3) e | (2) lerate |
| **14.** p (2) posely | (2) tentionally | de (3) erately |
| **15.** shr (2) k | (2) nce | rec (2) l |
| **16.** (2) liberation | cog (1) tation | (2) flec (4) |
| **17.** fr (2) ndliness | am (2) bility | (3) diality |
| **18.** agr (2) ment | tr (2) ty | (3) vention |
| **19.** l (1) mit | b (2) der | ex (3) mity |
| **20.** pre (2) ble | ex (2) dium | (3) face |

 **EXERCISE 1.27:** ANALOGIES

Which lettered pair of words—*a, b, c, d,* or *e*—most nearly expresses the same relationship as the capitalized pair? Write the letter of your answer on your answer paper.

1. CALAMITY : MISFORTUNE
   *a.* hill : mountain
   *b.* deluge : rainfall
   *c.* crime : misdemeanor
   *d.* brook : river
   *e.* lake : ocean
   *Hint:* A **calamity** is a great **misfortune**.

2. PREFACE : INDEX
    *a.* initiation : club          *b.* mouth : river
    *c.* appetizer : dessert        *d.* sunrise : noon
    *e.* lobby : edifice
    *Hint:* A **preface** is the first part of a book; an **index** is the last.

3. RELINQUISH : ABANDON
    *a.* wane : flourish            *b.* convene : adjourn
    *c.* submit : defy              *d.* repel : attract
    *e.* extinguish : quench

4. INVADER : AGGRESSION
    *a.* burglar : arson            *b.* lawbreaker : arrest
    *c.* liar : perjury             *d.* shoplifter : penalty
    *e.* swindler : greed
    *Hint:* An **invader** commits **aggression**.

5. CONGREGATE : DISPERSE
    *a.* hesitate : waver           *b.* prognosticate : foretell
    *c.* cow : coerce               *d.* flinch : wince
    *e.* commend : reprimand

6. LOATHSOME : RECOIL
    *a.* incredible : believe       *b.* irritating : relax
    *c.* spectacular : gasp         *d.* interesting : yawn
    *e.* illegible : understand
    *Hint:* Something that is **loathsome** makes us **recoil**.

7. ALTITUDE : DEPTH
    *a.* significance : importance  *b.* confidence : doubt
    *c.* anxiety : worry            *d.* mitigation : relief
    *e.* version : interpretation

8. INTOLERABLE : ENDURE
    *a.* intelligible : comprehend  *b.* complicated : simplify
    *c.* palatable : consume        *d.* inequitable : justify
    *e.* accessible : approach

9. COGITATION : BRAIN
   *a.* digestion : stomach       *b.* air : lungs
   *c.* perspiration : exertion    *d.* backbone : spine
   *e.* nutrition : food

10. HOST : MULTITUDE
    *a.* novice : veteran         *b.* masterpiece : reproduction
    *c.* crony : chum             *d.* cordiality : hostility
    *e.* guest : courtesy

 **EXERCISE 1.28:** COMPOSITION

Answer in a sentence or two.

1. Why don't people show cordiality to an aggressor?
2. What calamity might occur to an airplane flying at a low altitude?
3. Give an example of a host whom you could not tolerate.
4. Why wouldn't a crony deliberately intimidate you?
5. Describe a time you felt dubious about a decision after giving it some reflection.

# Commonsense Contexts

Do you know what *famished* means? If not, you should be able to tell from the following context:

> "The morning had passed away, and Rip felt *famished* for want of his breakfast."
>
> —WASHINGTON IRVING

How do you feel when the morning has gone by and you have not had breakfast? Very hungry, of course, even starved. Therefore, *famished* in the above context must mean "very hungry."

Note that the above context is different from those we have had so far. It has neither an opposite word nor a similar word to help with the meaning of *famished*. It does, however, offer a clue in the words "for want of his breakfast," so that you can get the meaning by using *common sense*.

Here is another commonsense context. Can you tell what *inundated* means in the sentence below?

> As a result of a break in the water main, many cellars in the area were *inundated*.

What happens to cellars when a nearby water main breaks? They become flooded, naturally. Therefore, *inundated* in the above context must mean "flooded."

## Pretest 5

Here are some more commonsense contexts. Each contains a clue or clues to the meaning of the italicized word. Discover the meaning by using common sense, as in the previous examples.

1. "Mrs. Linton's funeral was appointed to take place on the Friday after her *decease*."—EMILY BRONTË

2. The race ended in a tie when Paul and Abe crossed the finish line *simultaneously.*

3. If you stand up in the boat, it may *capsize,* and we'll find ourselves in the water.

4. I cannot tell you the secret unless you promise not to *divulge* it.

5. "I now made one or two attempts to speak to my brother, but in some manner which I could not understand the *din* had so increased that I could not make him hear a single word, although I screamed at the top of my voice in his ear."—EDGAR ALLAN POE

6. We had no use for our flashlights; the moon *illuminated* our path very clearly.

7. Sandra became *incensed* when I refused to return her library books for her, and she has not spoken to me since then.

8. The President heads our national government, the Governor our state government, and the Mayor our *municipal* government.

9. On February 12, 1809, in a Kentucky log cabin, there was born a boy who *subsequently* became the sixteenth President of the United States.

10. "All was dark within, so that I could *distinguish* nothing by the eye."—ROBERT LOUIS STEVENSON

11. There was a noise like the explosion of a firecracker when Karen *punctured* the balloon with a pin.

12. President Franklin D. Roosevelt died in 1945, and his wife, Eleanor, in 1962; she *survived* him by seventeen years.

13. Every time you cross a busy street against the light, you are putting your life in *jeopardy.*

14. By automobile, you can *traverse* the bridge in two minutes; on foot, it takes about half an hour.

15. "I was witness to events of a less peaceful character. One day when I went out to my woodpile, or rather my pile of stumps, I observed two large ants, the one red, the other much larger, nearly half an inch long, and black, fiercely *contending* with one another." —HENRY DAVID THOREAU

16. The microscope is of the utmost importance in the study of biology because it can *magnify* objects too small to be seen by the naked eye.

17. At one point during the hurricane, the winds reached a *velocity* of 130 miles an hour.

18. Farmers will be in trouble unless the *drought* ends soon; it hasn't rained in six weeks.

19. The speaker should have used the microphone. Her voice was *inaudible,* except to those near the platform.

20. "However, at low water I went on board, and though I thought I had *rummaged* the cabin so effectually, as that nothing more could be found, yet I discovered a locker with drawers in it, in one of which I found two or three razors, and one pair of large scissors, with some ten or a dozen of good knives and forks. . . ."
—DANIEL DEFOE

## Study Your Lesson Words, **Group 5**

| WORD | MEANING AND TYPICAL USE |
|---|---|
| **capsize** (*v.*)<br>'kap-,sīz or kap-'sīz | overturn; upset<br>When Sam's canoe *capsized,* I swam over to help him turn it right side up. |
| **contend** (*v.*)<br>kən-'tend | 1. compete; vie; take part in a contest; fight; struggle<br>Every spring some baseball writers try to predict which two teams will *contend* in the next World Series. |
| | 2. argue; maintain as true; assert<br>Don't argue with the umpire. If she says you are out, it's no use *contending* you are safe. |
| **contentious** (*adj.*) | quarrelsome; belligerent |
| **decease** (*n.*)<br>di-'sēs | death; demise<br>Shortly after President Kennedy's *decease,* Vice President Johnson was sworn in as the new chief executive. |
| **din** (*n.*)<br>'din | loud noise; uproar; clamor; racket<br>I couldn't hear what you were saying because the plane passing overhead made such a *din*. |
| **distinguish** (*v.*)<br>di-'stiŋ-(g)wish | tell apart; differentiate; recognize<br>The twins are so alike that it is hard to *distinguish* one from the other. |

**divulge** (*v.*)
də-'vəlj or dī-'vəlj

make known; reveal; disclose
Yesterday our teacher read us a composition without *divulging* the name of the writer.

**drought** (*n.*)
'draut

long period of dry weather; lack of rain; dryness
While some regions are suffering from *drought*, others are experiencing heavy rains and floods.

**famish** (*v.*)
'fa-mish

starve; suffer from extreme hunger; make extremely hungry
The missing hikers were *famished* when we found them; they had not eaten for more than twelve hours.

**illuminate** (*v.*)
i-'lü-mə-,nāt

light up; lighten; brighten
The bright morning sun *illuminated* the room; there was no need for the lights to be on.

**inaudible** (*adj.*)
i-'no-də-bəl

incapable of being heard; not audible
The only part of your answer I could hear was the first word; the rest was *inaudible*.

**incense** (*v.*)
in-'sen(t)s

make extremely angry; enrage; madden; infuriate
Some of the members were so *incensed* by the way Tamar opened the meeting that they walked right out.

**inundate** (*v.*)
'i-,nən-dāt

flood; swamp; deluge
The rainstorm *inundated* a number of streets in low-lying areas.

**jeopardy** (*n.*)
'je-pər-dē

danger; peril
If you arrive late for a job interview, your chances of being hired will be in serious *jeopardy*.

**jeopardize** (*v.*)

endanger; imperil

**magnify** (*v.*)
'mag-nə-,fī

cause to be or look larger; enlarge; amplify; exaggerate
The bacteria shown in your textbook have been greatly *magnified*; their actual size is considerably smaller.

**municipal** (*adj.*)
myü-'ni-sə-pəl

of a city or town
Your mother works for the city? How interesting! My father is also a *municipal* employee.

**puncture** (*v.*)
'pəŋk-chər

make a hole with a pointed object; pierce; perforate
Our neighbor swept a nail off his curb, and later it *punctured* one of his own tires.

**rummage** (*v.*)
'rə-mij

search thoroughly by turning over all the contents; ransack
Someone must have *rummaged* my desk; everything in it is in disorder.

**simultaneously** (*adv.*)
‚sī-məl-'tā-nē-əs-lē

at the same time; concurrently; together
The twins began school *simultaneously*, but they did not graduate at the same time.

**subsequently** (*adv.*)
'səb-si-‚kwənt-lē

later; afterward; next
When I first saw that dress, it was $49.95; *subsequently* it was reduced to $29.95; now it is on sale for $19.95.

**survive** (*v.*)
sər-'vīv

live longer than; outlive; outlast
After landing at Plymouth, the Pilgrims suffered greatly; about half of them failed to *survive* the first winter.

**traverse** (*v.*)
tra-'vərs

pass across, over, or through; cross
The Trans-Siberian Railroad, completed in 1905, *traverses* the Asian continent.

**velocity** (*n.*)
və-'lä-sə-tē

speed; swiftness; celerity; rapidity
Do you know that light travels at a *velocity* of 186,000 miles a second?

## *Apply What You Have Learned*

 **EXERCISE 1.29:** SENTENCE COMPLETION

Write the lesson word that best fits the meaning of the sentence.

1. If that beached whale is to __?__, we must get him back into the water.

2. At its maximum __?__ , the new high-speed train can __?__ the distance in less than two hours.

3. Though she has a strong voice, her words were almost __?__ d by the __?__ of the chanting crowd.

4. While Sal __?__ d the attic, I __?__ searched the basement, but we failed to find the old comic books.

5. After the boat __?__ d, we had to __?__ with the strong current as we swam shoreward.

6. The __?__ employees were __?__ d when the mayor refused to raise their salaries.

7. The doctor's __?__ put the health of the community in __?__ because no other physician was willing to practice in that remote area.

8. 1 know the Bakers well, but in their Halloween costumes I could not __?__ them from the other guests.

9. Driving is difficult on a moonless night when there are no street lights to __?__ the road.

10. The candidate attempted to __?__ his achievements, but his exaggerations were __?__ d by the reporter's sharp questioning.

 ## EXERCISE 1.30: SYNONYMS

Eliminate repetition by replacing the boldfaced word or words with a **synonym** from your lesson words.

1. Tanks can pass over terrain that civilian vehicles cannot **pass through**.

2. When he is in a rage, do not say anything that will **enrage** him further.

3. The forests are especially dry because we have had a **long period of dry weather**.

4. Those who drive today are putting their lives in **danger** because the roads are icy and dangerous.

5. If you lean over the side of the boat, you may **turn** it **over**.

6. Steve maintains that you started the fight, and you **maintain** that he did.

7. Even with flood control, the Mississippi will occasionally **flood** millions of acres.

8. The speeding vehicle was clocked at a **speed** of 90 miles an hour.

9. Many who had outlived previous earthquakes did not **outlive** this one.

10. The findings have not been disclosed; the committee will **disclose** them at the proper time.

 ## EXERCISE 1.31: ANTONYMS

On your answer paper, enter the lesson word that is most nearly the **opposite** of the boldfaced word or words.

1. People whose main concern is for the **safety** of their money may not want to put their savings in __?__ by investing in the stock market.

2. In the flood, eighty-four people **perished**, nine are missing, and eleven __?__d.

3. Let us neither __?__ our accomplishments nor **minimize** our failures.

4. The brightly __?__d business district was momentarily **darkened** by a sudden power outage.

5. Skills **previously** acquired may __?__ serve us in good stead.

6. I often **confuse** one twin with the other. How are you able to __?__ them?

7. Admirers of the late leader faithfully observe the anniversaries of his **birth** and __?__.

8. The **stillness** of the early morning was abruptly broken by the __?__ of wailing sirens.

9. Angela was so __?__d that she could not be **placated**.

10. The two letters were mailed **at different times**, but they arrived __?__.

 ## EXERCISE 1.32: CONCISE WRITING

Express the thought of each sentence in **no more than four words**.

1. The long period of dry weather has come to an end.

2. Burglars searched through the cabinets, turning over all the contents.

3. The charges that they were making made her extremely angry.

4. Someone made a hole in that tank with a pointed instrument.

5. Light from the moon lit up the path that we were following.

 **EXERCISE 1.33:** SYNONYM SUMMARY

Each line, when completed, should have three words similar in meaning. The parentheses indicate the number of missing letters. On your answer paper, write the *complete* words. Answers to the first line are **search**, **ransack**, and **rummage**.

| | | |
|---|---|---|
| **1.** s (2) rch | (3) sack | rum (4) |
| **2.** per (1) l | dan (3) | (3) pardy |
| **3.** sp (2) d | (2) lerity | (4) city |
| **4.** (2) set | (4) turn | caps (3) |
| **5.** quarrel (4) | bel (4) rent | conten (2) ous |
| **6.** d (2) th | (2) mise | (2) cease |
| **7.** (2) rage | in (3) se | (2) furi (3) |
| **8.** p (2) rce | per (6) | punc (4) |
| **9.** clam (1) r | (2) roar | (1) i (1) |
| **10.** bri (2) ten | (2) ghten | (2) lumin (3) |
| **11.** arg (2) | (3) tend | (2) sert |
| **12.** (2) gether | (3) currently | simul (4) ously |
| **13.** sw (1) mp | delu (2) | in (2) date |
| **14.** different (2) te | rec (2) nize | disting (2) sh |
| **15.** (3) live | out (2) st | surv (3) |
| **16.** di (3) ge | (3) close | rev (2) l |
| **17.** (2) terward | lat (2) | (3) sequently |
| **18.** (2) large | ampl (1) fy | magn (3) |
| **19.** (2) danger | imp (4) | j (2) pard (3) |
| **20.** t (2) n | (1) ity | muni (2) pal |

**EXERCISE 1.34:** ANALOGIES

Which lettered pair of words—*a, b, c, d,* or *e*—most nearly expresses the same relationship as the capitalized pair?

1. AMPLIFY : ENLARGE
   - *a.* ban : allow
   - *b.* survive : perish
   - *c.* censure : commend
   - *d.* imperil : jeopardize
   - *e.* specify : incense

2. DROUGHT : RAIN
   - *a.* curiosity : interest
   - *b.* famine : hunger
   - *c.* aloofness : privacy
   - *d.* indifference : concern
   - *e.* frankness : honesty

3. HARE : CELERITY
   - *a.* lion : timidity
   - *b.* chicken : courage
   - *c.* ant : industriousness
   - *d.* bat : vision
   - *e.* spider : impatience

4. DECEASE : INTERMENT
   - *a.* cloudburst : inundation
   - *b.* index : preface
   - *c.* inauguration : election
   - *d.* evening : afternoon
   - *e.* childhood : infancy

   *Hint:* **Decease** is followed by **interment.**

5. CAPSIZE : RIGHT
   - *a.* raze : demolish
   - *b.* suffice : do
   - *c.* perforate : puncture
   - *d.* madden : incense
   - *e.* damage : repair

   *Hint:* To **capsize** is the opposite of to **right.**

6. TRESPASSER : TRAVERSE
   - *a.* builder : construct
   - *b.* vendor : sell
   - *c.* pedestrian : walk
   - *d.* transient : travel
   - *e.* thief : take

   *Hint:* A **trespasser traverses** another's property illegally.

7. RUMMAGE : SEARCH
   a. vanquish : defeat
   b. scorch : burn
   c. simmer : boil
   d. chill : freeze
   e. whisper : shout

8. CONTENDER : VIE
   a. emissary : send
   b. aggressor : fear
   c. outcast : reject
   d. victim : assault
   e. dissenter : object

9. SECRET : DIVULGE
   a. promise : keep
   b. thorn : remove
   c. warning : ignore
   d. defect : correct
   e. debt : pay

10. DIN : NOISE
    a. garment : shirt
    b. vanilla : flavor
    c. coin : dime
    d. color : purple
    e. tool : saw
    *Hint:* A **din** is a **kind of noise.**

 **EXERCISE 1.35:** COMPOSITION

Answer in a sentence or two.

1. Why might people in an agricultural country be famished after a long drought?
2. What information, divulged in a newspaper, could jeopardize a politician's career?
3. Is a din ever inaudible? Explain
4. What might help you survive a capsizing craft?
5. Describe a situation in which a citizen and a municipal employee might become contentious.

## *Pretest 6*

By using the commonsense method, determine the meaning of the italicized words below.

21. "Now, the point of the story is this: Did the tiger come out of that door, or did the lady? The more we *reflect* upon this question, the harder it is to answer."—FRANK R. STOCKTON

22. According to the rules, as soon as you lose a match, you are *eliminated* from the tournament.

23. In the midst of waxing the car, I became so *fatigued* that I had to stop for a rest.

24. Realizing that I was going the wrong way on a one-way street, I quickly *reversed* direction.

25. "And he took care of me and loved me from the first, and I'll *cleave* to him as long as he lives, and nobody shall ever come between him and me."—GEORGE ELIOT

26. My father is a sales agent, but I plan to go into some other *vocation*.

27. Tenants usually do not stop complaining about the lack of heat until they are *content* with the temperature.

28. The speaker kept the audience laughing with one *facetious* remark after another.

29. Ms. Muldoon thought I was to blame for the whispering, unaware that the girl behind me was the true *culprit*.

30. "We set out with a fresh wind ... never dreaming of danger, for indeed we saw not the slightest reason to *apprehend* it."
—EDGAR ALLAN POE

31. In your sentence, "She refused to accept my invitation to the party," omit the words "to accept"; they are *superfluous*.

32. In New York City, Philadelphia, Chicago, Los Angeles, and most other large *urban* centers, traffic is a serious problem.

33. Room 109 is too small for our club; it can *accommodate* only 35, and we have 48 members.

34. Everyone makes a mistake once in a while; no one is *infallible*.

35. "Now, in the whale-ship, it is not every one that goes in the boats. Some few hands are reserved, called ship-keepers, whose *province* it is to work the vessel while the boats are pursuing the whale."
—HERMAN MELVILLE

36. Don't dive there! The water is too *shallow*! Do you want to fracture your skull?

37. The detectives continued their search of the apartment, believing that the missing letter was *concealed* somewhere in it.

38. There are no clothing shops in the *vicinity* of the school; the nearest one is about a mile away.

39. To halt the *pilfering* of construction materials, the builder has decided to hire security guards.

40. "Then he advanced to the stockade, threw over his crutch, got a leg up, and with great vigor and skill succeeded in *surmounting* the fence and dropping safely to the other side."
   —Robert Louis Stevenson

## *Study Your Lesson Words,* **Group 6**

| WORD | MEANING AND TYPICAL USE |
|---|---|
| **accommodate** (*v.*)<br>ə-'kä-mə-ˌdāt | 1. hold or contain without crowding or inconvenience; have room for<br>   The new restaurant will *accommodate* 128 persons.<br><br>2. oblige; do a favor for; furnish with something desired<br>   I'm sorry I have no pen to lend you. Ask Norman. Perhaps he can *accommodate* you. |
| **apprehend** (*v.*)<br>ˌa-pri-'hend | 1. anticipate (foresee) with fear; dread<br>   Now I see how foolish I was to *apprehend* the outcome of the test. I passed easily.<br><br>2. arrest<br>   The escaped prisoners were *apprehended* as they tried to cross the border. |
| **apprehension** (*n.*) | alarm; uneasiness |
| **apprehensive** (*adj.*) | fearful; afraid |
| **cleave** (*v.*)<br>'klēv | stick; adhere; cling; be faithful<br>   Some of the residents are hostile to new ways; they *cleave* to the customs and traditions of the past. |

**conceal** (*v.*)
kən-'sēl

keep secret; withdraw from observation; hide; secrete
I answered all questions truthfully, for I had nothing to *conceal*.

**content** (*adj.*)
kän-'tent

satisfied; pleased
If you are not *content* with the merchandise, you may return it for an exchange or a refund.

**culprit** (*n.*)
'kəl-prət

one guilty of a fault or crime; offender; wrongdoer
The last time we were late for the party, I was the *culprit*. I wasn't ready when you called for me.

**eliminate** (*v.*)
i-'li-mə-,nāt

drop; exclude; remove; get rid of; rule out
The new director hopes to reduce expenses by *eliminating* unnecessary jobs.

**facetious** (*adj.*)
fə-'sē-shəs

given to joking; not to be taken seriously; witty; funny
Bea meant it when she said she was quitting the team. She was not being *facetious*.

**fatigue** (*v.*)
fə-'tēg

tire; exhaust; weary
Why not take the elevator? Climbing the stairs will *fatigue* you.

   **fatigue** (*n.*)

exhaustion; weariness

**infallible** (*adj.*)
,in-'fa-lə-bəl

incapable of being in error; sure; certain; absolutely reliable
When Phil disputes my answer or I question his, we take it to our math teacher. We consider her judgment *infallible*.

**pilfer** (*v.*)
'pil-fər

steal (in small amounts); purloin
The shoplifter was apprehended after *pilfering* several small articles.

**province** (*n.*)
'prä-vən(t)s

1. proper business or duty; sphere; jurisdiction
If your brother misbehaves, you have no right to punish him; that is not your *province*.

2. territory; region; domain

**reflect** (*v.*)
ri-'flekt

think carefully; meditate; contemplate
I could have given a much better answer if I had had the time to *reflect*.

**reverse** (*v.*)
ri-'vərs

turn completely about; change to the opposite position; revoke; annul
If found guilty, a person may appeal to a higher court in the hope that it will *reverse* the verdict.

**reverse** (*n.*)

setback; defeat; reversal
In 1805, Napoleon's fleet met with a serious *reverse* at the Battle of Trafalgar.

**reversible** (*adj.*)

able to be worn with either side out

**shallow** (*adj.*)
'sha-,lō

1. not deep
Nonswimmers must use the *shallow* part of the pool.

2. lacking intellectual depth; superficial; uncritical

**superfluous** (*adj.*)
sủ-'pər-flü-əs

beyond what is necessary or desirable; surplus; needless
We already have enough volunteers; additional help would be *superfluous*.

**surmount** (*v.*)
sər-'maúnt

conquer; overcome; climb over
At the end of the third quarter, the visitors were ahead by 18 points, a lead that our team was unable to *surmount*.

**urban** (*adj.*)
'ər-bən

having to do with cities or towns
In the United States today, the *urban* population far outnumbers the farm population.

**vicinity** (*n.*)
və-'si-nə-tē

neighborhood; locality; region about or near a place
Katerina lost her keys in the *vicinity* of Pine Street and Wyoming Avenue.

**vocation** (*n.*)
vō-'kā-shən

occupation; calling; business; trade; profession
Ruth will be studying to be an engineer. Bob plans to enter teaching. I, however, have not yet chosen a *vocation*.

## *Apply What You Have Learned*

 **EXERCISE 1.36:** SENTENCE COMPLETION

Write the lesson word that best fits the meaning of the sentence.

1. Most __?__ residents are __?__ to live in the city, despite its many problems.
2. The warden's staff carefully searched the __?__ of the zoo, hoping to __?__ the escaped tiger.
3. Only after practicing law for three years did Deirdre realize that medicine was her true __?__.
4. If you want your writing to be concise, you must __?__ all __?__ words.
5. The new auditorium can __?__ three thousand people.
6. The police are empowered to arrest, but not to punish, an alleged __?__ because punishment is the __?__ of the courts.
7. The weary runner __?__ed her exhaustion with a final burst of speed to win the six-mile race.
8. If building supplies are left unattended at the construction site, someone may __?__ them.
9. After pausing to __?__, the speaker __?__d his position because he realized he had been completely wrong.
10. You shouldn't have taken me seriously when I boasted that my judgment is __?__, for I was only being __?__.

 **EXERCISE 1.37:** SYNONYMS

Eliminate repetition by replacing the boldfaced word or words with a **synonym** from your lesson words.

1. Teaching children is not solely the **duty** of the schools; it is also a parental duty.
2. The new buses are roomier; they **have room for** thirty-six passengers.
3. There are no food shops in this neighborhood, but there are several in the **neighborhood** of the railroad station.

4. Even the experts are sometimes in error; no one is **absolutely incapable of error.**

5. A century ago, children generally followed the occupation of their elders, instead of choosing an **occupation** of their own.

6. It is not enough to get rid of spelling errors in your writing; you must also **get rid of** unnecessary words.

7. Prior to today's **defeat**, we were the only undefeated team in the league.

8. Physical exercise makes us very tired, though it does not seem to **tire** our gym instructor.

9. Progress is slow on the section of the highway near the city because of heavy **city** traffic.

10. The person initially blamed for the offense was not the real **offender.**

 **EXERCISE 1.38:** ANTONYMS

On your answer paper, enter the lesson word that is most nearly the **opposite** of the boldfaced word.

1. Here, the water is __?__, but a few feet out it is quite **deep.**

2. Weather forecasters are sometimes **wrong**; they are not __?__.

3. Are more helpers **necessary**, or would they just be __?__?

4. I felt **refreshed** by our stroll along the beach, but my companion was __?__d.

5. Some are __?__ with the outcome; others are **dissatisfied.**

6. The lawmakers decided to __?__ some of the jobs they had just voted to **create.**

7. If you say you are famished after that filling seven-course dinner, you cannot be **serious**; you are being __?__.

8. Let us __?__ to the principles of law and justice; we cannot **abandon** them.

9. Facts that for years were __?__ed from the public are now being **revealed.**

10. When the suspect was __?__ed, her attorneys petitioned a judge to **release** her.

**EXERCISE 1.39:** CONCISE WRITING

Express the thought of each sentence in **no more than four words**.

1. Are these coats able to be worn with either side out?
2. The opinions that he expresses are lacking in intellectual depth.
3. Most of the hotels have rooms for guests staying for only a short time.
4. The remarks that she made were not intended to be taken seriously.
5. We made a complete about-face and embraced the opposite point of view.

 **EXERCISE 1.40:** SYNONYM SUMMARY

Each line, when completed, should have three words similar in meaning. The parentheses indicate the number of missing letters. On your answer paper, write the *complete* words. Answers to the first line are **tire**, **exhaust**, and **fatigue**.

| | | |
|---|---|---|
| 1. t (1) re | ex (1) aust | fati (3) |
| 2. conq (2) r | (4) come | (3) mount |
| 3. (2) raid | appre (3) sive | fear (3) |
| 4. occu (2) tion | (3) fession | (2) cation |
| 5. satisf (2) d | pl (2) sed | con (2) nt |
| 6. n (2) ghborhood | (2) cality | vi (3) ity |
| 7. med (1) tate | con (3) plate | (2) flect |
| 8. h (1) de | sec (2) te | con (1) eal |
| 9. wit (2) | fun (1) y | face (3) us |
| 10. (2) feat | (3) back | (2) verse |
| 11. (2) move | ex (3) de | e (3) inate |
| 12. st (2) l | (3) loin | pilf (2) |
| 13. need (4) | surp (2) s | su (3) fluous |
| 14. cl (1) ng | (2) here | cl (2) ve |

| 15. h (1) ld | cont (2) n | accom (2) date |
|---|---|---|
| 16. (2) critical | superfi (3) l | shal (3) |
| 17. s (1) re | cert (2) n | inf (3) ible |
| 18. of (3) der | wrongd (2) r | (3) prit |
| 19. d (1) ty | b (1) s (1) ness | prov (4) |
| 20. (1) larm | (2) easiness | ap (3) hension |

 **EXERCISE 1.41:** ANALOGIES

Which lettered pair of words—*a, b, c, d,* or *e*—most nearly expresses the same relationship as the capitalized pair?

**1.** SHALLOW : DEEP
  *a.* remote : distant
  *b.* frigid : cold
  *c.* scarce : abundant
  *d.* transient : brief
  *e.* depressing : sad

**2.** PROVINCE : COUNTRY
  *a.* story : edifice
  *b.* island : sea
  *c.* month : day
  *d.* hand : finger
  *e.* flock : bird

**3.** OBLIGING : ACCOMMODATE
  *a.* timorous : complain
  *b.* reticent : gossip
  *c.* industrious : loaf
  *d.* contentious : argue
  *e.* obstinate : yield

**4.** CULPRIT : REPRIMAND
  *a.* victim : suffer
  *b.* hostage : release
  *c.* tutor : instruct
  *d.* donor : give
  *e.* tenant : rent

**5.** SHOPLIFTER : PILFER
  *a.* dissenter : concur
  *b.* scofflaw : obey
  *c.* transient : remain
  *d.* perjurer : lie
  *e.* vagrant : reside

6. APPREHENSIVE : CONFIDENCE
   *a.* appreciative : gratitude
   *b.* cordial : warmth
   *c.* diplomatic : tact
   *d.* polite : manners
   *e.* spineless : determination

7. CONTENT : DISSATISFIED
   *a.* normal : atypical
   *b.* lukewarm : tepid
   *c.* rare : extraordinary
   *d.* enthusiastic : zealous
   *e.* despotic : authoritarian

8. URBAN : CITY
   *a.* metropolitan : town
   *b.* suburban : nation
   *c.* global : world
   *d.* national : region
   *e.* municipal : state

9. MEDITATE : MIND
   *a.* grope : eyes
   *b.* kneel : ground
   *c.* swelter : perspiration
   *d.* speak : tongue
   *e.* yell : din

10. REFLECT : CONTEMPLATION
    *a.* confront : timidity
    *b.* plan : confusion
    *c.* confess : guilt
    *d.* swerve : collision
    *e.* intimidate : coercion
    *Hint:* When we **reflect**, we engage in **contemplation**.

 **EXERCISE 1.42:** COMPOSITION

Answer in a sentence or two.

1. Why do stores try to apprehend people who pilfer?
2. Do workers feel apprehensive if their jobs may be eliminated? Why?
3. Tell what a culprit might try to conceal.
4. Why would it be superfluous to doubt an infallible person?
5. Does surmounting a problem make you feel content? Explain.

# Mixed Contexts

This section deals with all types of contexts studied so far—those containing a contrasting word, a similar word, or a commonsense clue. On your answer paper, write the meaning of the italicized word.

## Pretest 7

1. "You shall hear how Hiawatha/Prayed and fasted in the forest,/ Not for greater skill in hunting,/Not for greater *craft* in fishing. . . ."
   —HENRY WADSWORTH LONGFELLOW.

2. If you lose the key to your apartment, go to the superintendent. He has a *duplicate* of every key in our building.

3. Geri didn't notice me in the crowd, but she spotted my brother, who is *conspicuous* because of his red hair.

4. Children who do not want their cereal should not be required to finish it against their *volition.*

5. "Daring burglaries by armed men, and highway robberies, took place in the capital itself every night; families were publicly cautioned not to go out of town without removing their furniture to upholsterers' warehouses for *security.*"—CHARLES DICKENS

6. The team's uniforms were *immaculate* at the start of play, but by the end of the first quarter they were dirty with mud.

7. Let's wait. It's raining too hard now. As soon as it *abates,* we'll make a dash for the car.

8. Cows, pigs, and chickens are familiar sights to a *rural* youngster, but they are rarely seen by an urban child.

9. A pound of *miniature* chocolates contains many more pieces than a pound of the ordinary size.

10. "Stubb was the second mate. He was a native of Cape Cod; and hence, according to local usage, was called a Cape-Codman. A happy-go-lucky; neither *craven* nor valiant."—HERMAN MELVILLE

11. I expected the medicine to alleviate my cough, but it seems to have *aggravated* it.

12. After their quarrel, Cynthia and Warren didn't talk to each other until Ann succeeded in *reconciling* them.

13. "The Man Without a Country," by Edward Everett Hale, is not a true story; the incidents and characters are entirely *fictitious*.

14. When traveling in Canada, you may exchange American money for Canadian *currency* at any bank.

15. Some students would probably collapse if they had to run two miles; they don't have the *stamina*.

16. Donald was defeated in last year's election, but that won't *deter* him from running again.

17. Several neutral countries are trying to get the *belligerent* nations to stop fighting.

18. Company and union officials have been in conference around the clock in an attempt to reach an *accord* on wages.

19. The fight might have been serious if a passerby had not *intervened* and sent the participants on their way.

20. Our band now has four players and, if you join, it will become a *quintet*.

## Study Your Lesson Words, **Group 7**

| WORD | MEANING AND TYPICAL USE |
|---|---|
| **abate** (*v.*)<br>ə-'bāt | 1. become less; decrease; diminish; let up<br>　　The water shortage is *abating*, but it is still a matter of some concern. |
| | 2. make less; reduce; moderate<br>　　Helen's close defeat in the tennis tournament has not *abated* her zeal for the game. |
| **abatement** (*n.*) | slackening; letup |
| **accord** (*n.*)<br>ə-'kȯrd | agreement; understanding<br>　　If both sides to the dispute can be brought to the conference table, perhaps they can come to an *accord*. |

**accord** (*v.*)

agree; correspond
Check to see if your definition *accords* with the one in the dictionary.

**aggravate** (*v.*)
'a-grə-,vāt

make worse; worsen; intensify
If your sunburn itches, don't scratch; that will only *aggravate* it.

**belligerent** (*adj.*)
bə-'li-jə-rənt

fond of fighting; warlike; combative
Bert still has a tendency to settle his arguments with his fists. When will he learn that it's childish to be so *belligerent*?

**conspicuous** (*adj.*)
kən-'spi-kyə-wəs

noticeable; easily seen; prominent; striking
Among Manhattan's skyscrapers, the Empire State Building is *conspicuous* for its superior height.

**craft** (*n.*)
'kraft

1. skill; art; trade
The weavers of Oriental rugs are famous for their remarkable *craft*.

2. skill or art in a bad sense; guile
The Greeks took Troy by *craft*; they used the trick of the wooden horse.

**crafty** (*adj.*)

sly; cunning

**craven** (*adj.*)
'krā-vən

cowardly; dastardly; pusillanimous; gutless
Henry Fleming thought he would be a hero, but as the fighting began he fled from the field in *craven* fear.

**craven** (*n.*)

coward; dastard

**currency** (*n.*)
'kər-ən(t)-sē

something in circulation as a medium of exchange; money; coin; bank notes
Some New England tribes used beads as *currency*.

**deter** (*v.*)
di-'tər

turn aside through fear; discourage; hinder; keep back
The heavy rain did not *deter* people from coming to the play. Nearly every seat was occupied.

**duplicate** (*n.*)
'dü-pli-kət

one of two things exactly alike; copy; reproduction
If the photocopying machine had been working, I could have made a *duplicate* of my history notes for my friend who was absent.

**fictitious** (*adj.*)
fik-'ti-shəs

1. made up; imaginary; not real
In JOHNNY TREMAIN, there are *fictitious* characters like Johnny and Rab, as well as real ones, like Samuel Adams and Paul Revere.

2. false; pretended; assumed for the purpose of deceiving
The suspect said she lived at 423 Green Street, but she later admitted it was a *fictitious* address.

**immaculate** (*adj.*)
i-'ma-kyə-lət

spotless; without a stain; absolutely clean; unblemished
The curtains were spotless; the tablecloth was *immaculate,* too.

**intervene** (*v.*)
,in-tər-'vēn

1. occur between; be between; come between
More than two months *intervene* between a president's election and the day he takes office.

2. come between to help settle a quarrel; intercede; interfere
Ralph is unhappy that I stepped into the dispute between him and his brother. He did not want me to *intervene.*

**intervention** (*n.*)

interference; interposition

**miniature** (*adj.*)
'mi-nē-ə-,chủər

small; tiny
Kim has a *miniature* stapler in her bag. It takes up very little room.

**quintet** (*n.*)
kwin-'tet

group of five
A basketball team, because it has five players, is often called a *quintet.*

**reconcile** (*v.*)
're-kən-,sīl

1. cause to be friends again; restore to friendship or harmony
Pat and Tom are friends again. I wonder who *reconciled* them.

2. settle; resolve
We are friends again; we have *reconciled* our differences.

**rural** (*adj.*)
'rür-əl

having to do with the country (as distinguished from the city or town)
    Six inches of snow fell in the city and up to fourteen inches in the *rural* areas upstate.

**security** (*n.*)
si-'kyür-ə-tē

1. safety; protection
    Guests are advised to deposit their valuables in the hotel's vault for greater *security*.
    *Security* has been tightened at airports.

2. measures taken to assure protection against attack, crime, sabotage, etc.

**stamina** (*n.*)
'sta-mə-nə

strength; vigor; endurance
    Swimming the English Channel is a feat that requires considerable *stamina*.

**volition** (*n.*)
vō-'li-shən

act of willing or choosing; will; choice
    Did the employer dismiss him, or did he leave of his own *volition*?

## Apply What You Have Learned

 **EXERCISE 1.43:** SENTENCE COMPLETION

On your answer paper, write the lesson word that best fits the meaning of the sentence.

1. Only when the United Nations __?_d did the two __?__ nations agree to stop fighting.
2. It is almost certain that the bitter rivals would not have reached a(n) __?__ of their own __?__.
3. Geraldine still lacks the __?__ to go on a ski trip; her miserable cold has not __?_d.
4. Since the assassination attempt, the __?__ surrounding the prime minister has been particularly __?__.
5. The two singers should __?__ their differences; they made much better music together than they now do apart.
6. The jazz __?__ has a drummer, a saxophonist, a bassist, a trumpeter, and a pianist.

7. At auction, the 1856 British Guiana one-penny postage stamp will command a huge price because it has no ＿?＿.

8. The ＿?＿ of stained-glass painting flourished during the thirteenth century.

9. I fear that my intervention will only ＿?＿ an already difficult situation.

10. Residents of the farming county insist that the construction of a large airport will not ＿?＿ with the ＿?＿ life they are determined to preserve.

 **EXERCISE 1.44:** SYNONYMS

Eliminate repetition by replacing the boldfaced word or words with a **synonym** from your lesson words.

1. We can settle our dispute without interference; please do not **interfere**.

2. Some urban residents who move to the country find it hard to adjust to **country** life.

3. A few of the strikers do not agree with the **agreement** tentatively reached with their employer.

4. Insert the original into the copier, and in seconds you will have a clear **copy**.

5. Antitheft devices that discourage an amateur thief may not **discourage** a professional burglar.

6. I could barely notice the moon an hour ago, but now it is much more **noticeable**.

7. The dining room is a model of cleanliness; the tablecloths and the curtains are **spotlessly clean**.

8. Since his recent excuses have been shown to be false, we suspect his earlier ones may have been **false**, too.

9. What can be done to **make** these two ex-friends **friendly again**?

10. The Armed Forces protect us. Without them we would have no **protection** against aggression.

**EXERCISE 1.45:** ANTONYMS

On your answer paper, enter the lesson word that is most nearly the **opposite** of the boldfaced word or words.

1. By no stretch of the imagination can a(n) _?_ withdrawal be viewed as a **valorous** deed.
2. No _?_ was reached; the meeting ended in **dissension**.
3. With a worrier, _?_ problems sometimes assume **mammoth** proportions.
4. It is hard to understand why a **friendly** neighbor like Alicia should suddenly turn _?_.
5. By reducing the occupants' exposure to **danger**, buckled seatbelts provide a measure of _?_.
6. Employers began to **augment** their staffs as the recession _?_d.
7. The stop sign was not _?_; an overhanging tree limb made the warning sign **hard to see**.
8. At mealtime, an infant's _?_ bib soon becomes **full of stains**.
9. Weak security does not _?_ attack but tends to **encourage** it.
10. Intervention by outsiders may _?_, rather than **alleviate**, the tension between the foes.

 **EXERCISE 1.46:** CONCISE WRITING

Express the thought of each sentence in **no more than four words.**

1. The paper money that they have been using as a medium of exchange is not worth anything.
2. Hostile engagements are continuing to take place without any sign of letting up.
3. Living in the country does not cost a great deal of money.
4. The reputation that she has achieved with people in general does not have a single stain or blemish.
5. Are the measures that we have taken to protect ourselves against attack adequate to do the job?

**EXERCISE 1.47:** SYNONYM SUMMARY

Each line, when completed, should have three words similar in meaning. The parentheses indicate the number of missing letters. On your answer paper, write the *complete* words.

| | | |
|---|---|---|
| **1.** saf (1) ty | (3) tection | (2) curity |
| **2.** notic (2) ble | prom (1) nent | conspic (4) |
| **3.** stain (4) | (2) blemished | im (4) late |
| **4.** sett (2) | rec (3) ile | (2) solve |
| **5.** disc (2) rage | hind (2) | d (1) t (1) r |
| **6.** str (3) th | vig (2) | stam (3) |
| **7.** combat (3) | (3) like | bel (3) erent |
| **8.** let (1) p | slack (2) ing | (1) bat (1) ment |
| **9.** interf (3) | in (3) vene | (2) terc (3) |
| **10.** cr (2) ty | cun (4) | (1) ly |
| **11.** (1) gree | (3) respond | (2) cord |
| **12.** fal (2) | (3) ginary | ficti (5) |
| **13.** (1) ill | choi (2) | (2) lition |
| **14.** gutl (3) | (3) illanimous | (1) rave (1) |
| **15.** wors (2) | intens (3) | (2) grav (3) |
| **16.** sm (3) | (2) ny | min (2) ture |
| **17.** mon (2) | (1) oi (1) | curr (4) |
| **18.** (1) opy | (2) prod (2) tion | (4) icate |
| **19.** dast (3) | cow (3) | (3) ven |
| **20.** in (3) ference | (5) vention | (2) terpo (2) tion |

**EXERCISE 1.48:** ANALOGIES

Which lettered pair of words—*a, b, c, d,* or *e*—most nearly expresses the same relationship as the capitalized pair? Write the letter of your answer on your answer paper.

1. QUINTET : FIVE
   - *a.* decade : year
   - *b.* dozen : gross
   - *c.* score : twenty
   - *d.* liter : quart
   - *e.* ounce : pound

2. RURAL : COUNTRY
   - *a.* urban : population
   - *b.* local : vicinity
   - *c.* initial : conclusion
   - *d.* terminal : beginning
   - *e.* parallel : line

3. IMMACULATE : SPOT
   - *a.* infinite : end
   - *b.* significant : meaning
   - *c.* erroneous : fault
   - *d.* unanimous : support
   - *e.* mute : silence

4. SENTINEL : SECURITY
   - *a.* child : supervision
   - *b.* motorist : insurance
   - *c.* coach : competition
   - *d.* proprietor : risk
   - *e.* companion : company

5. PROMINENT : SEE
   - *a.* cumbersome : carry
   - *b.* complex : understand
   - *c.* fragile : break
   - *d.* inconspicuous : notice
   - *e.* faint : hear

6. AGGRAVATE : WORSE
   - *a.* facilitate : difficult
   - *b.* rectify : correct
   - *c.* nullify : valid
   - *d.* elucidate : obscure
   - *e.* complicate : simple

7. WRITING : CRAFT
   - *a.* skill : reading
   - *b.* science : biology
   - *c.* patience : virtue
   - *d.* education : ignorance
   - *e.* sobriety : fault

**8.** BELLIGERENT : CONTENTION
- *a.* craven : valor
- *b.* underhanded : deception
- *c.* frank : concealment
- *d.* reserved : conversation
- *e.* honest : fraud

**9.** RECONCILE : ESTRANGE
- *a.* succeed : precede
- *b.* vanquish : surmount
- *c.* abandon : neglect
- *d.* abate : moderate
- *e.* accommodate : oblige

**10.** CHICKEN : PUSILLANIMOUS
- *a.* hawk: timid
- *b.* tortoise : speedy
- *c.* swan : awkward
- *d.* dove : warlike
- *e.* bat : blind

 **EXERCISE 1.49:** COMPOSITION

Answer in a sentence or two.

1. Describe how being belligerent might aggravate an argument.
2. If two friends weren't speaking to each other, how might you intervene to reconcile them?
3. Would making miniature dollhouse furniture require special craft? Explain.
4. What might families in a rural area do to guard their security?
5. Would you be making a fictitious claim if you said your bedroom was immaculate? Why or why not?

## Pretest 8

Write the meaning of the italicized word.

21. "...I doubted not that I might one day, by taking a voyage, see with my own eyes the little fields, houses, and trees, the *diminutive* people, the tiny cows...."—CHARLOTTE BRONTË
22. Walter left, saying he would return *presently*, but he was gone for a long time.

23. If you miss the bus, you have the choice of walking or waiting an hour for the next bus. There is no other *alternative*.

24. My aim for this weekend is to finish my history and English assignments. I shall be disappointed if I cannot achieve this *objective*.

25. "In most books, the *I*, or first person, is omitted; in this it will be *retained*...."—HENRY DAVID THOREAU

26. The Goodmans don't mind leaving their children in your *custody* because you are an excellent babysitter.

27. Is it fair for the partner who made the smaller investment to receive the *major* share of the profits?

28. Most people will change their minds when shown they are wrong, but not Timothy. He is too *opinionated*.

29. Last year, I shared a gym locker with another student. Now I have one *exclusively* for myself.

30. "Perceiving myself in a *blunder*, I attempted to correct it."
—EMILY BRONTË

31. Some volcanoes have erupted in recent times; others have been *dormant* for many years.

32. Frequent absences will make you fall behind in your work and *imperil* your chances of passing.

33. There were no soft drinks. The only *beverages* on the menu were milk, coffee, tea, and hot chocolate.

34. Two girls at the next table started quarreling, but I couldn't learn what their *controversy* was about.

35. "As the news of my arrival spread through the kingdom, it brought *prodigious* numbers of rich, idle, and curious people to see me; so that the villages were almost emptied...."—JONATHAN SWIFT

36. Everyone in the class must take the final examination to pass the course. No student is *exempt*.

37. Don't put off what you should do today to "tomorrow," or "next week," or simply "later." Stop *procrastinating*.

38. My fears of the dentist were *dispelled* when I had a relatively painless first visit.

39. Dad fell behind in his work at the office because of a *protracted* illness lasting several weeks.

40. "For though Lorna's father was a nobleman of high and goodly *lineage*, her mother was of yet more ancient and renowned descent...."—RICHARD D. BLACKMORE

## *Study Your Lesson Words,* **Group 8**

| WORD | MEANING AND TYPICAL USE |
|---|---|
| **alternative** (*n.*)<br>òl-'tər-nə-tiv | 1. choice; one of two or more things offered for choice<br>If given the choice of making either an oral or a written report, I would pick the second *alternative*.<br><br>2. other or remaining choice |
| **beverage** (*n.*)<br>'bev-rij | drink; liquid for drinking<br>Orange juice is a healthful *beverage*. |
| **blunder** (*n.*)<br>'blən-dər | mistake or error caused by stupidity or carelessness<br>Have you ever committed the *blunder* of mailing a letter without a postage stamp? |
| **controversy** (*n.*)<br>'kän-trə-vər-sē | dispute; quarrel; debate; strife<br>The Republicans and the Democrats have been engaged in a *controversy* over which party is responsible for the increased taxes. |
| **controversial** (*adj.*) | arousing controversy; contentious; disputatious |
| **custody** (*n.*)<br>'kəs-tə-dē | care; safekeeping; guardianship<br>The treasurer has *custody* of our club's financial records. |
| **diminutive** (*adj.*)<br>də-'mi-nyə-tiv | below average size; small; tiny<br>To an observer in an airplane high over the city, even the largest buildings seem *diminutive*. |
| **dispel** (*v.*)<br>di-'spel | drive away by scattering; scatter; disperse<br>The two officers were commended for their skill in *dispelling* the mob and preventing violence. |
| **dormant** (*adj.*)<br>'dòr-mənt | inactive, as if asleep; sleeping; quiet; sluggish; resting<br>In early spring, new buds begin to appear on trees and shrubs that have been *dormant* all winter. |

**exclusively** (*adv.*)
iks-'klü-siv-lē

solely; without sharing with others; undividedly
    Mrs. Lopez had bought the computer for all of her children, but the oldest behaved as if it were *exclusively* his.

**exclusive** (*adj.*)

sole; single; unshared

**exempt** (*adj.*)
ig-'zem(p)t

freed or released from a duty, liability, or rule to which others are subject
    A certain portion of each person's income is legally *exempt* from taxation.

**exemption** (*n.*)

immunity; impunity

**imperil** (*v.*)
im-'per-əl

endanger; jeopardize
    The fishing vessel was *imperiled* by high winds, but it managed to reach port safely.

**lineage** (*n.*)
'li-nē-ij

descent (in a direct line from a common ancestor); ancestry; family; extraction
    A study of Franklin D. Roosevelt's *lineage* shows that he was descended from a Dutch ancestor who settled in America about 1638.

**major** (*adj.*)
'mā-jər

greater; larger; more important; principal
    When the *major* companies in an industry raise prices, the smaller ones usually follow suit.

**objective** (*n.*)
əb-'jek-tiv

aim or end (of an action); goal
    Our fund has already raised $650; its *objective* is $1000.

**objective** (*adj.*)

involving facts, rather than personal feelings or opinions
    College admissions committees consider two kinds of data: subjective evidence, such as letters of recommendation; and *objective* evidence, such as your scores on college-entrance tests.

**opinionated** (*adj.*)
ə-'pin-yə-,nā-təd

unduly attached to one's own opinion; obstinate; stubborn
    If you keep arguing that you are right, in the face of overwhelming objective evidence that you are wrong, you are *opinionated*.

**presently** (*adv.*)
'pre-z⁼nt-lē

in a little time; shortly; soon; before long
   We won't have to wait long for our bus. It will
be here *presently.*

**procrastinate** (*v.*)
prə-'kras-tə-,nāt

put things off; delay; postpone; defer; dawdle
   When a book is due, return it to the library
promptly. Otherwise you will be fined 10¢ for
every day you *procrastinate.*

**prodigious** (*adj.*)
prə-'di-jəs

extraordinary in size, quantity, or extent; vast;
enormous; huge; amazing
   The average American city requires a *prodigious*
amount of fresh milk daily.

**prodigy** (*n.*)

something extraordinary; wonder; phenomenon

**protract** (*v.*)
prō-'trakt

draw out; lengthen in time; prolong; extend
   The visitors had planned to stay for a few hours
only, but they were persuaded to *protract* their
visit.

**retain** (*v.*)
ri-'tān

keep; continue to have, hold, or use
   The corporation will close its restaurants but
*retain* its most profitable clothing stores.

**retentive** (*adj.*)

having the power to retain or remember;
tenacious
   Dora has a *retentive* memory.

## *Apply What You Have Learned*

 **EXERCISE 1.50:** SENTENCE COMPLETION

Write the lesson word that best fits the meaning of the sentence.

1. When Reuben learned Friday that the library would close for the
   weekend, he realized what a(n) __?__ it was to have __?__d with his
   research paper.

2. We must stop quarreling. If this committee spends another hour in
   __?__ it will be unable to achieve its __?__.

3. To __?__ the workers' apprehensions of losing their jobs, the new
   employer promised to __?__ all of them.

4. Most of the time, Pam has to share a swimming lane with others, but today she had one __?__ for herself.

5. Though many of the secondary roads are impassable, the __?__ highways have all been plowed.

6. Replacing the old bridge will cost a(n) __?__ amount of money, but there is no practical __?__.

7. Neither side is inclined to __?__ the dispute much longer; a settlement is expected __?__.

8. In the days of special privilege, individuals of royal __?__ were generally __?__ from taxation.

9. We stopped for a(n) __?__ to quench our thirst.

10. When the parents are at work, the children are in the __?__ of their grandparents.

 ## EXERCISE 1.51: SYNONYMS

Eliminate repetition by replacing the boldfaced word or words with a **synonym** from your lesson words.

1. You can leave the dogs in Antoine's **care**; he will take excellent care of them.

2. Elections with only one choice are a farce because the voters have no **other choice**.

3. Grace cannot be held solely responsible if the accident was not **solely** her fault.

4. People make the common **mistake** of mistaking one of the twins for the other.

5. Two quarrelsome members are responsible for most of the **quarreling** in the club.

6. We decided not to **prolong** our conversation since we had been on the telephone long enough.

7. When asked what I wanted to drink, I asked for a cold **drink**.

8. You may have the original, and we will **keep** the copy.

9. She traces her ancestors back several generations, but I know little about my own **ancestry**.

10. People with an enormous appetite for knowledge usually do an **enormous** amount of reading.

**EXERCISE 1.52:** ANTONYMS

On your answer paper, enter the lesson word that is most nearly the **opposite** of the boldfaced word or words.

1. In spring, many living things that have been __?__ all winter gradually become **active** again.

2. Unfortunately, __?__ has developed; there had been a period of total **absence of strife**.

3. The residents __?__ed by the flood are now **out of danger**.

4. When her term expires, she will **give up** the presidency but __?__ her seat on the executive board.

5. We were planning to __?__ our stay, when an unforeseen shortage of funds caused us instead to **curtail** it.

6. Some **minor** issues remain to be settled, but the __?__ ones have all been resolved.

7. When that __?__ blue spruce was planted a score of years ago, it was a **tiny** seedling.

8. Everything you buy is not necessarily **subject** to the sales tax; food purchases, for example, may be __?__.

9. In the search for truth, __?__ considerations are more reliable than those **based on feelings or opinions**.

10. For every person who does **not put off today's work to some other time**, there are many who __?__.

 **EXERCISE 1.53:** CONCISE WRITING

Express the thought of each sentence in **no more than four words**.

1. Does this belong to you alone and to no one else?

2. They will bring the meeting to a close in a little while.

3. What are the choices that are being offered to us?

4. The individuals on both sides are unduly attached to their own opinions.

5. We presented evidence that is based on fact, rather than on what people think or feel.

**EXERCISE 1.54:** SYNONYM SUMMARY

Each line, when completed, should have three words similar in meaning. The parentheses indicate the number of missing letters. On your answer paper, write the *complete* words.

| | | |
|---|---|---|
| 1. d (1) scent | an (1) estry | lin (2) ge |
| 2. prol (1) ng | (2) tend | (3) tract |
| 3. err (2) | (3) take | (2) under |
| 4. s (2) n | (2) ortly | (3) sently |
| 5. dr (1) nk | liq (2) d | (1) ever (3) |
| 6. go (1) l | (2) m | (2) jective |
| 7. s (1) le | (2) shared | ex (3) sive |
| 8. c (1) re | (2) ardianship | (1) us (4) |
| 9. d (1) lay | d (2) dle | (7) tinate |
| 10. d (1) sp (1) rse | (1) cat (3) | (2) spel |
| 11. (2) danger | (3) pardize | (2) peril |
| 12. extr (2) rdinary | (1) norm (3) | (3) dig (2) us |
| 13. (1) mall | t (1) ny | (2) min (1) tive |
| 14. h (1) ld | k (2) p | (2) tain |
| 15. (2) munity | imp (1) nity | (3) mption |
| 16. stub (4) | (2) stin (1) te | opin (2) nated |
| 17. r (1) sting | slug (2) sh | dorm (3) |
| 18. content (4) | dis (2) tatious | (3) troversial |
| 19. l (1) rger | princip (2) | (2) jor |
| 20. w (1) nder | (2) enomenon | (3) digy |

**EXERCISE 1.55:** ANALOGIES

Which lettered pair of words—*a, b, c, d,* or *e*—most nearly expresses the same relationship as the capitalized pair? Write the letter of your answer on your answer paper.

1. MILK : BEVERAGE
   - *a.* utensil : fork
   - *b.* spider : web
   - *c.* distance : mile
   - *d.* moccasin : shoe
   - *e.* metal : aluminum

2. CONTROVERSY : HARMONY
   - *a.* expertise : experience
   - *b.* shallowness : depth
   - *c.* wealth : means
   - *d.* tact : judgment
   - *e.* inundation : precipitation

3. OPINIONATED : LISTEN
   - *a.* docile : obey
   - *b.* extravagant : squander
   - *c.* alert : observe
   - *d.* submissive : yield
   - *e.* suspicious : trust

4. PRODIGIOUS : AMAZEMENT
   - *a.* irrational : admiration
   - *b.* subjective : infallibility
   - *c.* controversial : accord
   - *d.* inconspicuous : attention
   - *e.* outrageous : indignation

5. SCATTER : DISPEL
   - *a.* adjourn : convene
   - *b.* divulge : secrete
   - *c.* expel : admit
   - *d.* meddle : intervene
   - *e.* disoblige : accommodate

6. TENACIOUS : HOLD
   - *a.* belligerent : contend
   - *b.* permissive : ban
   - *c.* persistent : relinquish
   - *d.* disputatious : assent
   - *e.* reticent : inform

7. BLUNDER : IGNORANCE
   - *a.* infection : fever
   - *b.* flu : virus
   - *c.* needle : perforation
   - *d.* rumor : panic
   - *e.* explosion : din

8. EXEMPTION : PRIVILEGE
   - *a.* exclamation : sigh
   - *b.* asset : liability
   - *c.* interval : fortnight
   - *d.* reading : skill
   - *e.* vehicle : van

9. INDOLENT : PROCRASTINATE
   - *a.* implacable : forgive
   - *b.* conservative : change
   - *c.* curious : inquire
   - *d.* timid : protest
   - *e.* indifferent : care

10. SHIFTLESS : OBJECTIVE
    - *a.* crafty : cunning
    - *b.* wary : caution
    - *c.* disgruntled : complaint
    - *d.* partial : prejudice
    - *e.* callous : sympathy

 **EXERCISE 1.56:** COMPOSITION

Answer in a sentence or two.

1. Can procrastinating imperil a student's success in school? How?
2. Do great writers and artists have diminutive or prodigious talents? Explain.
3. Why do opinionated people often find themselves in controversies?
4. Describe one of the major blunders of your life.
5. Is it better to dispel or retain fears about your ability to succeed? Why?

*Chapter*

# 2

# Enlarging Vocabulary Through Central Ideas

## What is a central idea?

Examine these words: *devour, edible, glutton, luscious, palatable, voracious.*
What do they have in common?

As you may have guessed, these words revolve around the idea of
*eating.* We may therefore call *EATING* the central idea of this word
group.

Every central idea discussed in this book has several words that we
can associate with it. For example, under *DISAGREEMENT* we may
*include antagonize, discord, discrepancy, dissent, irreconcilable,* and *wrangle.*
Similarly, we may group *bulwark, dynamic, impregnable, invigorate, robust,*
and *vigor* under the central idea *STRENGTH.*

In this chapter you will enlarge your vocabulary by learning words
grouped under twenty central ideas like *EATING, DISAGREEMENT,* and
*STRENGTH.*

## Why study words through central ideas?

When you study vocabulary by the central-ideas method, you are dealing with groups of related words. Each word you learn helps you with
some other word, or words, in the group. Consider, for example, the
words *frugal* and *economize* that you will meet under POVERTY. *Frugal*
means "thrifty" or "avoiding waste." To *economize* is to "cut down
expenses" or to "be frugal." Notice that *economize* can strengthen your

grasp of *frugal,* and vice versa. As a result, you should be better able to understand, as well as use, both *frugal* and *economize.* By the interesting central-ideas method, you can effectively learn many words in a short time.

### How to use this vocabulary chapter

To get the most out of this chapter, follow these suggestions:

1. Notice the spelling. Then pronounce the word, using the pronunciation indicated below it.

2. Learn all the definitions in the MEANING column.

3. Pay particular attention to the TYPICAL USE column. Each sentence has been constructed to help you fix in mind the meaning and use of a new word. Follow up by constructing, at least in your mind, a similar sentence using your own context.

4. Do the exercises thoughtfully, not mechanically. Then review each word you have missed.

5. Make a point of *using* newly learned words whenever appropriate: in class discussions, informal conversations, compositions, and letters. A new word does not become a part of your vocabulary until you have *used* it a few times.

# CENTRAL IDEAS 1–5

## Pretest 1

Write the *letter* of the best answer.

1. If you are *versatile,* you __?__.
   (A) like sports   (B)  are easily angered
   (C)  can do many things well

**2.** You have no reason to be *apprehensive*. Stop __?__.

    (A) boasting   (B) worrying   (C) arguing

**3.** When you are *rash,* you are __?__.

    (A) taking risks   (B) not in a hurry   (C) too cautious

**4.** *Affluent* people are __?__.

    (A) polite   (B) poor   (C) very wealthy

**5.** Since we have __?__, we don't have to be *frugal*.

    (A) no means   (B) more than enough   (C) very little

---

THE ANSWERS ARE
**1.** C  **2.** B  **3.** A  **4.** C  **5.** B

---

As you work through Central Ideas 1–5, you will become familiar with several interesting and useful words, including the italicized words on which you have just been tested.

## 1. Skill

| WORD | MEANING AND TYPICAL USE |
|---|---|
| **adroit** (*adj.*)<br>ə-'dròit | expert in using the hands or mind; skillful; clever; deft; dexterous<br>    Our *adroit* passing enabled us to score four touchdowns. |
| **ambidextrous** (*adj.*)<br>ˌam-bi-'dek-strəs | able to use both hands equally well<br>    Ruth is an *ambidextrous* hitter; she can bat right-handed or left-handed. |
| **apprentice** (*n.*)<br>ə-'pren-təs | person learning an art or trade under a skilled worker; learner; beginner; novice; tyro<br>    Young Ben Franklin learned the printing trade by serving as an *apprentice* to his half brother James. |
| **aptitude** (*n.*)<br>'ap-tə-ˌtüd | natural tendency to learn or understand; bent; talent<br>    Cindy is not clumsy with tools; she has mechanical *aptitude*. |

**craftsperson** (*n.*)
'krafts-,pər-s°n

skilled worker; artisan
    To build a house, you need the services of carpenters, bricklayers, plumbers, and electricians; each one must be a skilled *craftsperson.*

**dexterity** (*n.*)
dek-'ster-ə-tē

skill in using the hands or mind; deftness; adroitness; expertise
    You can't expect an apprentice to have the same *dexterity* as a skilled worker.

**maladroit** (*adj.*)
,ma-lə-'droit

clumsy; inept; awkward
    A *maladroit* worker banged his thumb with a hammer.

**versatile** (*adj.*)
'vər-sə-t°l

capable of doing many things well; many-sided; all-around
    Leonardo da Vinci was remarkably *versatile.* He was a painter, sculptor, architect, musician, engineer, and scientist.

 **EXERCISE 2.1:** SKILL WORDS

Complete the partially spelled skill word. The parentheses indicate the number of missing letters.

1. If you have musical (3) **it** (3), you ought to learn to play an instrument.

2. A century ago, one learned a trade by serving as a(n) (3) **rent** (3).

3. Janet is a(n) (3) **sat** (3) athlete with letters in swimming, tennis, and volleyball.

4. When I injured my right hand, I realized what an advantage it must be to be (2) **bid** (4) **ous.**

5. A(n) (1) **raftspe** (4)'s dexterity with tools is the result of years of experience.

## 2. Poverty

**destitute** (*adj.*)
'des-tə-,tüt

not possessing the necessities of life, such as food, shelter, and clothing; needy; indigent
The severe earthquake killed hundreds of persons and left thousands *destitute*.

**economize** (*v.*)
i'kä-nə-,mīz

reduce expenses; be frugal
Consumers can *economize* by buying their milk in gallon containers.

**frugal** (*adj.*)
'frü-gəl

1. barely enough; scanty
The old man had nothing to eat but bread and cheese; yet he offered to share this *frugal* meal with his visitor.

2. avoiding waste; economical; sparing; saving; thrifty
My weekly allowance for lunches and fares isn't much, but I can get by on it if I am *frugal*.

**impoverish** (*v.*)
im-'päv-rish

make very poor; reduce to poverty; bankrupt; ruin; pauperize
The increase in dues of only a dollar a year will not *impoverish* anyone.

**indigence** (*n.*)
'in-di-jən(t)s

poverty; penury
By hard work, countless thousands of Americans have raised themselves from *indigence* to wealth.

## 3. Wealth

**affluent** (*adj.*)
'a-flü-ənt

very wealthy; rich; opulent
The new wing to the hospital is a gift from an *affluent* humanitarian.

**avarice** (*n.*)
'a-və-rəs

excessive desire for wealth; greediness; cupidity
If manufacturers were to raise prices without justification, they could be accused of *avarice*.

**avaricious** *(adj.)*
‚a-və-'ri-shəs

greedy; grasping; covetous
An *avaricious* person likes to get and keep, but not to give or share.

**covet** *(v.)*
'kə-vət

desire; long for; crave, especially something belonging to another
Jorge *coveted* his neighbor's farm but could not get her to sell it.

**dowry** *(n.)*
'daù-rē

money, property, etc., that a bride brings to her husband
The *dowry* that his wife brought him enabled the Italian engraver Piranesi to devote himself completely to art.

**financial** *(adj.)*
fə-'nan(t)-shəl

having to do with money matters; monetary; pecuniary; fiscal
People who keep spending more than they earn usually get into *financial* difficulties.

**fleece** *(v.)*
'flēs

(literally, to remove the wool from a sheep or a similar animal) deprive or strip of money or belongings by fraud; charge excessively for goods or services; rob; cheat; swindle
If your sister paid $9000 for that car, she was *fleeced*. The mechanic says it is worth $5500.

**hoard** *(v.)*
'hȯrd

save and conceal; accumulate; amass
Aunt Bonnie had a reputation as a miser who *hoarded* every penny she could get her hands on.

**lavish** *(adj.)*
'la-vish

1. too free in giving, using, or spending; profuse; prodigal
The young heir was warned that he would soon have nothing left if he continued to be *lavish* with money.

2. given or spent too freely; very abundant; extravagant; profuse
Vera's composition is good, but it doesn't deserve the *lavish* praise that Linda gave it.

**lucrative** *(adj.)*
'lü-krə-tiv

profitable; moneymaking
Because the gift shop did not produce a sufficient profit, the owner decided to go into a more *lucrative* business.

**means** (*n. pl.*)
'mēnz
wealth; property; resources
    To own an expensive home, a yacht, and a limousine, you have to be a person of *means*.

**opulence** (*n.*)
'ä-pyə-lən(t)s
wealth; riches; affluence
    Dickens contrasts the *opulence* of France's nobility with the indigence of her peasants.

**sumptuous** (*adj.*)
'səm(p)(t)-shə-wəs
involving large expense; luxurious; costly
    The car with the leather upholstery and thick rugs is beautiful but a bit *sumptuous* for my simple tastes.

 **EXERCISE 2.2:** POVERTY AND WEALTH WORDS

Complete the partially spelled poverty or wealth word. The parentheses indicate the number of missing letters.

1. As a(n) (2) **flu** (3) nation, the United States has given billions to aid the world's needy.

2. 18th-century France was impoverished by the (4) **use** spending of her royal family.

3. It is not surprising that needy people (2) **vet** the possessions of prosperous neighbors.

4. The bride is bringing her husband a large dowry, as her parents are people of (2) **an** (1).

5. If it does not begin to (1) **con** (5), the nation will be in serious financial trouble.

## 4. Fear

**apprehensive** (*adj.*)
,a-pri-'hen(t)-siv
expecting something unfavorable; afraid; anxious
    *Apprehensive* parents telephoned the school when the class was late in getting home from the museum.

**cower** (*v.*)
'kaů-ər
draw back tremblingly; shrink or crouch in fear; cringe; recoil
    If you stand up to your bullying sister instead of *cowering* before her, she may back down.

**dastardly** (*adj.*)
'das-tərd-lē

cowardly and mean
It was *dastardly* of the captain to desert the sinking vessel and leave the passengers to fend for themselves.

**intimidate** (*v.*)
in-'ti-mə-,dāt

make fearful or timid; frighten; force by fear; cow; bully
The younger children would not have given up the playing field so quickly if the older ones hadn't *intimidated* them.

**poltroon** (*n.*)
päl-'trün

thorough coward; dastard; craven
Like the *poltroon* that he was, Tonseten hid under a bed when he saw a fight coming.

**timid** (*adj.*)
'ti-məd

lacking courage or self-confidence; fearful; timorous; shy
If the other team challenges us, we should accept. Let's not be so *timid*!

**trepidation** (*n.*)
,tre-pə-'dā-shən

nervous agitation; fear; fright; trembling
I thought Carol would be nervous when she made her speech, but she delivered it without *trepidation*.

## 5. Courage

**audacious** (*adj.*)
ȯ-'dā-shəs

1. bold; fearlessly daring
The *audacious* sea captain set a course for uncharted waters.

2. too bold; insolent; impudent
After we had waited for about twenty minutes, an *audacious* latecomer strolled up and tried to get in at the head of our line.

**audacity** (*n.*)
ȯ-'da-sə-tē

nerve; rashness; temerity
Oliver Twist, nine-year-old poorhouse inmate, was put into solitary confinement when he had the *audacity* to ask for a second helping of porridge.

**dauntless** (*adj.*)
'dȯnt-ləs

fearless; intrepid; very brave; valiant
The frightened sailors wanted to turn back, but their *dauntless* captain urged them to sail on.

**exploit** (*n.*)
'ek-,splȯit

heroic act; daring deed; feat
Amelia Earhart won worldwide fame for her *exploits* as an aviator.

**fortitude** (*n.*)
'fȯr-tə-,tüd

courage in facing danger, hardship, or pain; endurance; bravery; pluck; backbone; valor
The officer showed remarkable *fortitude* in remaining on duty despite a painful wound.

**indomitable** (*adj.*)
in-'dä-mə-tə-bəl

incapable of being subdued; unconquerable; invincible
The bronco that would not be broken threw all its riders. It had an *indomitable* will to be free.

**plucky** (*adj.*)
'plə-kē

courageous; brave; valiant; valorous
After two days on a life raft, the *plucky* survivors were rescued by a helicopter.

**rash** (*adj.*)
'rash

overhasty; foolhardy; reckless; impetuous; taking too much risk
When you lose your temper, you may say or do something *rash* and regret it afterward.

 **EXERCISE 2.3:** FEAR AND COURAGE WORDS

Complete the partially spelled fear or courage word.

1. Don't think you can (6) **date** us by shaking your fists at us!

2. Queen Elizabeth I knighted Francis Drake for his (5) **its** at sea.

3. The champions looked (6) **tab** (2) when they took the field, but we beat them.

4. Who would have thought that a(n) (2) **mid** sophomore like Sophie would have had the courage to address so large an audience?

5. It would be (1) **as** (1) to drop out of school because of failure in a single test.

# Review Exercises

 **REVIEW 1:** SENTENCE COMPLETION

On your answer paper, write the word from the list below that best fits the context. Use each word only once.

| | | |
|---|---|---|
| affluent | apprehensive | apprentice |
| aptitude | avarice | craftsperson |
| destitute | economize | exploit |
| financial | fortitude | frugal |
| hoard | impoverish | indigence |
| indomitable | intimidate | lavish |
| lucrative | opulence | |

1. Many unprofitable businesses have been made __?__ by immigrants who were __?__ when they first arrived in this country.

2. Sir Edmund Hillary and Tenzing Norgay showed amazing __?__ in 1953 when they climbed Mt. Everest, a peak that had been __?__.

3. Why are some people inclined to __?__ even when they have accumulated more than enough? Can it be __?__?

4. No one would expect a(n) __?__ to have the expertise of a(n) __?__.

5. Gertrude Ederle's early __?__ for swimming marked her for future greatness. When she swam the English Channel—the first woman to do so—she broke the men's speed record for that swim. What a(n) __?__!

6. The Wall Street crash of 1929 reduced countless investors from __?__ to __?__.

7. When __?__ spenders suddenly lose their jobs, they may wish that they had been more __?__ in managing their money.

8. The violent storm did not seem to __?__ the crew, but it made the passengers __?__.

9. Soaring outlays for employee pension and medical benefits can bring a(n) __?__ corporation to the brink of __?__ ruin.

10. If we do not __?__ in the use of our precious natural resources, we will __?__ our country.

**REVIEW 2:** SYNONYMS

Avoid repetition by replacing the boldfaced word with a **synonym** from the following list. The answer to question 1 is **bent**.

anxious         bent         indigent
fleece          pluck        pauperize
invincible      cow          lucrative
affluence

1. Cheryl is talented in many areas, but she has no **talent** for dramatics.
2. In a time of need, the **needy** look to the government for help.
3. Wealthy people tend to associate with people of **wealth**.
4. Conquerors often commit the blunder of believing they are **unconquerable**.
5. Don't let that bully **bully** you.
6. A sales tax is no way to fight poverty because it will more deeply **impoverish** whose who are already impoverished.
7. It has not been a **profitable** year. Profits are way down.
8. Don't be **afraid**. There is nothing to be afraid of.
9. The press lauded the courageous rescuers for their **courage**.
10. Know with whom you are dealing if you do not want to be cheated. A reputable firm will not **cheat** you.

 **REVIEW 3:** ANTONYMS

Write the word from the following list that is most nearly the **opposite** of the boldfaced word or words. The first answer is **enrich**.

adroit          dastardly        destitute
economize       undercharge      frugal
enrich          unprofitable     rash
sumptuous

1. Dictators __?__ themselves but **impoverish** their subjects.
2. An **inept** person cannot provide the __?__ leadership that we need.
3. This is a time to __?__, rather than to **increase expenses**.

4. When funds are low, one must be __?__ to survive; **wasteful** spending cannot be tolerated.

5. Under questioning, the accused tend to be **cautious**, knowing that _____ answers can make problems for them.

6. Attacking unarmed civilians is a(n) __?__ deed, but the aggressor considered it a **daring** act.

7. At first the thief claimed he stole from the **opulent** only to aid the __?__.

8. The purchase of Alaska, which many had regarded as __?__, turned out to be quite **lucrative**.

9. Investigation showed that the customers who thought they had been **fleeced** were in fact __?__d.

10. Most gift shoppers look for items **that involve little expense**; they cannot afford __?__ merchandise.

 **REVIEW 4:** CONCISE WRITING

Express the thought of each sentence below in **no more than four words.**

1. There are millions of people who lack the basic necessities of life, such as food, shelter, and clothing.

2. Employees who are in the process of learning a trade under the guidance of a skilled worker do not receive very high salaries.

3. Those who practice the art of swindling charge their victims excessively for goods and services.

4. There are occasions when people are inclined to do things that entail altogether too much risk.

5. Those who have no confidence in themselves lack the courage to face danger, hardship, or pain.

**REVIEW 5:** SYNONYM SUMMARY

Each line, when completed, should have three words similar in meaning. The parentheses indicate the number of missing letters. On your answer paper, write the *complete* words. Answers to the first line are **pauperize, bankrupt,** and **impoverish.**

1. p (2) perize      bankr (1) pt      (2) poverish

2. f (2) lhardy      impet (1) ous      (1) ash

3. mon (1) tary      pec (1) niary      finan (2) al

4. n (1) vice      t (1) ro      apprent (1) ce

5. n (1) rve      tem (1) rity      (2) dacity

6. pr (1) f (1) se      prod (1) gal      lav (3)

7. (2) kward      in (1) pt      maladr (2) t

8. (1) mass      accum (1) late      h (2) rd

9. val (2) nt      (2) trepid      d (2) ntless

10. pov (1) rty      pen (1) ry      ind (1) gence

11. cr (1) ve      d (1) sire      c (1) v (1) t

12. cr (1) nge      (2) coil      cow (2)

13. t (1) lent      b (1) nt      (2) titude

14. gr (2) diness      cup (1) dity      av (1) r (1) ce

15. trem (1) ling      (1) right      tr (1) p (1) dation

16. l (1) x (1) rious      cost (2)      sum (2) uous

17. unconq (2) rable      invin (2) ble      ind (1) mit (1) ble

18. gr (1) sping      covet (2) s      ava (2) cious

19. (2) rifty      (3) nomical      fr (1) g (1) l

20. adr (2) tness      exp (1) rtise      dex (2) rity

 **REVIEW 6:** ANALOGIES

Which lettered pair of words—*a, b, c, d,* or *e*—most nearly expresses the same relationship as the capitalized pair?

1. PECUNIARY : MONEY
   - *a.* lunar : sun
   - *b.* meteorological : weather
   - *c.* toxic : waste
   - *d.* urban : nation
   - *e.* vocational : leisure

2. BUNGLER : MALADROIT
   - *a.* scapegoat : blameworthy
   - *b.* windbag : silent
   - *c.* flatterer : sincere
   - *d.* maverick : submissive
   - *e.* jack-of-all-trades : versatile

3. INTIMIDATE : COW
   - *a.* ignore : badger
   - *b.* praise : nag
   - *c.* harass : hound
   - *d.* outfox : help
   - *e.* offend : please

4. ASTRONAUT : INTREPID
   - *a.* fact finder : objective
   - *b.* apprentice : inattentive
   - *c.* chauffeur : intoxicated
   - *d.* custodian : unwary
   - *e.* mediator : partial

5. AUDACIOUS : MANNERS
   - *a.* dauntless : courage
   - *b.* vigorous : stamina
   - *c.* indigent : means
   - *d.* ambitious : goal
   - *e.* competent : skill

6. EXPLOIT : ADMIRATION
   - *a.* blunder : self-esteem
   - *b.* setback : prestige
   - *c.* felony : crime
   - *d.* repetition : interest
   - *e.* calamity : dismay

   *Hint:* An **exploit** arouses **admiration**.

7. ECONOMIZE : THRIFTY

   *a.* annoy : helpful

   *b.* sympathize : lukewarm

   *c.* worry : apprehensive

   *d.* bully : cordial

   *e.* tarry : punctual

8. DEXTERITY : TRAIT

   *a.* whale : fish

   *b.* arrow : missile

   *c.* utensil : shovel

   *d.* beverage : thirst

   *e.* bird : sparrow

9. AVARICE : PRODIGALITY

   *a.* enmity : hostility

   *b.* reluctance : unwillingness

   *c.* confidence : trust

   *d.* security : anxiety

   *e.* yearning : desire

10. PALACE : OPULENCE

    *a.* prison : liberty

    *b.* hovel : comfort

    *c.* paradise : discord

    *d.* dove : belligerence

    *e.* sweatshop : drudgery

 **REVIEW 7:** COMPOSITION

Answer in a sentence or two.

1. Would you prefer an adroit or maladroit craftsperson to build your new house? Why?

2. Why is it difficult for destitute people to economize?

3. Are avaricious parents likely to lavish money on their children? Why or why not?

4. Why would a timid child be more likely to cower than an audacious child?

5. If you were a soldier, would you prefer a leader who was plucky or rash? Why?

# CENTRAL IDEAS 6–10

## Pretest 2

Write the *letter* of the best answer.

1. An *estranged* friend is a friend __?__.

   (A) you hardly know   (B) with whom you have quarreled
   (C) who has moved away

2. If a criminal's name is *divulged,* it is __?__.

   (A) made public   (B) kept secret   (C) legally changed

3. The two nations are old __?__ because their goals almost always *correspond.*

   (A) allies   (B) rivals   (C) enemies

4. __?__ is not a *condiment.*

   (A) Pepper   (B) Lettuce   (C) Mustard

5. Anything that is *latent* cannot be __?__.

   (A) present   (B) hidden   (C) visible

> **THE ANSWERS ARE**
> **1.** B   **2.** A   **3.** A   **4.** B   **5.** C

The italicized words on which you were tested are a sample of the new vocabulary you are about to meet in Central Ideas 6–10.

## 6. Concealment

**alias** (*n.*)
'ā-lē-əs

assumed name
Inspector Javert discovered that Monsieur Madeleine was not the mayor's real name but an *alias* for Jean Valjean, the ex-convict.

**alias** (*adv.*)

otherwise called; otherwise known as
Jean Valjean, *alias* Monsieur Madeleine, was arrested by Inspector Javert.

**clandestine** (*adj.*)
klan-'des-tən

carried on in secrecy and concealment; secret; covert; underhand; undercover
Before the Revolutionary War, a patriot underground organization used to hold *clandestine* meetings in Boston.

**enigma** (*n.*)
i-'nig-mə

puzzling statement; riddle; mystery; puzzling problem or person
I have read the sentence several times but cannot understand it. Maybe you can help me with this *enigma*.

**enigmatic** (*adj.*)
e-,nig-'ma-tik

mysterious; puzzling; obscure
Her statement is *enigmatic*; we cannot make head or tail of it.

**latent** (*adj.*)
'lā-t°nt

present but not showing itself; hidden but capable of being brought to light; dormant; potential
A good education will help you discover and develop your *latent* talents.

**lurk** (*v.*)
'lərk

1. be hidden; lie in ambush
Katherine called the police when she noticed a stranger *lurking* behind her neighbor's garage.

2. move stealthily; sneak; slink

**seclude** (*v.*)
si-'klüd

shut up apart from others; confine in a place hard to reach; hide; cloister; sequester
To find a quiet place to study, Amy had to *seclude* herself in the attic.

| | |
|---|---|
| **stealthy** (*adj.*)<br>'stel-thē | secret in action or character; catlike; sly; furtive<br>The spy had to be very *stealthy* to get past the two guards without being noticed. |

## 7. Disclosure

| | |
|---|---|
| **apprise** (*v.*)<br>ə-'prīz | inform; notify; advise<br>The magazine has *apprised* its readers of an increase in rates beginning May 1. |
| **avowal** (*n.*)<br>ə-'vau̇-əl | open acknowledgment; frank declaration; admission; confession<br>The white flag of surrender is an *avowal* of defeat. |
| **divulge** (*v.*)<br>də-'vəlj | make public; disclose; reveal; tell<br>I told my secret only to Margaret because I knew she would not *divulge* it. |
| **elicit** (*v.*)<br>i-'li-sət | draw forth; bring out; evoke; extract<br>By questioning the witness, the attorney *elicited* that it was raining at the time of the accident. |
| **enlighten** (*v.*)<br>in-'lī-tᵊn | shed the light of truth and knowledge upon; free from ignorance; inform; instruct<br>The newcomer was going in the wrong direction until someone *enlightened* him that his room was at the other end of the hall. |
| **manifest** (*v.*)<br>'ma-nə-ˌfest | show; reveal; display; evidence<br>I am surprised that Harriet is taking an art course because she has never, to my knowledge, *manifested* any interest in the subject. |
| **manifest** (*adj.*) | plain; clear; evident; not obscure; obvious<br>It is now *manifest* that the family across the street intends to move. |
| **overt** (*adj.*)<br>ō-'vərt | open to view; not covert or hidden; public; manifest<br>The concealed camera recorded the *overt* acceptance of the bribe. |

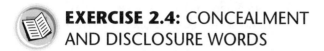 **EXERCISE 2.4:** CONCEALMENT
AND DISCLOSURE WORDS

Complete the partially spelled concealment or disclosure word.

1. Price fluctuations are often (4) **mat** (2); we cannot tell why they occur.
2. Can I call without (5) **gin** (1) my identity?
3. He is confused. Will you please (2) **light** (2) him?
4. Two large companies were suspected of having made a **cove** (2) agreement to fix prices.
5. It takes time for (2) **tent** talents to show themselves.

## 8. *Agreement*

| | |
|---|---|
| **accede** (*v.*)<br>ak-'sēd | (usually followed by *to*) agree; assent; consent; acquiesce<br>    When I asked my teacher if I might change my topic, he readily *acceded* to my request. |
| **accord** (*n.*)<br>ə-'kòrd | agreement; harmony<br>    Though we are in *accord* on what our goals should be, we differ on the means for achieving them. |
| **compact** (*n.*)<br>'käm-,pakt | agreement; understanding; accord; covenant<br>    The states bordering on the Delaware River have entered into a *compact* for the sharing of its water. |
| **compatible** (*adj.*)<br>kəm-'pa-tə-bəl | able to exist together harmoniously; in harmony; agreeable; congenial<br>    Arthur and I can't be on the same committee. We're not *compatible*. |
| **compromise** (*n.*)<br>'käm-prə-,mīz | settlement reached by a partial yielding on both sides<br>    At first, the union and management were far apart on wages, but they finally came to a *compromise*. |

**conform** (*v.*)
kən-'fòrm

be in agreement or harmony with; act in accordance with accepted standards or customs; comply; obey
When a new style in clothes appears, do you hasten to *conform*?

**consistent** (*adj.*)
kən-'sis-tənt

keeping to the same principles throughout; showing no contradiction; in accord; compatible; consonant
By bringing up an unrelated matter you are not being *consistent* with your previous statement that we should stick to the topic.

**correspond** (*v.*)
,kär-ə-'spänd

be in harmony; match; fit; agree; be similar
The rank of second lieutenant in the Army *corresponds* to that of ensign in the Navy.

**dovetail** (*v.*)
'dəv-,tāl

to fit together with, so as to form a harmonious whole; interlock with
Gilbert's skill as a writer *dovetailed* with Sullivan's talent as a composer, resulting in the famous Gilbert and Sullivan operettas.

**reconcile** (*v.*)
're-kən-,sīl

cause to be friendly again; bring back to harmony
After their quarrel, Althea and Pat refused to talk to each other until I *reconciled* them.

**relent** (*v.*)
ri-'lent

become less harsh, severe, or strict; soften in temper; yield
Serena gave her parents so many good reasons for letting her borrow the car that they finally *relented*.

# 9. Disagreement

**altercation** (*n.*)
,ol-tər-'kā-shən

noisy, angry dispute; quarrel, wrangle
We halted the *altercation* by separating the two opponents before they could come to blows.

**antagonize** (*v.*)
an-'ta-gə-,nīz

make an enemy of; arouse the hostility of
The official *antagonized* the leader of her own party by not campaigning for him.

**cleavage** (*n.*)
'klē-vij

split; division; schism; chasm
We hope compromise will repair the *cleavage* in our ranks.

**discord** (*n.*)
'dis-,kȯrd

disagreement; dissension; strife
Billy Budd put an end to the *discord* aboard the "Rights-of-Man." He was an excellent peacemaker.

**discrepancy** (*n.*)
dis-'kre-pən-sē

difference; disagreement; variation; inconsistency
Eighty people were at the dance but only seventy-four tickets were collected at the door. What accounts for this *discrepancy?*

**dissent** (*v.*)
di-'sent

differ in opinion; disagree; object
The vote approving the amendment was far from unanimous; six members *dissented.*

**embroil** (*v.*)
im-'brȯil

draw into a conflict
My enthusiastic support for Lynette's candidacy soon *embroiled* me in a debate with her opponents.

**estrange** (*v.*)
is-'trānj

turn (someone) from affection to dislike or enmity; make unfriendly; separate; alienate
A quarrel over an inheritance *estranged* the brothers for many years.

**friction** (*n.*)
'frik-shən

conflict of ideas between persons or parties of opposing views; disagreement
At the budget hearing, there was considerable *friction* between the supporters and the opponents of higher taxes.

**irreconcilable** (*adj.*)
i-,re-kən-'sī-lə-bəl

unable to be brought into friendly accord or understanding; hostile beyond the possibility of reconciliation; not reconcilable; incompatible
It is doubtful whether anyone can make peace between the estranged partners; they have become *irreconcilable.*

**litigation** (*n.*)
,li-tə-'gā-shən

lawsuit; act or process of carrying on a lawsuit
Some business disputes can be settled out of court; others require *litigation.*

**at variance**
ˌat ˈver-ē-ən(t)s

in disagreement; at odds
    Cynthia is an independent thinker. Her opinions are often *at variance* with those of the rest of our group.

**wrangle** (*v.*)
ˈraŋ-gəl

quarrel noisily; dispute angrily; brawl; bicker
    When I left, two neighbors were quarreling noisily. When I returned an hour later, they were still *wrangling*.

## EXERCISE 2.5: AGREEMENT AND DISAGREEMENT WORDS

Complete the partially spelled agreement or disagreement word.

1. We tried to (2) **con** (4) the two friends who had quarreled, but we failed.
2. If our bus and train schedules (4) **tail**, we won't have to sit around in the waiting rooms.
3. Both sides must give in a little if there is to be a(n) (4) **act**.
4. Our dog and cat are (3) **pat** (4); they get along well.
5. There is no reason for you to (4) **oil** yourself in their altercation.

# 10. Eating

**condiment** (*n.*)
ˈkän-də-mənt

something (such as pepper or spices) added to or served with food to enhance its flavor; seasoning
    There is a shelf in our kitchen for pepper, salt, mustard, catsup, and other *condiments*.

**devour** (*v.*)
di-ˈvau̇(ə)r

eat up greedily; feast upon like an animal or a glutton; dispatch
    The hikers were so hungry that they *devoured* the food as fast as it was served.

**edible** (*adj.*)
ˈe-də-bəl

fit for human consumption; eatable; comestible; nonpoisonous
    Never eat wild mushrooms, even though they look *edible*. They may be poisonous.

**glutton** (*n.*)
'glə-t°n

1. greedy eater; person in the habit of eating too much
 Andrea had a second helping and would have taken a third except that she didn't want to be considered a *glutton*.

2. person with a great capacity for enduring or doing something
 He is a *glutton* for punishment.

**luscious** (*adj.*)
'lə-shəs

delicious; juicy and sweet; delectable
 Ripe watermelon is *luscious*. Everyone will want a second slice.

**palatable** (*adj.*)
'pa-lə-tə-bəl

agreeable to the taste; pleasing; savory
 The main dish had little flavor, but I made it more *palatable* by adding condiments.

**slake** (*v.*)
'slāk

(with reference to thirst) bring to an end through refreshing drink; satisfy; quench
 On a sultry afternoon, there is a long line of people at the drinking fountain, waiting to *slake* their thirst.

**succulent** (*adj.*)
'sə-kyə-lənt

full of juice; juicy
 The steak will be dry if you leave it in the oven longer. Take it out now if you want it to be *succulent*.

**voracious** (*adj.*)
vȯ-'rā-shəs

having a huge appetite; greedy in eating; gluttonous; ravenous
 If Chester skips breakfast, he is *voracious* by lunchtime.

 **EXERCISE 2.6:** EATING WORDS

Complete the partially spelled eating word.

 **1.** There will be a choice of beverages for (3) **king** your thirst.

 **2.** Please leave some of that pie for us; don't be (4) **ton** (6).

 **3.** These oranges have too much pulp; they are not (5) **lent**.

4. We have plenty of food on hand when our relatives come for dinner because they have **(1)** or **(6)** appetites.

5. Some prefer their food served unseasoned so that they themselves may add the **(3)** **dim** **(3)**.

# Review Exercises

 **REVIEW 8:** SENTENCE COMPLETION

On your answer paper, write the word from the list below that best fits the context. Use each word only once.

| | | |
|---|---|---|
| accord | antagonize | apprise |
| at variance | clandestine | compatible |
| condiment | devour | divulge |
| elicit | embroil | enigma |
| estrange | glutton | litigation |
| palatable | reconcile | relent |
| slake | succulent | |

1. When the water in her canteen was consumed, the hiker __?_d her thirst on some __?__ berries that she found along the trail.

2. The reason for the treasurer's resignation was never __?_d. To this day, it remains a(n) __?__ .

3. Gulliver was __?_d of the king's plot to kill him by a daring friend who visited him __?_ly.

4. Neither party could afford the high cost of __?__, so they reached a(n) __?__ out of court.

5. By intense questioning, the lawyer __?_ed from the witness that her testimony was __?__ with what she had told the police.

6. Though I sprinkled a heavy dose of __?_s on the food I was served, I could not make it __?__ .

7. Several of us tried to __?__ the two __?_d cronies, but we succeeded only in making them more hostile to each other.

8. Mark __?_d so many of his coworkers that the boss had to lecture him on the importance of being __?__ .

9. If she had not had to skip lunch, Sara would not have __?_ed her dinner. Ordinarily, she is no __?__.

10. The two neighboring countries have been __?_ed with each other for centuries, and it is unlikely they will soon __?__ in their hatreds.

 **REVIEW 9:** SYNONYMS

Avoid repetition by replacing the boldfaced word or expression with a **synonym** from the list.

| | | |
|---|---|---|
| compact | correspond | covert |
| discrepancy | dovetail | edible |
| enlighten | luscious | manifest |
| wrangle | | |

1. It was a delicious meal; the food was **delicious**.

2. Can you **inform** us about how the Johnsons are doing? We have had no information from them since they moved.

3. The truth is now **obvious** to everyone but Jack, who is obviously still confused.

4. It was no secret to our military experts that the ruthless dictator was making **secret** preparations for war.

5. Both sides agree to the truce and are ready to sign a(n) **agreement** to respect its conditions.

6. It takes an expert to distinguish poisonous mushrooms from those that are **nonpoisonous**.

7. They **quarrel noisily** all the time. They are unusually quarrelsome.

8. Here are two pieces of the picture puzzle that I cannot **fit together**. Can you help me make them fit?

9. We agree on most matters, but there are times when our views do not **agree**.

10. There is a difference between the price we paid and the price we should have paid, but fortunately it is only a slight **difference**.

**REVIEW 10:** ANTONYMS

Write the word from the list below that is most nearly the **opposite** of the boldfaced word or words.

|  |  |  |
|---|---|---|
| acquiesce | alienate | altercation |
| avoid | fit | inedible |
| latent | lurk | overt |
| unpalatable |  |  |

1. Some of the catch was **fit for human consumption**; the rest was __?__.

2. We had hoped for an **accord**, but the session ended in a(n) __?__.

3. No sooner were they **reconciled** than they became __?__d again.

4. Many now __?__ fatty foods that they used to **devour**.

5. With condiments, this dish is **agreeable to my taste**; otherwise it is __?__.

6. Nobody **objected** to the proposal; all of us __?__d.

7. Counterintelligence operations are **closed to public scrutiny**; they cannot be __?__.

8. Some details telephoned by civilians about strangers in their vicinity **dovetail** with the description of the escapee; others do not __?__.

9. There is more to be feared from foes who __?__ in the shadows than from those who **are in open view**.

10. Some of the child's talents are already **visible**; others are __?__ and may emerge later.

 **REVIEW 11:** CONCISE WRITING

Express the thought of each sentence below in **no more than four words**.

1. The process of carrying on a lawsuit may cost a great deal of money.

2. Lack of flexibility prevented a settlement from being reached in which each side would have yielded a little in its demands.

3. The negotiations that had been carried on in secrecy failed to get anywhere.

4. A conflict of ideas between parties of opposing views threatens to break up the alliance.

5. The practice of lying can turn friends from affection to dislike for each other.

 **REVIEW 12:** SYNONYM SUMMARY

Each line, when completed, should have three words similar in meaning.

| | | |
|---|---|---|
| **1.** f (1) t | m (1) tch | (6) pond |
| **2.** sep (1) rate | al (2) nate | (3) range |
| **3.** sat (2) fy | q (2) nch | (1) lake |
| **4.** y (2) ld | sof (1) en | (2) lent |
| **5.** (5) cover | c (1) vert | clan (7) |
| **6.** sl (1) | f (1) rtive | st (2) lthy |
| **7.** inconsisten (1) y | var (2) tion | (3) crepancy |
| **8.** glut (2) nous | raven (3) | (2) racious |
| **9.** dorm (1) nt | potent (2) l | late (2) |
| **10.** str (1) fe | (3) sension | (3) cord |
| **11.** sh (1) w | (3) play | m (1) n (1) fest |
| **12.** delic (3) s | (2) lectable | l (1) s (1) ious |
| **13.** sn (2) k | (2) ink | l (1) rk |
| **14.** agr (3) ble | congen (2) l | comp (1) t (1) ble |
| **15.** ass (1) nt | (2) quiesce | a (1) cede |
| **16.** extr (2) t | (1) voke | el (1) c (1) t |
| **17.** seq (2) ster | cl (2) ster | (2) clude |
| **18.** c (1) mply | ob (1) y | (3) form |
| **19.** a (1) c (1) rd | coven (1) nt | (3) pact |
| **20.** spl (1) t | s (1) hism | cl (2) v (1) ge |

**REVIEW 13:** ANALOGIES

Which lettered pair of words—*a, b, c, d,* or *e*—most nearly expresses the same relationship as the capitalized pair?

**1.** ENIGMA : BEWILDERMENT
   *a.* pain : swelling
   *b.* irritability : fatigue
   *c.* conservation : scarcity
   *d.* blunder : embarrassment
   *e.* skid : icing

**2.** GLUTTON : FOOD
   *a.* alcoholic : beverages
   *b.* miser : hoarding
   *c.* aggressor : restraint
   *d.* workaholic : whiskey
   *e.* gossip : secrecy

**3.** CLANDESTINE : SECRET
   *a.* gutless : dastardly
   *b.* equitable : oppressive
   *c.* initial : terminal
   *d.* evasive : frank
   *e.* atypical : customary

**4.** STEALTHY : CAT
   *a.* gentle : mule
   *b.* deliberate : hare
   *c.* timid : panther
   *d.* lumbering : elephant
   *e.* blind : eagle

**5.** COMESTIBLE : CONSUME
   *a.* unforgivable : condone
   *b.* permissible : allow
   *c.* enigmatic : understand
   *d.* transient : remain
   *e.* intolerable : endure

**6.** MUSTARD : CONDIMENT
   *a.* cinnamon : appetite
   *b.* bulb : socket
   *c.* oak : evergreen
   *d.* saw : tool
   *e.* shrub : tree

**7.** SLAKE : QUENCH
   *a.* acquiesce : object
   *b.* deluge : inundate
   *c.* impede : expedite
   *d.* ignite : extinguish
   *e.* squander : conserve

8. SAVORY : TONGUE
   - *a.* distinct : voice
   - *b.* wavy : hair
   - *c.* melodious : ear
   - *d.* acute : vision
   - *e.* desirous : fingers

9. LATENT : INCONSPICUOUS
   - *a.* manifest : invisible
   - *b.* toxic : nonpoisonous
   - *c.* final : unalterable
   - *d.* rational : illogical
   - *e.* tasty : unpalatable

10. ALIAS : NAME
    - *a.* wig : hair
    - *b.* arrow : direction
    - *c.* razor : beard
    - *d.* detergent : dirt
    - *e.* reply : inquiry

 **REVIEW 14:** COMPOSITION

Answer in a sentence or two.

1. Why do people involved in clandestine activity often move in a stealthy way?
2. Is it necessary to divulge information that is already manifest? Why or why not?
3. Is a compromise more likely to lead to accord or discord? Explain.
4. Can you explain why people with irreconcilable differences often resort to litigation?
5. Describe a time you were embroiled in an altercation.

# CENTRAL IDEAS 11–15

## Pretest 3

Write the *letter* of the best answer.

1. A wait of __?__ before being served is *inordinate.*

   (A) five minutes   (B) two hours   (C) thirty seconds

2. *Cogent* arguments are __?__.

   (A) illogical   (B) preventable   (C) convincing

3. A *scrupulous* person has a high regard for __?__.

   (A) what is right   (B) those in authority   (C) what is beautiful

4. If you feel *enervated,* you are not so __?__ as usual.

   (A) bored   (B) nervous   (C) strong

5. A team that *defaults* __?__ the game.

   (A) delays   (B) loses   (C) wins

> **THE ANSWERS ARE**
> **1. B   2. C   3. A   4. C   5. B**

How well did you do? Any questions that you may have missed or are uncertain about will be cleared up for you as you work through Central Ideas 11–15, which follow immediately.

## 11. Size, Quantity

**colossal** (*adj.*)   huge; enormous; gigantic; mammoth; vast
kə-'lä-səl   The game was played in a *colossal* sports arena with a seating capacity of more than 60,000.

**commodious** (*adj.*)
kə-'mō-dē-əs

spacious and comfortable; roomy; ample; not confining
It will be easy to move in the equipment because the halls and stairways are *commodious.*

**gamut** (*n.*)
'ga-mət

entire range of anything, as of musical notes, emotions, etc.
First I thought I had done very well, then well, and finally, poorly. I ran the *gamut* from confidence to despair.

**infinite** (*adj.*)
'in-fə-nət

without ends or limits; boundless; endless; inexhaustible
We do not know whether space is bounded or *infinite.*

**infinitesimal** (*adj.*)
,in-fi-nə-'te-sə-məl

so small as to be almost nothing; immeasurably small; very minute
If there is any salt in this soup, it must be *infinitesimal.* I can't taste it.

**inflate** (*v.*)
in-'flāt

swell with air or gas; expand; puff up
Since one of the tires had lost air, we stopped at a gas station to *inflate* it.

**inordinate** (*adj.*)
i-'nȯr-dᵊn-ət

much too great; not kept within reasonable bounds; excessive; immoderate
If you eat an *inordinate* amount of sweets, you are likely to gain weight.

**iota** (*n.*)
ī-'ō-tə

(ninth and smallest letter of the Greek alphabet) very small quantity; infinitesimal amount; bit
If you make the same mistake again, despite all my warnings, I will not have one *iota* of sympathy for you.

**magnitude** (*n.*)
'mag-nə-,tüd

size; greatness; largeness; importance
To supervise eight hundred employees is a responsibility of considerable *magnitude.*

**picayune** (*adj.*)
,pi-kē-'yün

concerned with trifling matters; petty; small; of little value
In studying, don't spend too much time on *picayune* details. Concentrate on the really important matters.

| | |
|---|---|
| **pittance** (*n.*)<br>'pi-t°n(t)s | small amount; meager wage or allowance<br>At those low wages, few will apply for the job.<br>Who wants to work for a *pittance*? |
| **puny** (*adj.*)<br>'pyü-nē | slight or inferior in size, power, or importance;<br>weak; insignificant<br>The skyscraper dwarfs the surrounding<br>buildings. By comparison to it, they seem *puny*. |
| **superabundance** (*n.*)<br>‚sü-pər-ə-'bən-dən(t)s | great abundance; surplus; excess<br>Ronald's committee doesn't need any more<br>assistance. He has a *superabundance* of helpers. |

 **EXERCISE 2.7:** SIZE AND QUANTITY WORDS

Complete the partially spelled size or quantity word.

1. The homes from which students come run the **(1) am (2)** from affluence to indigence.

2. This **(3) mod (4)** sofa can accommodate four people comfortably.

3. There was a(n) **(3) era (8)** of food. We could have had several more guests for dinner.

4. The spare tire needs to be **(3) late (1)**; it has too much air.

5. Management regards the demand for an immediate twenty percent increase in wages as **(4) din (3)**.

## 12. Weakness

| | |
|---|---|
| **debilitate** (*v.*)<br>di-'bi-lə-‚tāt | impair the strength of; enfeeble; weaken<br>The fever had so *debilitated* the patient that she<br>lacked the strength to sit up. |
| **decadent** (*adj.*)<br>'de-kə-dənt | marked by decay or decline; falling off; declining;<br>deteriorating<br>When industry moves away, a flourishing town<br>may quickly become *decadent*. |

**decrepit** (*adj.*)
di-'kre-pət

broken down or weakened by old age or use; worn out

    Billy Dawes rode past the redcoats on a horse that looked *decrepit* and about to collapse.

**dilapidated** (*adj.*)
də-'la-pə-,dā-təd

falling to pieces; decayed; partly ruined or decayed through neglect

    Up the road was an abandoned farmhouse, partially in ruins, and near it a barn, even more *dilapidated*.

**enervate** (*v.*)
'e-nər-,vāt

lessen the vigor or strength of; weaken; enfeeble

    The extreme heat had *enervated* us. We had to rest under a shady tree until our strength was restored.

**flimsy** (*adj.*)
'flim-zē

lacking strength or solidity; frail; unsubstantial

    Judy understands algebra well, but I have only a *flimsy* grasp of the subject.

**frail** (*adj.*)
'frā(ə)l

not very strong; weak; fragile

    Mountain climbing is for the robust, not the *frail*.

**incapacitate** (*v.*)
,in-kə-'pa-sə-'tāt

render incapable or unfit; disable; paralyze

    Ruth will be absent today. A sore throat has *incapacitated* her.

**infirmity** (*n.*)
in-'fər-mə-tē

weakness; feebleness; frailty

    On leaving the hospital, John felt almost too weak to walk, but he soon overcame this *infirmity*.

## 13. Strength

**bulwark** (*n.*)
'bùl-wərk

wall-like defensive structure; rampart; defense; protection; safeguard

    For centuries the British regarded their navy as their principal *bulwark* against invasion.

**citadel** (*n.*)
'si-tə-dᵊl

fortress; stronghold

    The fortified city of Singapore was once considered unconquerable. In 1942, however, this *citadel* fell to the Japanese.

**cogent** (*adj.*)
'kō-jənt

forcible; compelling; powerful; convincing
A request for a raise is more likely to succeed if supported with *cogent* reasons.

**dynamic** (*adj.*)
dī-'na-mik

forceful; energetic; active
Audrey represents us forcefully and energetically. She is a *dynamic* speaker.

**formidable** (*adj.*)
'fȯr-mə-də-bəl

exciting fear by reason of strength, size, difficulty, etc.; hard to overcome; to be dreaded
The climbers gasped when they caught sight of the *formidable* peak.

**forte** (*n.*)
'fȯrt

strong point; that which one does with excellence
I am better than Jack in writing but not in math; that is his *forte.*

**impregnable** (*adj.*)
im-'preg-nə-bəl

incapable of being taken by assault; unconquerable; invincible
Before World War II, the French regarded their Maginot Line fortifications as an *impregnable* bulwark against a German invasion.

**invigorate** (*v.*)
in-'vi-gə-,rāt

give vigor to; fill with life and energy; strengthen; enliven
If you feel enervated by the heat, try a swim in the cool ocean. It will *invigorate* you.

**robust** (*adj.*)
rō-'bəst

strong and healthy; vigorous; sturdy; sound
The lifeguard was in excellent physical condition. I had never seen anyone more *robust.*

**tenacious** (*adj.*)
tə-'nā-shəs

holding fast or tending to hold fast; unyielding; stubborn; strong
After the dog got the ball, I tried to dislodge it from her *tenacious* jaws, but I couldn't.

**vehement** (*adj.*)
'vē-ə-mənt

showing strong feeling; forceful; violent; furious
Your protest was too mild. If it had been more *vehement,* the supervisor might have paid attention to it.

**vigor** (*n.*)          active strength or force; energy
'vi-gər                The robust young pitcher performed with
                       extraordinary *vigor* for seven innings, but
                       weakened in the eighth and was removed from
                       the game.

 **EXERCISE 2.8:** WEAKNESS AND
STRENGTH WORDS

Complete the partially spelled weakness or strength word.

1. It will be difficult to defeat the faculty players; they certainly do not look  (5) **pit**.

2. Ed was quite  (2) **ail** until the age of twelve, but then he developed into a robust youth.

3. I doubt you can beat Ann in tennis. It happens to be her  (1) **or** (2).

4. A sprained ankle may sideline you for several weeks, but a fractured ankle will  (2) **cap** (7)  you for months.

5. Laziness, luxury, and a lack of initiative are some of the characteristics of a  (2) **cad** (3)  society.

## *14. Neglect*

**default** (*n.*)        failure to do something required; neglect;
di-'fòlt                negligence; failure to meet a financial obligation
                        The Royals must be on the playing field by
                        4 P.M. If they do not appear, they will lose the
                        game by *default*.

**default** (*v.*)        fail to pay or appear when due
                        The finance company took away Mr. Lee's car
                        when he *defaulted* on the payments.

**heedless** (*adj.*)     not taking heed; inattentive; careless;
'hēd-ləs                thoughtless; unmindful; reckless
                        If you drive in a blizzard, *heedless* of the
                        weather bureau's warnings, you may not reach
                        your destination.

**ignore** (*v.*)  refuse to take notice of; disregard; overlook
ig-'nȯr  Justin was given a ticket for *ignoring* a stop sign.

**inadvertent** (*adj.*)  (used to describe blunders, mistakes, etc., rather
ˌi-nəd-'vər-t°nt  than people) heedless; thoughtless; careless
Unfortunately, I made an *inadvertent* remark in
Irma's presence about her losing the election.

**neglect** (*v.*)  give little or no attention to; leave undone;
ni-'glekt  disregard
Most members of the cast *neglected* their studies
during rehearsals, but after the performance they
caught up quickly.

**neglect** (*n.*)  lack of proper care or attention; disregard;
negligence
For leaving his post, the guard was charged
with *neglect* of duty.

**remiss** (*adj.*)  negligent; careless; lax
ri-'mis  The owner of the stolen car was *remiss* in
having left the keys in the vehicle.

**sloven** (*n.*)  untidy person
'slə-vən  Cleanup is easy at our lunch table if there are
no *slovens*.

**slovenly** (*adj.*)  negligent of neatness or order in one's dress,
'slə-vən-lē  habits, work, etc.; slipshod; sloppy
You would not expect anyone so neat in
personal appearance to be *slovenly* in
housekeeping.

## 15. Care

**discreet** (*adj.*)  showing good judgment in speech and action;
di-'skrēt  wisely cautious
You were *discreet* not to say anything about our
plans when Harry was here. He can't keep a
secret.

**heed** (*v.*)
'hēd

take notice of; give careful attention to; mind
   I didn't *heed* the warning that the pavements were icy. That's why I slipped.

**meticulous** (*adj.*)
mə-'ti-kyə-ləs

extremely or excessively careful about small details; fussy
   Before signing a contract, read it carefully, including the fine print. This is one case where it pays to be *meticulous*.

**scrupulous** (*adj.*)
'skrü-pyə-ləs

having painstaking regard for what is right; conscientious; honest; strict; precise
   My instructor refuses to be a judge because two of her former students are contestants. She is very *scrupulous*.

**scrutinize** (*v.*)
'skrü-tᵊn-ˌīz

examine closely; inspect
   The gatekeeper *scrutinized* Harvey's pass before letting him in, but he just glanced at mine.

**solicitude** (*n.*)
sə-'li-sə-ˌtüd

anxious or excessive care; concern; anxiety
   My sister's *solicitude* over getting into college ended when she received word that she had been accepted.

**vigilance** (*n.*)
'vi-jə-lən(t)s

alert watchfulness to discover and avoid danger; alertness; caution; watchfulness
   The security guard who apprehended the thief was praised for *vigilance*.

**wary** (*adj.*)
'war-ē

on one's guard against danger, deception, etc.; cautious; vigilant
   General Braddock might not have been defeated if he had been *wary* of an ambush.

 **EXERCISE 2.9:** NEGLECT AND CARE WORDS

Complete the partially spelled neglect or care word.

1. Before handing in my paper, I (2) **rut** (5) **d**  it to see if there were any errors.

2. When Mom scolded Jeffrey for the (2) **oven** (2)  appearance of his room, he promised to make it more tidy.

3. If you (2) **nor** (1) the warning, you may have to suffer the consequences.

4. My aunt would have lost her case by (2) **fault** if she had failed to appear in court.

5. Deborah is (3) **up** (5) about returning books to the library on time. She has never had to pay a fine.

## *Review Exercises*

 **REVIEW 15:** SENTENCE COMPLETION

On your answer paper, write the word from the list below that best fits the context. Use each word only once.

| | | |
|---|---|---|
| colossal | debilitate | decrepit |
| default | discreet | formidable |
| forte | frail | heed |
| ignore | impregnable | inadvertent |
| invigorate | iota | puny |
| remiss | scrupulous | vehement |
| vigilance | vigor | |

1. Milly regrets that she __?_d your directions. She could have saved a great deal of time and trouble if she had __?_ed them.

2. Undercover detectives must be exceptionally __?_. If they make one __?_ remark, they may risk death.

3. Although Nathan, our __?_ linebacker, is only of average size, he is so quick and strong that he has made our defense __?_. Not one team has scored a touchdown against us.

4. In Lilliput, where people were six inches tall, Gulliver was __?_, but in Brobdingnag, the land of the giants, he looked __?_.

5. There is not one __?_ of truth in the rumor that Barbara has misused club funds. She is the most __?_ person I have ever met.

6. Her brother's __?_ is carpentry. He can rebuild a(n) __?_ house in a few weeks.

7. Despite their __?_ protests, the farmer and his family were forced to vacate their property because they had __?_ed on their mortgage.

8. Bart's long illness has left him so __?__ that he has to postpone his return to the team to regain his __?__ .

9. The convict got away because his guards were __?__ . If they had exercised proper __?__ , he would not have escaped.

10. Pam felt __?__d on Friday, after working fourteen hours at her office, but she hoped that the relaxation of the weekend would __?__ her.

## REVIEW 16: SYNONYMS

Avoid repetition by replacing the boldfaced word or expression with a **synonym** from the following words.

| | | |
|---|---|---|
| bulwark | cogent | commodious |
| dynamic | flimsy | incapacitate |
| magnitude | robust | slovenly |
| solicitude | | |

1. The Armed Forces protect our freedom. They are our principal **protection** against foreign aggression.

2. Arthritis is his most important ailment. He has other problems, too, but they are of lesser **importance**.

3. We are concerned about my sister's health, and when we don't hear from her our **concern** increases.

4. You seem to lack energy today. Usually, you are much more **energetic**.

5. The locker I was assigned to had been used by an untidy person; it was very **untidy**.

6. Injuries sustained in practice often **disable** athletes and put them on the disability list.

7. There is not too much room in this closet; that one is more **roomy**.

8. I am convinced you are in error, unless you can offer **convincing** proof to the contrary.

9. Eileen was not very strong before her appendectomy, but she will soon be **strong and healthy** again.

10. Most of the excuses that were given had almost no substance whatsoever; they were very **unsubstantial**.

**REVIEW 17:** ANTONYMS

Write the word from the list below that is most nearly the **opposite** of the boldfaced word or words.

| | | |
|---|---|---|
| confining | heedless | ignore |
| infinite | inflate | meticulous |
| picayune | scrutinize | sloven |
| wary | | |

1. Most of the salesclerks were **not fussy about small details**, but one was truly __?__ .

2. Thoughtless consumers behave as if our water supplies were __?__ , when in fact they are quite **limited**.

3. It is unlikely that a(n) __?__ will quickly acquire the habits of a **neat person**.

4. The __?__ driver slows down and looks in all directions before crossing an intersection; the **foolhardy** one speeds right through.

5. Hardly anyone **took notice of** the latecomers; most of the audience __?__ d them.

6. People used to **commodious** accommodations may find the ship's cabins too __?__ .

7. Customs officials do **not closely examine** every piece of a traveler's luggage, but they may select one suitcase and __?__ its contents.

8. Smoking by visitors in a patient's room is a **major** violation of hospital rules; it is not a(n) __?__ matter.

9. The driver was __?__ of the altercation at the back of the bus because she had to be **attentive** to the road.

10. Try to have an even temper. Do not let one victory __?__ , or one defeat **deflate**, your self-esteem.

 **REVIEW 18:** CONCISE WRITING

Express the thought of each sentence below in **no more than four words**.

1. The expenses that we had were so small that they came to almost nothing.

2. Addicts are subject to cravings that they are unable to keep within reasonable bounds.

3. Those who do proofreading have to be extremely careful about small details.

4. Many people pay little or no attention to the responsibilities that they are supposed to carry out.

5. There is no fortress in the whole wide world that is not capable of being taken by assault.

 **REVIEW 19:** SYNONYM SUMMARY

Each line, when completed, should have three words similar in meaning.

| | | |
|---|---|---|
| 1. stren (1) then | (2) liven | invig (1) r (1) te |
| 2. l (1) x | car (1) less | (2) miss |
| 3. con (1) ern | (2) xiety | soli (1) itude |
| 4. (1) well | exp (1) nd | (2) flate |
| 5. dis (1) ble | paral (1) ze | inca (2) citate |
| 6. f (1) rceful | (2) ergetic | (2) namic |
| 7. st (1) rdy | (2) gorous | (2) bust |
| 8. decl (1) ning | (2) teriorating | dec (1) dent |
| 9. (3) regard | (4) look | (2) nore |
| 10. (2) gantic | mamm (1) th | c (1) l (1) ss (1) l |
| 11. (2) nest | consc (2) nt (1) ous | scr (1) p (1) lous |
| 12. w (2) k | insigni (2) cant | p (1) ny |
| 13. (2) fense | r (1) mpart | bulw (2) k |
| 14. fr (2) l | (2) substantial | flim (1) y |
| 15. (2) cessive | (2) moderate | in (1) rd (1) nate |
| 16. (2) attentive | c (3) less | heed (4) |
| 17. s (1) rpl (1) s | (2) cess | (5) abundance |
| 18. r (2) my | (1) mple | (3) modious |
| 19. strongh (2) d | fort (4) | c (1) t (1) del |
| 20. (2) feeble | weak (2) | (1) nervate |

**REVIEW 20:** ANALOGIES

Which lettered pair of words—*a, b, c, d,* or *e*—most nearly expresses the same relationship as the capitalized pair?

1.  DEBILITATE : VIGOR
    *a.* pauperize : penury
    *b.* jeopardize : danger
    *c.* incarcerate : liberty
    *d.* economize : conservation
    *e.* fortify : courage

2.  INFINITE : END
    *a.* vital : life
    *b.* significant : meaning
    *c.* immortal : existence
    *d.* commodious : room
    *e.* anonymous : name

3.  PITTANCE : ABUNDANCE
    *a.* sprinkle : deluge
    *b.* smidgen : trace
    *c.* conflagration : flame
    *d.* pity : compassion
    *e.* mountain : hill

4.  SLOVEN : IMMACULATE
    *a.* glutton : voracious
    *b.* despot : domineering
    *c.* craven : pusillanimous
    *d.* bigot : unprejudiced
    *e.* buffoon : ridiculous

5.  TENACIOUS : YIELD
    *a.* remorseful : repent
    *b.* unforgiving : relent
    *c.* wary : heed
    *d.* voracious : devour
    *e.* contentious : fight

6.  SCRUTINIZE : EXAMINE
    *a.* saunter : walk
    *b.* skim : read
    *c.* ape : copy
    *d.* mumble : talk
    *e.* doze : sleep

7.  IGNORE : OVERLOOK
    *a.* hoard : squander
    *b.* learn : instruct
    *c.* abate : intensify
    *d.* initiate : terminate
    *e.* acknowledge : avow

8. COLOSSAL : ELEPHANT
   - *a.* puny : whale
   - *b.* gentle : lamb
   - *c.* microscopic : ameba
   - *d.* extinct : dinosaur
   - *e.* infectious : virus

   *Hint:* **Colossal** describes the size of an **elephant**.

9. DRUNKENNESS : FRAILTY
   - *a.* tomato : vegetable
   - *b.* award : excellence
   - *c.* diploma : document
   - *d.* gas : oxygen
   - *e.* condiment : appetite

   *Hint:* Note that **tomato** is not a **vegetable**.

10. DECADENT : FLOURISHING
    - *a.* picayune : invaluable
    - *b.* avaricious : greedy
    - *c.* slipshod : untidy
    - *d.* lax : remiss
    - *e.* scrupulous : precise

 **REVIEW 21:** COMPOSITION

Answer in a sentence or two.

1. Tell why it is foolish to spend inordinate amounts of time on picayune matters.
2. Is a football team with puny players likely to beat a team with colossal players? Why or why not?
3. Why is an impregnable castle easier to defend than a dilapidated one?
4. Would you prefer to have a meticulous or slovenly appearance? Explain your answer.
5. What might a person, debilitated by disease, do to reinvigorate himself?

# CENTRAL IDEAS 16–20

## Pretest 4

Write the *letter* of the best answer.

**1.** When you *defer* to someone, you are __?__ .

(A) wasting time   (B) being rude   (C) showing respect

**2.** Conditions were bad both __?__ and *abroad.*

(A) on land   (B) at home   (C) below deck

**3.** A *perennial* danger is one that is __?__ .

(A) constant   (B) avoidable   (C) temporary

**4.** __?__ is a serious *infraction.*

(A) Losing your wallet   (B) Forgery   (C) Testifying under oath

**5.** Anything that is *incumbent* on you is __?__ .

(A) unpleasant   (B) not your business   (C) your duty

> **THE ANSWERS ARE**
> **1.** C   **2.** B   **3.** A   **4.** B   **5.** C

Question 1 may have puzzled you, since *defer* was used in a way not yet studied. This is one of the vocabulary skills you will learn about in the final Central Ideas section, numbered 16–20.

## 16. Residence

**abroad** (*adv.*)
ə-'brȯd

in or to a foreign land or lands
After living *abroad* for a time, Robert Browning became homesick for his native England.

**commute** (*v.*)
kə-'myüt

travel back and forth daily, as from a home in the suburbs to a job in the city
Large numbers of suburban residents regularly *commute* to the city.

**commuter** (*n.*)

person who commutes
Many a *commuter* spends as much as three hours a day in getting to and from work.

**denizen** (*n.*)
'de-nə-zən

inhabitant; dweller; resident; occupant
On their safari, the tourists photographed lions, leopards, and other ferocious *denizens* of the jungle.

**domicile** (*n.*)
'dä-mə-ˌsīl

house; home; dwelling; residence; abode
Soon after they moved, the Coopers invited us to visit them at their new *domicile*.

**inmate** (*n.*)
'in-ˌmāt

person confined in an institution, prison, hospital, etc.
When the warden took charge, the prison had fewer than 100 *inmates*.

**migrate** (*v.*)
'mī-ˌgrāt

1. move from one place to settle in another
Because they were persecuted in England, the Puritans *migrated* to Holland.

2. move from one place to another with the change of season
In winter, many European birds *migrate* to the British Isles in search of a more temperate climate.

**native** (*n.*)
'nā-tiv

person born in a particular place
His entire family are *natives* of New Jersey except the grandparents, who were born abroad.

**native** (*adj.*)

born or originating in a particular place
Tobacco, potatoes, and tomatoes are *native* American plants that were introduced into Europe by explorers returning from the New World.

| | |
|---|---|
| **nomad** (*n.*)<br>'nō-,mad | member of a tribe that has no fixed abode but wanders from place to place; wanderer<br>   *Nomads* have no fixed homes but move from region to region to secure their food supply. |
| **nomadic** (*adj.*)<br>nō-'ma-dik | roaming from place to place; wandering; roving<br>   Mobile homes appeal to people with *nomadic* inclinations. |
| **sojourn** (*n.*)<br>'sō-,jərn | temporary stay<br>   On her trip home, Geraldine will stop in St. Louis for a two-day *sojourn* with relatives. |

 ## EXERCISE 2.10: RESIDENCE WORDS

Complete the partially spelled residence word. The parentheses indicate the number of missing letters.

1. Many Northerners **(2) grate** to Florida in the winter.

2. Humans are vastly outnumbered by the other **den (5)** of this earth.

3. Most people are not affluent enough to have a summer residence in the country and a permanent **(2) mi (4)** in the city.

4. These are not native melons; they are shipped from **(2) road**.

5. The regulations permit **(2) ma (3)** to receive visitors on Sunday.

## 17. Disobedience

| | |
|---|---|
| **defiance** (*n.*)<br>di-'fī-ən(t)s | refusal to obey authority; disposition to resist; state of opposition<br>   The union showed *defiance* of the court order against a strike by calling the workers off their jobs. |
| **infraction** (*n.*)<br>in-'frak-shən | breaking (of a law, regulation, etc.); violation; breach<br>   Unless the driver has a permit, parking in a handicapped space is an *infraction* of the law. |

**insubordinate** (*adj.*)
,in(t)-sə-'bòr-d'n-ət

not submitting to authority; disobedient; mutinous; rebellious
Had the cabinet officer ignored the President's instructions, he would have been *insubordinate* and would have been asked to resign.

**insurgent** (*n.*)
in-'sər-jənt

person who rises in revolt; rebel
When the revolt broke out, the government ordered its troops to arrest the *insurgents*.

**insurrection** (*n.*)
,in(t)-sə-'rek-shən

uprising against established authority; rebellion; revolt
Troops had to be used in 1794 to put down an *insurrection* in Pennsylvania known as the Whiskey Rebellion.

**malcontent** (*n.*)
'mal-kən-tent

discontented person; rebel
The work stoppage was caused by a few *malcontents* who felt they had been ignored when promotions were made.

**perverse** (*adj.*)
pər-'vərs

obstinate (in opposing what is right or reasonable); willful; wayward
Though I had carefully explained the shorter route to him, the *perverse* young man came by the longer way.

**sedition** (*n.*)
si-'di-shən

speech, writing, or action seeking to overthrow the government; treason
During World War I, about 1500 persons who spoke or wrote against our form of government or the war effort were arrested for *sedition*.

**transgress** (*v.*)
trans-'gres

go beyond set limits of; violate, break, or overstep a command or law
The coach imposed strict training rules on the soccer team, and he scolded any player who *transgressed*.

**trespass** (*v.*)
'tres-pəs

encroach on another's rights, privileges, property, etc.
The owner erected a "Keep Off" sign to discourage people from *trespassing* on her land.

## 18. *Obedience*

**acquiesce** (*v.*)
ˌa-kwē-ˈes

accept by keeping silent; submit quietly; comply
   When Tom suggested that we go to the movies, I *acquiesced* because there seemed nothing else to do.

**allegiance** (*n.*)
ə-ˈlē-jən(t)s

loyalty; devotion; faithfulness; fidelity
   When aliens become American citizens, they must pledge *allegiance* to the United States.

**defer** (*v.*)
di-ˈfər

yield to another out of respect, authority, or courtesy; submit politely
   I thought my answer was correct, but I *deferred* to the teacher's opinion because of her superior knowledge.

**discipline** (*v.*)
ˈdi-sə-plən

train in obedience; bring under control
   The Walkers should not complain that their son does not obey because they never tried to *discipline* him.

**docile** (*adj.*)
ˈdä-səl

easily taught; obedient; tractable; submissive
   Diane listens when you explain something to her, but her sister is much less *docile.*

**meek** (*adj.*)
ˈmēk

submissive; yielding without resentment when ordered about or hurt by others; acquiescent
   About a third of the commuters protested the fare hike. The rest were too *meek* to complain.

**pliable** (*adj.*)
ˈplī-ə-bəl

easily bent or influenced; yielding; adaptable
   We tried to get Joe to change his mind, but he was not *pliable.* Perhaps you can influence him.

**submit** (*v.*)
səb-ˈmit

yield to another's will, authority, or power; yield; surrender
   Though he had boasted he would never be taken alive, the fugitive *submitted* without a struggle when the police arrived.

| tractable (*adj.*) | easily controlled, led, or taught; docile |
| 'trak-tə-bəl | George III wanted the thirteen colonies to be *tractable*. |

 ## **EXERCISE 2.11:** DISOBEDIENCE AND OBEDIENCE WORDS

Complete the partially spelled disobedience or obedience word.

1. Dictators want their subjects to be **me** (2).

2. Mrs. Farrell often leaves her children in our care because they are very **do** (4)  with us.

3. The insurgents were ordered to yield, but they will never  (4)  **it.**

4. When I asked my brother to turn down his radio, he made it even louder. I couldn't understand why he was so  (3)  **verse.**

5. If the neighbors complain about your playing your saxophone after 10 P.M., you should, as a matter of courtesy, **de** (3)  to their wishes.

# *19. Time*

| chronic (*adj.*) | 1. marked by long duration or frequent recurrence |
| 'krä-nik | Carl's sore arm is not a new development but the return of a *chronic* ailment. |
| | 2. having a characteristic, habit, disease, etc., for a long time; confirmed; habitual |
| | Some people are *chronic* complainers. They are always dissatisfied. |
| concurrent (*adj.*) | occurring at the same time; simultaneous; contemporary |
| kən-'kər-ənt | When the strike is settled, there will probably be an increase in wages and a *concurrent* increase in prices. |
| dawdle (*v.*) | waste time; loiter; idle |
| 'dȯ-dᵊl | Let's get going. If we *dawdle* we'll be late for dinner. |

**imminent** (*adj.*)
'i-mə-nənt

about to happen; threatening to occur soon; near at hand
The sudden darkening of the skies and the thunder in the distance apprised us that rain was *imminent*.

**incipient** (*adj.*)
in-'si-pē-ənt

beginning to show itself; commencing; in an early stage; initial
Certain serious diseases can be successfully treated if detected in an *incipient* stage.

**intermittent** (*adj.*)
,in-tər-'mi-tənt

coming and going at intervals; stopping and beginning again; recurrent; periodic
The showers were *intermittent*; there were intervals when the sun broke through the clouds.

**perennial** (*adj.*)
pə-'re-nē-əl

1. lasting indefinitely; incessant; enduring; permanent; constant; perpetual; everlasting
Don't think that war has plagued only modern times. It has been a *perennial* curse.

2. (of plants) continuing to live from year to year
Marigolds last only one season, but *perennial* plants such as lillies return year after year.

**procrastinate** (*v.*)
prə-'kras-tə-'nāt

put off until later things that should be done now; defer; postpone
Most of the picnickers took cover when rain seemed imminent. The few that *procrastinated* got drenched.

**protract** (*v.*)
prō-'trakt

draw out; lengthen in time; prolong; continue; extend
We had planned to stay only for lunch but, at our host's insistence, we *protracted* our visit until after dinner.

**sporadic** (*adj.*)
spə-'ra-dik

occurring occasionally or in scattered instances; isolated; infrequent
Though polio has been practically wiped out, there have been *sporadic* cases of the disease.

**EXERCISE 2.12:** TIME WORDS

Complete the partially spelled time word.

1. My sister is perverse. If I ask her when she will be through with the phone, she will deliberately (1) **rot** (4) her conversation.

2. There are two excellent TV programs tonight but, unfortunately, they are (3) **cur** (4).

3. If public utilities provided (2) **term** (6) service, consumers would not stand for it.

4. Hay fever is a(n) (3) **on** (2) sickness that affects millions, particularly in the spring and fall.

5. The complaints, (2) **or** (4) at first, have become quite frequent.

## 20. *Necessity*

**compulsory** (*adj.*)
kəm-'pəl-sə-rē
required by authority; obligatory
State law makes attendance at school *compulsory* for children of certain ages.

**entail** (*v.*)
in-'tā(ə)l
involve as a necessary consequence; impose; require
A larger apartment will of course *entail* greater expense.

**essence** (*n.*)
'e-sⁿ(t)s
most necessary or significant part, aspect, or feature; fundamental nature; core
The union and management held a lengthy meeting without getting to the *essence* of the dispute—wages.

**gratuitous** (*adj.*)
grə-'tü-ə-təs
uncalled for; unwarranted
Were it not for her *gratuitous* interference, the opposing sides would have quickly settled their dispute.

**imperative** (*adj.*)
im-'per-ə-tiv
not to be avoided; urgent; necessary; obligatory; compulsory
To maintain a good credit rating, it is *imperative* that you pay your bills on time.

**incumbent** (*adj.*)
in-'kəm-bənt

(with *on* or *upon*) imposed as a duty; obligatory
    Arlo felt it *incumbent* on him to pay for the window, since he had hit the ball that broke it.

**indispensable** (*adj.*)
ˌin-di-'spen(t)-sə-bəl

absolutely necessary; essential
    If we have to, we can do without luxuries and entertainment. However, food, shelter, and clothing are *indispensable*.

**necessitate** (*v.*)
ni-'se-sə-ˌtāt

make necessary; require; demand
    The sharp increase in the cost of fuel *necessitated* a rise in the bus fare.

**oblige** (*v.*)
ə-'blīj

compel; force; put under a duty or obligation
    The law *obliges* the police to secure a warrant before making a search.

**obviate** (*v.*)
'äb-vē-ˌāt

make unnecessary; preclude
    Karen has agreed to lend me the book I need. This *obviates* my trip to the library.

**prerequisite** (*n.*)
prē-'re-kwə-zət

something required beforehand
    A satisfactory grade in Basic Art is a *prerequisite* for Advanced Art.

**pressing** (*adj.*)
'pre-siŋ

requiring immediate attention; urgent
    Before rearranging my furniture, I have some more *pressing* matters to attend to, such as finishing my research paper.

**superfluous** (*adj.*)
sü-'pər-flü-əs

more than what is enough or necessary; surplus; excessive; unnecessary
    Our town already has enough gas stations; an additional one would be *superfluous*.

 **EXERCISE 2.13:** NECESSITY WORDS

Complete the partially spelled necessity word.

1. Since our trunk is rather small, we can take along only things that are **(5) pens (4)**.

2. Since they are your guests, isn't it **(4) mbent** on you to make them feel at home?

3. Increased use of robots and computers in factories may (2) **via** (2) the hiring of additional employees.

4. The **ess** (4) of the Bill of Rights is that it protects us against tyranny.

5. I was surprised to hear the team needs me because I had thought I was **super** (6).

## Review Exercises

 **REVIEW 22:** SENTENCE COMPLETION

Write the word from the list below that best fits the context. Use each word only once.

| | | |
|---|---|---|
| abroad | chronic | commute |
| defer | denizen | docile |
| domicile | entail | imperative |
| incumbent | insubordinate | insurrection |
| migrate | nomad | oblige |
| obviate | prerequisite | pressing |
| procrastinate | protract | |

1. If the __?__s of this community want better street lighting, it is __?__ on them to contribute to the expense of additional lampposts.

2. When her fans applauded so enthusiastically, the fatigued singer felt __?__d to __?__ her concert for an additional thirty minutes.

3. Because Andrea's job commands a high salary, she is willing to __?__ three hours a day between her __?__ and the company's headquarters.

4. Being a professional basketball player __?__s living the life of a(n) __?__, as pro teams have to travel from city to city across the country.

5. Unlike his predecessor, who was usually __?__, Major obeys my every command. I am lucky to have such a(n) __?__ dog.

6. Your research paper is due in three days, so it is __?__ that you start working on it. Why do you always __?__?

7. Renata has decided to __?__ to a drier climate because of her __?__ asthma.

8. A(n) __?__ in his country required the president of the new democracy to end his travels __?__ and return home immediately.

9. The reporter had to __?__ her story on the museum exhibit when she was given a more __?__ assignment.

10. Herman was told that his year of study in France will __?__ his taking Introductory French, the __?__ for Second-Year French.

 ## REVIEW 23: SYNONYMS

Avoid repetition by replacing the boldfaced word or expression with a **synonym** from the following words.

| | | |
|---|---|---|
| acquiesce | allegiance | dawdle |
| discipline(d) | indispensable | insurgent(s) |
| pliable | perennial | sojourn |
| trespass | | |

1. Some youngsters fail to obey regulations because they have never been **trained in obedience**.

2. The **rebels** refuse to end their rebellion unless their terms are met.

3. They stupidly took along unnecessary equipment, but forgot a few small items that were **absolutely necessary**.

4. Anyone who complains constantly about trivial matters is bound to be regarded as a **constant** nuisance.

5. We enjoyed our **temporary stay** with you; we regret we could not stay longer.

6. When unreasonable demands were made, we did not **submit quietly**. Why were you quiet?

7. The military leaders say they are loyal to the central government, but questions nevertheless remain about their **loyalty**.

8. We never encroached on their property. Why did they **encroach on ours**?

9. Let's not **waste time**. Time is precious.

10. The mayors have considerable influence with the governor, but sometimes he is not **easily influenced**.

**REVIEW 24:** ANTONYMS

Write the word from the list below that is most nearly the **opposite** of the boldfaced word or words.

| | | |
|---|---|---|
| alien | indispensable | intermittent |
| meek | native | perennial |
| pliable | protract | submit |
| tractable | | |

1. Some of the fruits and vegetables we buy are **imported**. Others are of __?__ origin.

2. **Curtail** your introductory remarks. If you __?__ them, you may bore the audience.

3. __?__ individuals consider themselves dispensable; they would never be so **arrogant** as to say they are irreplaceable.

4. There would have been no room for compromise if the negotiators were **obstinate**; fortunately, they were __?__.

5. Freedom-loving people would rather **resist** injustice than __?__ to it.

6. The rain was **continuous**. If it were __?__ I could have been outdoors briefly without getting drenched.

7. People whose **native** tongue is English may not understand conversations spoken in __?__ languages.

8. With adequate security, a large crowd is __?__; otherwise it may become **unruly**.

9. **Annual** plants die at the end of the growing season, but __?__ ones flower year after year.

10. Americans consume some foods that are __?__ for nutrition, and some that definitely are **not essential**.

 **REVIEW 25:** CONCISE WRITING

Express the thought of each sentence below in **no more than four words**.

1. Every workday, Beverly travels from her home in the suburbs to the city.

2. The noise would stop for a while, and then it would start up all over again.

3. Going to court either to sue someone or to resolve a dispute involves a great deal of expense as a necessary consequence.

4. Tribes that used to roam from province to province were a threat to the continued existence of Rome.

5. Europe was plagued by wars that went on and on for long periods of time.

 **REVIEW 26:** SYNONYM SUMMARY

Each line, when completed, should have three words similar in meaning. Supply the missing letters.

1. pr (1) l (1) ng      (2) tend      (3) tract

2. w (2) dering      (2) ving      (2) madic

3. f (1) rce      c (1) mp (1) l      (2) lige

4. y (2) lding      ad (1) pt (1) ble      pl (2) ble

5. rev (1) lt      (2) rising      in (3) rection

6. (1) weller      (2) habitant      den (4)

7. nec (3) ary      obl (1) g (1) tory      (2) per (1) tive

8. hab (1) t (1) al      (3) firmed      (2) ronic

9. v (2) lation      br (2) ch      (2) fraction

10. (2) frequent      is (1) l (1) ted      sp (1) r (1) dic

11. loyal (2)      (2) votion      alleg (2) nce

12. const (1) nt      (2) during      (3) ennial

13. obst (1) n (1) te      w (2) lful      p (1) rv (1) rse

14. (3) ecessary      s (1) rpl (1) s      s (1) p (1) rfl (1) ous

15. (2) quiescent      s (2) missive      m (2) k

16. rebe (2) ious      m (1) t (1) nous      (2) sub (1) rd (1) nate

17. commen (1) ing      in (1) t (2) l      incip (2) nt

18. per (2) dic      rec (2) ring      in (3) mittent

19. sim (1) ltan (1) ous      con (2) mporary      (3) current

20. ab (1) de      (2) sidence      (3) icile

**REVIEW 27:** ANALOGIES

Which lettered pair of words—*a, b, c, d,* or *e*—most nearly expresses the same relationship as the capitalized pair?

1. INDISPENSABLE : REPLACE
   - *a.* insignificant : ignore
   - *b.* edible : devour
   - *c.* foreseeable : avoid
   - *d.* incomprehensible : grasp
   - *e.* inconsequential : disregard

   *Hint:* Something that is **indispensable** cannot be **replaced**.

2. NOMAD : ROVE
   - *a.* nonconformist : acquiesce
   - *b.* hoarder : consume
   - *c.* drudge : toil
   - *d.* obstructionist : cooperate
   - *e.* transient : remain

3. JAYWALKING : INFRACTION
   - *a.* opinion : fact
   - *b.* silk : fiber
   - *c.* homicide : misdemeanor
   - *d.* sole : shoe
   - *e.* moon : planet

4. DOCILE : DEFIANCE
   - *a.* intelligent : curiosity
   - *b.* apprehensive : alarm
   - *c.* discreet : caution
   - *d.* fair-minded : partiality
   - *e.* appreciative : gratitude

   *Hint:* A **docile** person does not show **defiance**.

5. PROTRACT : CURTAIL
   - *a.* obviate : preclude
   - *b.* extend : abbreviate
   - *c.* lengthen : broaden
   - *d.* resist : withstand
   - *e.* dawdle : procrastinate

6. SOJOURN : STAY
   - *a.* lull : cessation
   - *b.* monument : reminder
   - *c.* superabundance : supply
   - *d.* age : time
   - *e.* odyssey : trip

7. SPORADIC : FREQUENT

 *a.* distant : remote
 *b.* ordinary : commonplace
 *c.* frugal : economical
 *d.* scrupulous : honest
 *e.* initial : terminal

8. INSUBORDINATE : OBEY

 *a.* cooperative : hinder
 *b.* flexible : adapt
 *c.* shy : withdraw
 *d.* meek : conform
 *e.* extravagant : waste

9. MALCONTENT : COMPLAINER

 *a.* acquaintance : crony
 *b.* defendant : plaintiff
 *c.* competitor : rival
 *d.* adversary : ally
 *e.* alien : citizen

10. MANSION : DOMICILE

 *a.* vehicle : limousine
 *b.* cottage : castle
 *c.* banquet : meal
 *d.* warehouse : storage
 *e.* hobby : vocation

 **REVIEW 28:** COMPOSITION

Answer in a sentence or two.

1. Why might it be difficult to send a package to the domicile of a nomad?

2. Are docile people likely to become insurgents? Explain.

3. Give an example of how society disciplines people who transgress its laws.

4. Is it incumbent on a student to show allegiance to his or her school? Why or why not?

5. Would you rather have sporadic or chronic headaches? Explain why.

# Enlarging Vocabulary Through Anglo-Saxon Prefixes

## *What is a prefix?*

A prefix is a sound (or combination of sounds) placed before and connected to a word or root to form a new word. Examples:

| PREFIX | | WORD OR ROOT | | NEW WORD |
|---|---|---|---|---|
| FORE (Anglo-Saxon prefix meaning "beforehand") | + | SEE | = | FORESEE (meaning "see beforehand") |
| DIS (Latin prefix meaning "apart") | + | SECT (root meaning "cut") | = | DISSECT (meaning "cut apart") |
| HYPER (Greek prefix meaning "over") | + | CRITICAL | = | HYPERCRITICAL (meaning "overcritical") |

## *Why study prefixes?*

A knowledge of prefixes and their meanings can help you enlarge your vocabulary. The number of English words beginning with prefixes is considerable, and it keeps increasing. Once you know what a particular prefix means, you have a clue to the meaning of every word beginning with that prefix. For example, when you learn that the Latin prefix *bi* means "two," you will understand—and remember—the meaning of *bipartisan* ("representing two political parties"), *bilingual* ("speaking two languages"), *bisect* ("cut in two"), etc.

Our prefixes come mainly from Anglo-Saxon (Old English), Latin, and Ancient Greek.

## *Purpose of this chapter*

This chapter has a double purpose: (1) to acquaint you with important Anglo-Saxon prefixes, and (2) to help you add to your vocabulary a number of useful words beginning with these prefixes.

# ANGLO-SAXON PREFIXES 1–4

## *Pretest 1*

Write the *letter* of the best answer.

1. An *outspoken* person is not likely to be __?__.

    (A) bold   (B) frank   (C) shy

2. When you have a *foreboding*, you feel that something __?__ is going to happen.

    (A) unimportant   (B) unfortunate   (C) good

3. *Misgivings* result from __?__.

    (A) doubts and suspicions   (B) selfishness   (C) increased output

4. *Forebears* are associated mainly with the __?__.

    (A) present   (B) past   (C) future

5. If you __?__, you are being *overconfident*.

(A) strike while the iron is hot   (B) count your chickens before they are hatched   (C) lock the barn after the horses are stolen

| THE ANSWERS ARE | | | | |
|---|---|---|---|---|
| 1. C | 2. B | 3. A | 4. B | 5. B |

In the following pages you will learn many more words formed with the prefixes you have just met, namely, *fore-, mis-, out-,* and *over-*.

# 1. FORE-: "beforehand," "front," "before"

| WORD | MEANING AND TYPICAL USE |
|---|---|
| **forearm** (*n.*)<br>'fȯr-ˌärm | (literally, "front part of the arm") part of the arm from the wrist to the elbow<br>A weightlifter has well-developed *forearms*. |
| **forebear** (*n.*)<br>'fȯr-ˌber | (literally, "one who has been or existed before") ancestor; forefather<br>Do you know from whom you are descended? Who were your *forebears*? |
| **foreboding** (*n.*)<br>fȯr-'bō-diŋ | feeling beforehand of coming trouble; misgiving; presentiment; omen<br>The day before the accident, I had a *foreboding* that something would go wrong. |
| **forecast** (*n.*)<br>'fȯr-ˌkast | estimate beforehand of a future happening; prediction; prophecy<br>Have you listened to the weather *forecast* for the weekend? |
| **forefront** (*n.*)<br>'fȯr-ˌfrənt | (literally, "front part of the front") foremost place or part; vanguard<br>The mayor is at the *forefront* of the drive to attract new industry to the city. |
| **foregoing** (*adj.*)<br>'fȯr-ˌgō-iŋ | going before; preceding; previous<br>Carefully review the *foregoing* chapter before reading any further. |

**foremost** (*adj.*)      standing at the front; first; most advanced;
'fòr-,mōst                 leading; principal; chief
                           Marie Curie was one of the *foremost* scientists of
                           the twentieth century.

**foreshadow** (*v.*)      indicate beforehand; augur; portend
fòr-'sha-,dō               Our defeat in the championship game was
                           *foreshadowed* by injuries to two of our star players
                           in a previous game.

**foresight** (*n.*)       act of looking forward; prudence; power of seeing
'fòr-,sīt                  beforehand what is likely to happen
                           *Foresight* is better than hindsight.

**foreword** (*n.*)        front matter preceding the text of a book; preface;
'fòr-,wərd                 introduction; prologue
                           Before Chapter 1, there is a brief *foreword* in
                           which the author explains the aims of the book.

 **EXERCISE 3.1:** *FORE-* WORDS

Write the most appropriate *fore-* word.

1. When asked if she thought we would win, the coach refused to
   make a __?__ .

2. Instead of cramming for a test the night before, be sensible and
   spread your review over several of the __?__ days.

3. These plastic gloves cover the hand, the wrist, and part of the __?__ .

4. I should have had the __?__ to buy a sweater before it got too cold;
   now all the best ones have been sold.

5. As the spacecraft rose toward the sky, the astronaut had a __?__ that
   he might not return.

## 2. MIS-: "bad," "badly," "wrongly"

**misbelief** (*n.*)       wrong or erroneous belief
,mis-bə-'lēf               People generally believed the
                           earth was flat until Columbus' momentous
                           voyage corrected that *misbelief*.

**misdeed** (*n.*)
,mis-'dēd

bad act; wicked deed; crime; offense
> The criminals were punished for their *misdeeds* by fines and prison terms.

**misfire** (*v.*)
,mis-'fīr

(literally, "fire wrongly") fail to fire or explode properly
> The soldier's weapon *misfired* during target practice.

**misgiving** (*n.*)
,mis-'gi-viŋ

uneasy feeling; feeling of doubt or suspicion; foreboding; lack of confidence
> With excellent weather and a fine driver, we had no *misgivings* about the trip.

**mishap** (*n.*)
'mis-,hap

bad happening; misfortune; unlucky accident; mischance
> Right after the collision, each driver blamed the other for the *mishap*.

**mislay** (*v.*)
,mis-'lā

put or lay in an unremembered place; lose
> Yesterday I *mislaid* my keys, and
it took me about a half hour to find them.

**mislead** (*v.*)
,mis-'lēd

lead astray (in the wrong direction); deceive; delude; beguile
> Some labels are so confusing that they *mislead* shoppers.

**misstep** (*n.*)
,mis-'step

wrong step; slip in conduct or judgment; blunder
> Quitting school is a *misstep* that you may regret for the rest of your life.

 **EXERCISE 3.2:** *MIS-* WORDS

Write the most appropriate *mis-* word.

1. Luckily, no one was seriously hurt in the __?__.
2. Where is your pen? Did you lose it or __?__ it?
3. I hated to lend Marie my notes because of a __?__ that she might not return them in time.
4. There is always the likelihood that a rifle may __?__.
5. Consumer groups have been attacking advertisements that __?__ the public.

## 3. OUT-: "beyond," "out," "more than," "longer (faster, better) than"

**outgrow** (*v.*)
,aut-'grō

grow beyond or too large for
The jacket I got last year is too small. I have *outgrown* it.

**outlandish** (*adj.*)
,aut-'lan-dish

looking or sounding as if it belongs to a (foreign) land beyond ours; strange; fantastic
Costume parties are amusing because people come in such *outlandish* costumes.

**outlast** (*v.*)
,aut-'last

last longer than; outlive; survive
The table is more solidly constructed than the chairs and will probably *outlast* them.

**outlook** (*n.*)
'aut-,luk

looking ahead or beyond; prospect for the future
The *outlook* for unskilled laborers is not bright.

**output** (*n.*)
'aut-,put

(literally, what is "put out") yield or product; amount produced
The *output* of the average American factory increases as new equipment is introduced.

**outrun** (*v.*)
,aut-'rən

run faster than
The thief thought he could *outrun* his pursuers.

**outspoken** (*adj.*)
,aut-'spō-kən

speaking out freely or boldly; frank; vocal; not reserved
Alma sometimes hurts others when she criticizes their work because she is too *outspoken*.

**outwit** (*v.*)
,aut-'wit

get the better of by being more clever; outsmart; outfox
The fictional detective Sherlock Holmes manages to *outwit* the cleverest criminals.

**EXERCISE 3.3:** *OUT-* WORDS

Write the most appropriate *out-* word.

1. I know I shall get the truth when I ask Alice because she is very __?__.
2. Where did you get that __?__ hat? I never saw anything like it.
3. My little brother suffers from shyness, but Mom hopes he will __?__ it.
4. These sneakers are the best I have ever had. They will __?__ any other brand.
5. Our prospects of avoiding a deficit are good, but the __?__ may change if we have unforeseen expenses.

## 4. OVER-: "too," "excessively," "over," "beyond"

**overbearing** (*adj.*)
,ō-vər-'ber-iŋ

domineering; bossy; inclined to dictate
    Once Jason was given a little authority, he began to issue orders in an *overbearing* manner.

**overburden** (*v.*)
,ō-vər-'bər-dᵊn

place too heavy a load on; burden excessively; overtax; overload
    It would *overburden* me to go shopping Thursday because I have so much homework that day.

**overconfident** (*adj.*)
,ō-vər-'kän-fə-dənt

too sure of oneself; excessively confident
    I was so sure of passing that I wasn't going to study, but Dave advised me not to be *overconfident*.

**overdose** (*n.*)
'ō-vər-,dōs

quantity of medicine beyond what is to be taken at one time or in a given period; too big a dose
    Do not take more of the medicine than the doctor ordered; an *overdose* may be dangerous.

**overestimate** (*v.*)
,ō-vər-'es-tə-māt

make too high an estimate (rough calculation) of the worth or size of something or someone; overvalue; overrate

Joe *overestimated* the capacity of the bus. He thought it could hold 60; it has room for only 48.

**overgenerous** (*adj.*)
,ō-vər-'jen-ə-rəs

too liberal in giving; excessively openhanded

Because the service was poor, Gina thought I was *overgenerous* in leaving a 15% tip.

**overshadow** (*v.*)
,ō-vər-'sha-dō

1. cast a shadow over; overcloud; obscure

Gary's errors in the field *overshadowed* his good work at the plate.

2. be more important than; outweigh

Don's game-saving catch *overshadowed* his previous errors in the outfield.

**oversupply** (*n.*)
,ō-vər-sə-'plī

too great a supply; an excessive supply

There is a shortage of skilled technicians but an *oversupply* of unskilled workers.

**overwhelm** (*v.*)
,ō-vər-'hwelm

cover over completely; overpower; overthrow; crush

The security guards were nearly *overwhelmed* by the crowds of shoppers waiting for the sale to begin.

 **EXERCISE 3.4:** *OVER-* WORDS

Write the most appropriate *over-* word.

1. There will be much food left if you seriously __?__ the number who will attend the party.

2. Frances would have been our first choice, but she already has too many responsibilities and we did not want to __?__ her.

3. Why did you buy more Ping-Pong balls? Don't you know we have an __?__?

4. I think my English teacher was __?__ when he gave me 99 because I didn't deserve it.

5. At first the new supervisor was very domineering, but as she got to know the staff, she became less __?__.

## *Review Exercises*

 **REVIEW 1:** WORD-BUILDING WITH *FORE-,
MIS-, OUT-,* AND *OVER-*

Change each of the following expressions to a single word. **Foreseen** is
the answer to the first question.

1. seen beforehand
2. badly matched
3. grown to excess
4. use wrongly
5. cooked too much
6. person beyond the law
7. wrong interpretation
8. doom beforehand
9. ride faster than
10. inform incorrectly
11. too cautious
12. bad calculation
13. front feet (of a four-legged animal)
14. too simplified
15. swim better than
16. govern badly
17. stay too long
18. one who runs before
19. wrong statement
20. shout louder than

**REVIEW 2:** SENTENCE COMPLETION

Write the word from the list below that best fits the context.

| | | |
|---|---|---|
| forearm | forecast | foremost |
| foreword | misgiving | mislaid |
| misled | misstep | outgrow |
| outlandish | output | outrun |
| outspoken | outwit | overbearing |
| overconfident | overdose | overestimate |
| oversupply | overwhelm | |

1. The __?__ of "sunny with a high in the 70s" __?__ me into scheduling the picnic for today. How was I to know it would rain?

2. Many of us, no matter how old we get, will never __?__ our love for circus clowns and their __?__ costumes.

3. Jim didn't practice because he thought he could easily __?__ his competitors. After the race, he realized he had been __?__.

4. The master criminal __?__d his own cleverness when he thought he could __?__ Sherlock Holmes.

5. After the interview, Frank had few, if any, __?__s. He thought he had said all the correct things and could not recall a single __?__.

6. One reason our representative was reelected by a(n) __?__ing margin is that she has always been __?__ in her defense of the environment.

7. One thing that impressed me as I watched the __?__ tennis player in the world win his third straight championship was the huge size of his right __?__.

8. Ed did not read the book. He couldn't get beyond the first paragraph of the __?__ because he disliked the writer's __?__ attitude.

9. When she realized there was a(n) __?__ of shoes on the market, the company president ordered __?__ to be cut back at all her plants.

10. Andy wondered if he had lost his watch or just __?__ it. He had been sleepy all day, perhaps because of a(n) __?__ of his flu medicine.

 **REVIEW 3:** SYNONYMS

Avoid repetition by replacing the boldfaced word or expression with a **synonym** from the following words.

| | | |
|---|---|---|
| forebear(s) | foreboding | forecast |
| misbelief | misdeed(s) | mishap |
| outlast(ed) | overburden(ed) | overgenerous |
| overshadow | | |

1. When it comes to tipping for exceptional service, some people are **inclined to be exceptionally liberal.**

2. I had a **feeling beforehand** that we would lose. What did you feel the outcome would be?

3. Your recent successes are important. They **are more important than** your earlier mistakes.

4. Some criminals show no remorse for their **crimes.**

5. I thought the replacement soles would not last long, but they **lasted longer than** the original ones.

6. Unfortunately, they had one **misfortune** after another.

7. You are already **bearing too heavy a load.** We must not add to your load.

8. A visit to the land of our **ancestors** can teach us much about our ancestry.

9. The pollsters are predicting that the governor will be reelected. Do you agree with that **prediction?**

10. I awoke on a holiday in the **mistaken belief** that it was a school day and was halfway to the bus stop before realizing my mistake.

**REVIEW 4:** ANTONYMS

Write the word from the list below that is most nearly the **opposite** of the boldfaced word or words.

| | | |
|---|---|---|
| forebear | foregoing | foremost |
| foresight | foreword | misdeed |
| mislead | overcautious | overestimate |
| undercook | | |

1. Most of us are pretty good in **hindsight** but deficient in __?__ .

2. Some works have not only a(n) __?__ , or prologue, but also a(n) **afterword**, or epilogue.

3. People who lack self-confidence **underestimate** themselves and __?__ their opponents.

4. If Adam and Eve were our __?__ s, then all of us are their **descendants**.

5. In a eulogy, the speaker dwells on the **positive achievements**, rather than the __?__ s, of the departed person.

6. Why is it that protection of the environment, which should be one of our __?__ concerns, so often gets the **least** attention?

7. In matters where your own judgment may __?__ you, seek out someone who can **enlighten** you.

8. Certain foods must not be served unless they have been **thoroughly cooked**; if __?__ ed, they may cause food poisoning.

9. The character who appeared briefly in the __?__ scene will be seen again in one of the **subsequent** episodes.

10. After realizing that I had been **too careless**, I went to the extreme of becoming __?__ .

 **REVIEW 5:** CONCISE WRITING

Express the thought of each sentence below in **no more than four words**.

1. Most people do not have the power of seeing beforehand what is likely to happen.

2. Doses of medicine that exceed the prescribed amount are capable of killing people.

3. Which spark plug is it that failed to fire in a proper way?

4. Grandma broke the part of her arm from her wrist to her elbow.

5. Percy managed to get the better of his enemies by being more clever than they were.

 **REVIEW 6:** SYNONYM SUMMARY

Each line, when completed, should have three words similar in meaning. Supply the missing letters.

1. ch (2) f             princip (2)            (4) most

2. (2) fense            cr (1) me              (3) deed

3. (4) father           (2) cestor             (4) b (2) r

4. (3) fortune          (3) chance             mish (2)

5. str (1) nge          (3) tastic             (3) land (3)

6. fr (1) nk            v (1) c (1) l          (3) spoke (1)

7. (2) under            (1) lip                (3) step

8. boss (1)             (2) mineering          (4) bear (3)

9. cr (1) sh            (4) throw              (5) helm

10. (3) diction         prophe (1) y           (4) cast

11. overval (2)         (4) rate               (4) es (2) mate

12. (1) men             (3) sentiment          (4) boding

13. (4) mart            (3) fox                (2) twit

14. overt (2)           (4) load               (4) b (2) den

15. (3) face            in (3) duction         (4) word

16. pre (1) eding       prev (4)               fore (5)

17. (3) vive            (3) live               (3) last

18. overcl (2) d        (3) cure               (4) shad (2)

19. dec (2) ve          beg (2) le             (3) lead

20. a (1) g (1) r       p (1) rtend            (6) ado (1)

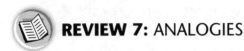

# REVIEW 7: ANALOGIES

Which lettered pair of words—*a, b, c, d,* or *e*—most nearly expresses the same relationship as the capitalized pair?

1. OVERBEARING : DOMINEER
   - *a.* meek : complain
   - *b.* nomadic : rove
   - *c.* immaculate : litter
   - *d.* submissive : defy
   - *e.* scrupulous : deceive

2. GRANDPARENT : FOREBEAR
   - *a.* bowl : vessel
   - *b.* officer : lieutenant
   - *c.* civilian : combatant
   - *d.* ship : frigate
   - *e.* native : alien

3. FOREWORD : TEXT
   - *a.* dessert : dinner
   - *b.* book : encyclopedia
   - *c.* climax : play
   - *d.* dawn : sunrise
   - *e.* toll : tax

4. MISDEED : PENALIZE
   - *a.* infraction : overlook
   - *b.* offense : tolerate
   - *c.* obligation : forget
   - *d.* promise : break
   - *e.* feat : acclaim

5. FOREBODING : APPREHENSION
   - *a.* truce : hostility
   - *b.* confession : guilt
   - *c.* recovery : ecstasy
   - *d.* rumor : confidence
   - *e.* impasse : settlement

6. HOAX : MISLEAD
   - *a.* threat : intimidate
   - *b.* definition : confuse
   - *c.* duty : perform
   - *d.* enigma : resolve
   - *e.* fine : pay

7. OVERGENEROSITY : BANKRUPTCY

    *a.* illiteracy : enlightenment    *b.* gluttony : indigestion

    *c.* penury : riches    *d.* avarice : pity

    *e.* impetuosity : patience

8. FOREARM : ELBOW

    *a.* ankle : wrist    *b.* muscle : nerve

    *c.* leg : knee    *d.* lip: mouth

    *e.* knuckle : hand

9. OVERDOSE : FATALITY

    *a.* mishap : blunder    *b.* covenant : disagreement

    *c.* famine : drought    *d.* surplus : scarcity

    *e.* thaw : avalanche

 **REVIEW 8:** COMPOSITION

Answer in a sentence or two.

1. Describe a time when you had a foreboding that a mishap might occur.

2. What misgivings would you have about making friends with an overbearing person?

3. What might a writer foreshadow with a description of an army that was far too confident of victory?

4. What is one way in which the police try to outwit those who would do misdeeds?

5. If you were to meet your forebears today, might they seem outlandish in some way? Explain.

# ANGLO-SAXON PREFIXES 5–8

## Pretest 2

Write the *letter* of the best answer.

1. An *understudy* is not a __?__ performer.

   (A) prepared    (B) substitute        (C) regular

2. Cars with a high *upkeep* __?__.

   (A) use less costly fuels    (B) are often in the repair shop
   (C) pick up speed rapidly

3. A *withdrawal* is the same as __?__.

   (A) a retreat    (B) a deposit        (C) an attack

4. When you wish to __?__ something in a sentence, *underscore* it.

   (A) stress    (B) correct            (C) erase

5. An *unabridged* dictionary __?__.

   (A) is not complete    (B) has no illustrations    (C) has not been
   shortened

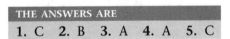

THE ANSWERS ARE
1. C   2. B   3. A   4. A   5. C

The material that follows will introduce you to many additional words formed with the prefixes *un-, under-, up-,* and *with-*.

## 5. UN-: "not," "lack of," "do the opposite of," "remove or release from"

**unabridged** (*adj.*)
,ən-ə-'brijd

not abridged; not made shorter; uncut; complete
Though an abridged dictionary is convenient to use, it contains far fewer definitions than an *unabridged* dictionary.

**unbiased** (*adj.*)
,ən-'bi-əst

not biased; not prejudiced in favor of or against; fair
Don't ask the mother of a contestant to serve as a judge because it may be hard for her to remain *unbiased*.

**unconcern** (*n.*)
,ən-kən-'sərn

lack of concern, anxiety, or interest; indifference; apathy
The audience was breathless with anxiety during the daring tightrope act, though the acrobats themselves performed with seeming *unconcern* for their own safety.

**undeceive** (*v.*)
,ən-di-'sēv

free from deception or mistaken ideas; set straight; disabuse
If you think I can get Mrs. Owens to hire you because she is my cousin, let me *undeceive* you. I have no influence with her.

**ungag** (*v.*)
,ən-'gag

remove a gag from; release from censorship
With the dictator's downfall, the censorship decrees were abolished, and the press was *ungagged*.

**unnerve** (*v.*)
,ən-'nərv

deprive of nerve or courage; cause to lose self-control; upset; enervate
The harassing noises of hostile fans so *unnerved* our star player that he missed two foul shots in a row.

**unquenchable** (*adj.*)
,ən-'kwen-chə-bəl

not quenchable; not capable of being satisfied; insatiable; inextinguishable
As a teenager, Jules had an *unquenchable* thirst for adventure stories; he read one after another.

**unscramble** (*v.*)
,ən-'skram-bəl

do the opposite of scramble; restore to intelligible form
    The previous secretary had mixed up the files so badly that it took me a week to *unscramble* them.

**unshackle** (*v.*)
,ən-'shak-əl

release from a shackle (anything that confines the legs or arms); set free; liberate
    When a captain put mutinous sailors in irons in the olden days, nobody was allowed to *unshackle* them.

**unwary** (*adj.*)
,ən-'war-ē

not wary; not alert; heedless; rash
    An *unwary* pedestrian is much more likely to be struck by a car than one who looks both ways and crosses with the light.

 **EXERCISE 3.5:** *UN-* WORDS

Write the most appropriate *un-* word.

1. Some baseball fans never miss a home game; they have an __?__ appetite for the sport.

2. The guards were warned that their prisoner was desperate and would try to escape if they were the least bit __?__.

3. I visited Grandma every day she was in the hospital. I can't understand why you accuse me of __?__ about her health.

4. For a reliable definition of a technical word, consult an __?__ dictionary.

5. Both the strikers and their employers want the mayor to arbitrate their dispute because they consider him __?__.

## 6.  UNDER-: "'beneath," "lower," "insufficient(ly)"

**underbrush** (n)
'ən-dər-ˌbrəsh

shrubs, bushes, etc., growing beneath large trees in a wood; undergrowth
   On its way through the dense jungle, the patrol had to be constantly wary of enemy soldiers who might be lurking in the *underbrush*.

**underdeveloped** (*adj.*)
ˌən-dər-di-'ve-ləpt

insufficiently developed because of a lack of capital and trained personnel for exploiting natural resources; backward; behindhand
   The United States has spent billions to help the *underdeveloped* nations improve their standard of living.

**undergraduate** (*n.*)
ˌən-dər-'gra-jə-wət

(literally, "lower than a graduate")
a student in a college or university who has not yet earned a bachelor's degree
   Full-time *undergraduates* can earn a bachelor's degree in four years.

**underpayment** (*n.*)
ˌən-dər-'pā-mənt

insufficient payment
   If too little is deducted from your weekly wages for income tax, the result is an *underpayment* at the end of the year.

**underprivileged** (*adj.*)
ˌən-dər-'priv-lijd

insufficiently privileged; deprived through social or economic oppression of some fundamental rights supposed to belong to all; disadvantaged; deprived
   The goal of the fund is to give as many *underprivileged* children as possible an opportunity for a vacation away from the city next summer.

**underscore** (*v.*)
'ən-dər-skȯr

draw a line beneath; emphasize; stress
   When you take notes, *underscore* items that are especially important.

**undersell** (*v.*)
ˌən-dər-'sel

sell at a lower price than
   The expression "You can't get it anywhere else for less" means about the same as "We will not be *undersold*."

**undersigned** (*n.*)
'ən-dər-,sīnd

person or persons who sign at the end of (literally, "under") a letter or document

Among the *undersigned* in the petition to the governor were some of the most prominent persons in the state.

**understatement** (*n.*)
'ən-dər-,stāt-mənt

a statement below the truth; a restrained statement in mocking contrast to what might be said

Frank's remark that he was "slightly bruised" in the accident is an *understatement*; he suffered two fractured ribs.

**understudy** (*n.*)
'ən-dər-,stə-dē

one who "studies under" and learns the part of a regular performer so as to be a substitute if necessary

While Madeline is recuperating from her illness, her role will be played by an *understudy*.

 **EXERCISE 3.6:** *UNDER-* WORDS

Write the most appropriate *under-* word.

1. The advanced course is for students with a bachelor's degree, but a qualified __?__ may enroll if the instructor approves.

2. An __?__ must master long and difficult roles, yet has no assurance of ever being called on to perform.

3. Arline told me she "passed," but that's an __?__; she got the highest mark in the class.

4. Mike's tee shot disappeared after hitting one of the trees, and he had to hunt for the ball in the __?__.

5. Because they buy in larger quantities at lower prices, chain-store operators are usually able to __?__ small merchants.

## 7. UP-: "up," "upward"

**upcoming** (*adj.*)
'əp-ˌkə-miŋ

coming up; being in the near future;
forthcoming; approaching
A monthly bulletin mailed to each customer
gives news of *upcoming* sales.

**update** (*v.*)
'əp-ˌdāt

bring up to date; modernize; renovate
New highway construction requires auto clubs
to *update* their road maps annually.

**upgrade** (*v.*)
'əp-ˌgrād

raise the grade or quality of; improve
Many employees attend evening courses to
*upgrade* their skills and improve their chances for
promotion.

**upheaval** (*n.*)
ˌəp-'hē-vəl

violent heaving up, as of the earth's crust;
commotion; violent disturbance; outcry
The prime minister's proposal for new taxes
created such an *upheaval* that his government fell.

**upkeep** (*n.*)
'əp-ˌkēp

maintenance ("keeping up"); cost of operating
and repairing
Susan traded in her old car because the *upkeep*
had become too high.

**uplift** (*v.*)
əp-'lift

lift up; elevate; raise
The news that employers are rehiring has
*uplifted* the hopes of many of the unemployed.

**upright** (*adj.*)
'əp-ˌrīt

standing up straight on the feet; erect; honest;
scrupulous
When knocked to the canvas, the boxer waited
till the count of nine before resuming an *upright*
position.

**uproot** (*v.*)
ˌəp-'rüt

pull up by the roots; remove completely;
eradicate; annihilate
The love of liberty is so firmly embedded in
people's hearts that no tyrant can hope to
*uproot* it.

| | |
|---|---|
| **upstart** (*n.*)<br>'əp-ˌstärt | person who has suddenly risen to wealth and power, especially if he or she is conceited and unpleasant<br>   When the new representative entered the legislature, some older members regarded her as an *upstart*. |
| **upturn** (*n.*)<br>'əp-'tərn | upward turn toward better conditions<br>   Most merchants report a slowdown in sales for October, but confidently expect an *upturn* with the approach of Christmas. |

 **EXERCISE 3.7:** *UP-* WORDS

Write the most appropriate *up-* word.

1. Perhaps today's victory, the first in four weeks, marks an __?__ in the team's fortunes.

2. To improve her book, the author will have to __?__ the last chapter to include the events of the past ten years.

3. If practicable, __?__ weeds by hand, instead of destroying them with chemicals that might damage the environment.

4. What is the name of the city agency responsible for the __?__ of our roads?

5. To stay in business, manufacturers must improve the quality of their products whenever their competitors __?__ theirs.

## 8. *WITH-:* "back," "away," "against"

| | |
|---|---|
| **withdraw** (*v.*)<br>with-'drȯ | 1. take or draw back or away; take out from a place of deposit<br>   The community association is her principal backer; if it *withdraws* its support, I don't see how she can be elected.<br><br>2. leave; retreat<br>   The invaders were ordered to *withdraw*. |

**withdrawal** (*n.*)
wi<u>th</u>-'drȯ-əl

1. act of taking back or drawing out from a place of deposit
When I am short of cash, I make a *withdrawal* from my bank account.

2. retreat; exit; departure
The invaders made a hasty *withdrawal*.

**withdrawn** (*adj.*)
wi<u>th</u>-'drȯn

drawn back or removed from easy approach; socially detached; unresponsive, introverted
Lola's brother keeps to himself and hardly says anything, though we try to be friendly; he seems *withdrawn*.

**withhold** (*v.*)
wi<u>th</u>-'hōld

hold back; keep from giving; restrain; curb
I would appreciate it if you would please *withhold* your comment until I have finished speaking.

**withholding tax** (*n.*)
wi<u>th</u>-'hōl-diŋ 'taks

sum withheld or deducted from wages for tax purposes
Your employer is required to deduct a certain amount from your salary as a *withholding tax* payable to the federal government.

**withstand** (*v.*)
wi<u>th</u>-'stand

stand up against; hold out; resist; endure
The walls of a dam must be strong enough to *withstand* tremendous water pressure.

**notwithstanding**
(*prep.*)
ˌnät-wi<u>th</u>-'stan-diŋ

(literally, "not standing against")
in spite of; despite
*Notwithstanding* their advantage of height, the visitors were unable to beat our basketball team.

 **EXERCISE 3.8:** *WITH-* WORDS

Write the most appropriate *with-* word.

1. Electronic banking lets you make a deposit or a __?__ at any time.

2. Whenever you get a raise, your __?__ goes up.

3. Construction of the new roadway has been approved, __?__ the protests from residents of the area.

4. Because of a disagreement with her partners, the lawyer announced that she would __?__ from the firm and open an office of her own.

5. The training that astronauts receive equips them to __?__ the hazards of space exploration.

## *Review Exercises*

 **REVIEW 9:** WORD-BUILDING WITH *UN-*, *UNDER-*, *UP-*, AND *WITH-*

Change each of the following expressions to a single word. The first answer is **underlying**.

1. lying beneath
2. not able to be avoided
3. holds back
4. insufficiently paid
5. act or instance of rising up
6. do the opposite of lock
7. lower (criminal) part of the world
8. standing up against
9. one who holds up, supports, or defends
10. sum taken (drawn) back from a bank account
11. not sociable
12. upward stroke
13. charged lower than the proper price
14. drew back or away
15. lack of reality
16. lifted upward
17. one who holds back
18. released from a leash
19. beneath the surface of the sea
20. upward thrust

**REVIEW 10:** SENTENCE COMPLETION

Write the word from the list below that best fits the context.

| | | |
|---|---|---|
| notwithstanding | unabridged | unbiased |
| unconcern | undeceive | underbrush |
| underscore | undersell | undersigned |
| understudy | unnerve | unquenchable |
| unshackle | unwary | upcoming |
| upgrade | uplift | upright |
| withdrawn | withhold | |

1. The parents of the __?__ boy took him to the circus, hoping that it might help to __?__ his spirits.

2. If you expect to find this extremely technical word in that little dictionary of yours, let me __?__ you. Only a(n) __?__ dictionary will have it.

3. A(n) __?__ camper, walking barefoot in the __?__, was bitten by a snake.

4. The new electronics store is using heavy TV advertising to __?__ its claim that it will __?__ all competitors.

5. Spurred by their __?__ desire for freedom, the prisoners managed to __?__ their wrists.

6. Maxine's __?__ about the __?__ test contrasts sharply with my own anxiety over it.

7. The prospect of suddenly being called upon to be the star does not __?__ an experienced __?__ familiar with the role.

8. The petition reads: "We, the __?__ XYZ Club members, are willing to pay higher dues to __?__ the refreshments served after meetings."

9. __?__ rumors to the contrary, the candidate insists that she is __?__, and she pledges that she will be fair to everyone.

10. The dealer who sold us the used car was a(n) __?__ person. He did not __?__ information from us about the true condition of the vehicle.

**REVIEW 11:** ANTONYMS

Write the word from the list below that is most nearly the **opposite** of the boldfaced word.

| | | |
|---|---|---|
| unabridged | unbiased | unconcern |
| underdeveloped | undergraduate | underpayment |
| understatement | unscrambled | unwary |
| upgraded | | |

1. Be **cautious** this morning. You may slip on the ice if you are __?__.

2. Once you receive your bachelor's degree, you are no longer an __?__ but a **graduate.**

3. Only __?__ persons should be on the jury. No one **prejudiced** in favor of or against the defendant should be chosen to serve.

4. Be accurate in describing your injuries when you file an accident report. Avoid both **exaggeration** and __?__.

5. It is a fact that **industrial** nations enjoy a higher standard of living than those that are __?__.

6. Someone **jumbled** up the pieces of the picture puzzle after I had finally __?__ them.

7. If you have made an **overpayment**, you will receive a refund; but if you have made an __?__, you still owe some money.

8. People who look with __?__ on the proposed legislation might show some **anxiety** if they knew how it might affect them.

9. An advantage an **abridged** dictionary has over one that is __?__ is that it is much less cumbersome.

10. If the winds diminish, the storm will be **downgraded** to a gale, but if they increase to 74 miles an hour, it will be __?__ to a hurricane.

 **REVIEW 12:** SYNONYMS

Avoid repetition by replacing the boldfaced word or expression with a **synonym** from the following words.

| | | |
|---|---|---|
| eradicate | understudy | ungag |
| update(d) | upheaval | upkeep |
| upturn | withdraw | withdrawal |
| withstand | | |

1. What caused the **disturbance**? Why were the people disturbed?

2. Though the new ruler has promised to **free** the press **from censorship**, he is now tightening censorship controls.

3. Jackie is learning the dispatcher's duties to qualify as his **substitute**, should substitution ever be necessary.

4. It is hard to **uproot** a weed that is deeply rooted.

5. The invaders were supposed to retreat to their own lines. What is delaying their **retreat**?

6. It cost $1400 to maintain our old car last year, and next year the **maintenance** may be even more expensive.

7. Our neighbors have **modernized** their kitchen. It now has a decidedly modern look.

8. Parents can hold their own against most complaints from children, but they cannot **hold out against** continual nagging.

9. It takes just a few seconds to **take out** money from your savings account when you use an automated teller machine.

10. Business is improving. There has been an encouraging **improvement** in retail sales.

 **REVIEW 13:** CONCISE WRITING

Express the thought of each sentence below in **no more than four words**.

1. Houdini succeeded in getting out of the shackles that were restraining his arms and legs.

2. There are people who through no fault of their own are deprived of some of the fundamental rights that all human beings are supposed to have.

3. Conceited individuals who have suddenly come into wealth and power can be bossy and domineering over others.

4. Those who referee games must not show any favoritism to one side or the other.

5. Sally has learned the ins and outs of my job and can take over my duties in the event of an emergency.

## REVIEW 14: SYNONYM SUMMARY

Each line, when completed, should have three words similar in meaning.

1. end (1) re     res (1) st     (4) stand

2. r (1) sh     heed (4)     (2) wary

3. h (1) nest     scrup (1) lous     up (5)

4. st (1) ess     (2) phasize     under (5)

5. retr (2) t     l (2) ve     with (4)

6. f (2) r     unpre (2) diced     (2) biased

7. l (1) berate     fr (2)     (2) shack (2)

8. comm (1) tion     (3) cry     (2) heav (2)

9. inextin (2) ishable     (2) satiable     (2) quench (1) ble

10. ex (1) t     depart (1) re     (4) draw (2)

11. compl (1) te     (2) cut     (3) bridged

12. m (1) dernize     (2) novate     (2) date

13. erad (1) cate     annihil (3)     (2) root

14. (3) advantaged     (2) prived     underpr (1) v (1) l (1) ged

15. (2) difference     ap (1) thy     (2) concern

16. appr (2) ching     f (1) rthcoming     up (6)

17. backw (1) rd     b (1) hindhand     (5) developed

18. restr (2) n     c (2) b     (4) hold

19. r (2) se     impr (1) ve     (2) grade

20. (2) set     en (1) rvate     (2) nerve

**REVIEW 15:** ANALOGIES

Which lettered pair of words—*a, b, c, d,* or *e*—most nearly expresses the same relationship as the capitalized pair?

1. UNGAG : CENSOR
   - *a.* overlook : neglect
   - *b.* liberate : unshackle
   - *c.* abandon : retain
   - *d.* inform : undeceive
   - *e.* hesitate : waver

2. WARY : HEED
   - *a.* acquiescent : rebel
   - *b.* infallible : err
   - *c.* lavish : economize
   - *d.* voracious : devour
   - *e.* opinionated : compromise

3. UNDERSTUDY : INSURANCE
   - *a.* exercise : circulation
   - *b.* privacy : door
   - *c.* guest : hospitality
   - *d.* bodyguard : security
   - *e.* bore : excitement

4. SHACKLES : HANDCUFFS
   - *a.* tree : birch
   - *b.* legs : limbs
   - *c.* measles : disease
   - *d.* fence : barrier
   - *e.* flavor : condiments

   *Hint:* **Shackles** is the category to which **handcuffs** belongs.

5. WITHDRAWN : SOCIABILITY
   - *a.* arrogant : humility
   - *b.* unassertive : timidity
   - *c.* outgoing : warmth
   - *d.* intrepid : valor
   - *e.* immaculate : tidiness

6. UPDATE : MODERNIZE
   - *a.* soothe : infuriate
   - *b.* invalidate : approve
   - *c.* yield : defer
   - *d.* expedite : procrastinate
   - *e.* bury : disinter

7. UPRIGHT : TRUST

    *a.* corrupt : contempt     *b.* domineering : obedience

    *c.* indolent : promotion     *d.* inhumane : sympathy

    *e.* gossipy : credence

    *Hint:* An **upright** person is worthy of **trust**.

8. UNDERSCORE : EMPHATIC

    *a.* simplify : complex     *b.* overshadow : inconspicuous

    *c.* rectify : inequitable     *d.* decontaminate : impure

    *e.* legalize : unlawful

9. UNCONCERN : INTEREST

    *a.* cordiality : friendliness     *b.* perseverance : ambition

    *c.* fervor : enthusiasm     *d.* honesty : virtue

    *e.* mediocrity : excellence

10. INTREPID : UNNERVE

    *a.* pliable : influence     *b.* audible : hear

    *c.* timorous : scare     *d.* outspoken : silence

    *e.* avaricious : share

    *Hint:* An **intrepid** person cannot be **unnerved**.

 ## REVIEW 16: WORD-BUILDING WITH EIGHT ANGLO-SAXON PREFIXES

Replace the italicized words with one word beginning with *fore-, mis-, out-, over-, un-, under-, up-,* or *with-*. **Foretell** is the answer to question 1.

1. If you study your opponent's habits, you may be able to *tell beforehand* what his or her next move will be.

2. We won because we *played better than* our opponents.

3. After the hike, we rested because we were *excessively tired.*

4. It is a mistake to exaggerate your abilities and talents, but it is just as bad *to set too low an estimate on* them.

5. The dispute has been *wrongly handled* from the very beginning.

6. Harry is usually *too critical* when he judges somebody else's work.

7. You will not get a good picture if the film is *exposed for less than the time needed.*

8. The will provided that all of the property was to go to the wife if she *lived longer than* her husband.

9. As a courteous guest, you should know when to leave; do not *stay beyond* your welcome.

10. The district attorney promised to *remove the mask of* the criminals posing as respectable citizens.

11. By stressing scholarship, our principal has succeeded in *lifting* the reputation of our school *up to a higher level.*

12. The early snowfall gave us a *taste beforehand* of the bitter winter to come.

13. A captain *has a higher rank than* a lieutenant.

14. We spoke in *lower tones* so as not to be overheard.

15. As I passed the kitchen, I caught a *glimpse beforehand* of what we are having for dinner.

16. Abe Lincoln had the *bad fortune* to lose his mother when he was only nine.

17. The hospital has beds for 90 patients; in addition, it provides daily treatment for hundreds of *patients who live beyond the hospital grounds.*

18. I have never heard you utter a single *statement lacking in accuracy.*

19. From the prisoners' outward appearance, it did not seem that they had been mistreated or *insufficiently fed.*

20. Lauren wanted to go on the overnight camping trip, but her father *held back* his consent, saying she was still too young.

 **REVIEW 17:** COMPOSITION

Answer in a sentence or two.

1. What is one way society tries to upgrade the lives of the underprivileged?

2. Describe an upcoming event in your life that could prove to be unnerving.

3. Why is it hard for a tree to withstand uprooting?

4. Would an upright business owner withhold money owed to his employees? Explain.

5. What might an underdeveloped nation do to gain an upturn in its economy?

# Enlarging Vocabulary Through Latin Prefixes

## LATIN PREFIXES 1–6

### Pretest 1

Write the *letter* of the best answer.

**1.** *Postscripts* are especially helpful to the letter writer who __?__ .

(A) forgets to answer   (B) answers too late   (C) makes omissions

**2.** *Bicameral* legislatures __?__ .

(A) serve for two years   (B) consist of two houses
(C) meet twice a year

3. There is more excitement over the *advent* of spring than over its
   _?_.

   (A) departure   (B) onset   (C) arrival

4. You *antedate* me as a member because you joined the club _?_ me.

   (A) after   (B) with   (C) before

5. A *semidetached* building touches _?_ other building(s).

   (A) one   (B) no   (C) two

6. Was the story *absorbing* or _?_?

   (A) true to life   (B) interesting   (C) boring

THE ANSWERS ARE

1. C   2. B   3. A   4. C   5. A   6. C

In the following pages you will learn additional words formed with
the six Latin prefixes involved in the pretest: *ab-, ad-, ante-, post-, bi-,*
and *semi-.*

# 1. AB-, A-, ABS-: "from," "away," "off"

The prefix *ab* (sometimes written *a* or *abs*) means "from," "away," or
"off." Examples:

| PREFIX | | ROOT | | NEW WORD |
|--------|---|------|---|----------|
| AB ("off") | + | RUPT ("broken") | = | ABRUPT ("broken off"; "sudden") |
| A ("away") | + | VERT ("turn") | = | AVERT ("turn away") |
| ABS ("from") | + | TAIN ("hold") | = | ABSTAIN ("hold from"; "refrain") |

| WORD | MEANING AND TYPICAL USE |
|------|-------------------------|
| **abdicate** (*v.*)<br>'ab-di-,kāt | formally remove oneself from; give up; relinquish; renounce; resign<br>    The aging monarch *abdicated* the throne and went into retirement. |
| **abduct** (*v.*)<br>ab-'dəkt | carry off or lead away by force; kidnap<br>    The Greeks attacked Troy to recover Helen, who had been *abducted* by the Trojan prince Paris. |

**abhor** (*v.*)
ab-'hòr

shrink from; detest; loathe; hate
Janet is doing her best to pass the course because she *abhors* the thought of having to repeat it in summer school.

**abnormal** (*adj.*)
ab-'nòr-məl

deviating from the normal; unusual; irregular
We had three absences today, which is *abnormal*. Usually, everyone is present.

**abrasion** (*n.*)
ə-'brā-zhən

scraping or wearing away of the skin by friction; irritation
The automobile was a total wreck, but the driver, luckily, escaped with minor cuts and *abrasions*.

**abrupt** (*adj.*)
ə-'brəpt

broken off; sudden; unexpected
Today's art lesson came to an *abrupt* end when the gongs sounded for a fire drill.

**abscond** (*v.*)
ab-'skänd

steal off and hide; depart secretly; flee; escape
A wide search is under way for the manager who *absconded* with the company's funds.

**absolve** (*v.*)
əb-'zälv

1. set free from some duty or responsibility; exempt; excuse
Ignorance of the law does not *absolve* a person from obeying it.

2. declare free from guilt or blame; exculpate; exonerate
Of the three suspects, two were found guilty, and the third was *absolved*.

**absorbing** (*adj.*)
əb-'sòr-biŋ

fully taking away one's attention; extremely interesting; engrossing
That was an *absorbing* book. It held my interest from beginning to end.

**abstain** (*v.*)
əb-'stān

withhold oneself deliberately from doing something; refrain; desist
My dentist said I would have fewer cavities if I *abstained* from sweets.

**averse** (*adj.*)
ə-'vərs

(literally, "turned from") opposed; disinclined; unwilling
> I am in favor of the dance, but I am *averse* to holding it on May 25.

**avert** (*v.*)
ə-'vərt

turn away; ward off; prevent; forestall
> The mayor tried to *avert* a strike by municipal employees.

**avocation** (*n.*)
ˌa-və-'kā-shən

occupation away from one's customary occupation; hobby
> My aunt, a pediatrician, composes music as an *avocation*.

 **EXERCISE 4.1:** *AB-, A-,* AND *ABS-* WORDS

Write the most appropriate word from group 1.

1. Some love spinach; others __?__ it.
2. A snowstorm in late May is __?__ for Chicago.
3. My father plays golf. What is your father's __?__?
4. The dictator refused to __?__ and was eventually overthrown.
5. Gene said the movie was interesting, but I didn't find it too __?__.
6. It was very decent of Marge to __?__ me of blame by admitting she was at fault.
7. The kidnapper was arrested when he tried to __?__ the executive.
8. I nominate Harriet for treasurer. She knows how to keep records and can be trusted not to __?__ with our dues.
9. The owner must raise $20,000 in cash at once if she is to __?__ bankruptcy.
10. We are __?__ to further increases in the sales tax. It is too high already.

# 2. AD-: "to," "toward," "near"

**adapt** (*v.*)
ə-'dapt

1. (literally, "fit to") adjust; suit; fit
   People who work at night have to *adapt* themselves to sleeping in the daytime.

2. make suitable for a different use; modify
   Lorraine Hansberry's hit Broadway play, A RAISIN IN THE SUN, was later *adapted* for the screen.

**addicted** (*adj.*)
ə-'dik-təd

given over (to a habit); habituated; devoted
You will not become *addicted* to smoking if you refuse cigarettes when they are offered.

**adequate** (*adj.*)
'a-di-kwət

equal to, or sufficient for, a specific need; enough; sufficient
The student who arrived ten minutes late did not have *adequate* time to finish the test.

**adherent** (*n.*)
ad-'hir-ənt

one who sticks to a leader, party, etc.; follower; faithful supporter
You can count on Martha's support in your campaign for reelection. She is one of your most loyal *adherents*.

**adjacent** (*adj.*)
ə-'jā-sᵊnt

lying near; nearby; neighboring; bordering
The island of Cuba is *adjacent* to Florida.

**adjoin** (*v.*)
ə-'jȯin

be next to; be in contact with; border; abut
Mexico *adjoins* the United States.

**adjourn** (*v.*)
ə-'jərn

put off to another day; suspend a meeting to resume at a future time; defer; recess
The judge *adjourned* the court to the following Monday.

**advent** (*n.*)
'ad-,vent

a "coming to"; arrival; approach
The weather bureau gave adequate warning of the *advent* of the hurricane.

**adversary** (*n.*)
'ad-vər-,ser-ē

person "turned toward" or facing another as an opponent; foe; antagonist
Before the contest began, the champion and her *adversary* shook hands.

| **adverse** (*adj.*)<br>ad-'vərs | in opposition to one's interests; hostile;<br>unfavorable |
|---|---|

Because of *adverse* reviews, the producer announced that the play will close with tonight's performance.

 **EXERCISE 4.2:** *AD-* WORDS

Write the most appropriate word from group 2.

1. With the __?__ of autumn, the days become shorter.
2. England was our __?__ in the War of 1812.
3. Is it very expensive to __?__ a summer home for year-round living?
4. We have sweets, but only occasionally. We are not __?__ to them.
5. The candidate has few supporters in the rural areas; most of his __?__s are in the cities.

## 3. *ANTE-:* "before"
## 4. *POST-:* "after"

| **antecedents** (*n. pl.*)<br>,an-tə-'sē-dənts | ancestors; forebears; predecessors |
|---|---|

Ronald's *antecedents* came to this country more than a hundred years ago.

| **antedate** (*v.*)<br>'an-ti-,dāt | 1. assign a date before the true date |
|---|---|

If you used yesterday's date on a check written today, you have *antedated* the check.

2. come before in date; predate; precede
Alaska *antedates* Hawaii as a state, having gained statehood on January 3, 1959, seven months before Hawaii.

| **postdate** (*v.*)<br>'pōst-,dāt | assign a date after the true date |
|---|---|

I *postdated* the check; it has tomorrow's date on it.

| **ante meridiem** (*adj.*)<br>,an-ti mə-'ri-dē-əm | before noon |
|---|---|

In 9 A.M., A.M. stands for *ante meridiem,* meaning "before noon."

**post meridiem** (*adj.*)
ˌpōst mə-ˈri-dē-əm

after noon
    In 9 P.M., P.M. stands for *post meridiem,* meaning "afternoon."

**anteroom** (*n.*)
ˈan-ti-ˌrüm

room placed before and forming an entrance to another; antechamber; waiting room
    If the physician is busy when patients arrive, the nurse asks them to wait in the *anteroom.*

**postgraduate** (*adj.*)
ˌpōst-ˈgra-jə-wət

having to do with study after graduation, especially after graduation from college
    After college, Nina hopes to do *postgraduate* work in law school.

**postmortem** (*n.*)
ˈpōst-ˈmȯr-təm

1. thorough examination of a body after death; autopsy
    The purpose of a *postmortem* is to discover the cause of death.

2. detailed analysis or discussion of an event just ended
    In a *postmortem* after a defeat, we discuss what went wrong and what we can do to improve.

**postscript** (*n.*)
ˈpōst-ˌskript

note added to a letter after it has been written
    After signing the letter, I noticed I had omitted an important fact, and I had to add a *postscript.*

 **EXERCISE 4.3:** *ANTE-* AND *POST-* WORDS

Write the most appropriate word from groups 3 and 4.

1. After graduating from the College of the City of New York, Jonas Salk did __?__ study at New York University to earn an M.D. degree.

2. Mr. Sims told me to put tomorrow's date on the letter, but I forgot to __?__ it.

3. The __?__ showed that the patient had died of natural causes.

4. In some areas, the peasants still use the same methods of farming as their __?__ did centuries ago.

5. You will not need a(n) __?__ if you plan your letter carefully.

## 5. BI-: "two"
## 6. SEMI-: "half," "partly"

**bicameral** (*adj.*)
bī-'kam-rəl

consisting of two chambers or legislative houses
Our legislature is *bicameral;* it consists of the House of Representatives and the Senate.

**bicentennial** (*n.*)
,bī-sen-'te-nē- əl

two-hundredth anniversary
Our nation's *bicentennial* was celebrated in 1976.

**biennial** (*adj.*)
bī-'e-nē-əl

occurring every two years
A defeated candidate for the House of Representatives can run again in two years because the elections are *biennial.*

**semiannual** (adi.)
,se-mē-'an-yə-wəl

occurring every half year, or twice a year; semiyearly
Promotion in our school is *semiannual,* occurring in January and June.

**bimonthly** (*adj.*)
bī-'mənth-lē

occurring every two months
We receive only six utility bills a year because we are billed on a *bimonthly* basis.

**semimonthly** (*adj.*)
,se-mē-'mənth-lē

occurring every half month, or twice a month
Employees paid on a *semimonthly* basis receive two salary checks per month.

**bilateral** (*adj.*)
bī-'la-t(ə)-rəl

having two sides
French forces joined the Americans in a *bilateral* action against the British at the Battle of Yorktown in 1781.

**bilingual** (*adj.*)
bī-'liŋ-gwəl

1. speaking two languages equally well
New York has a large number of *bilingual* citizens who speak English and a foreign language.

2. written in two languages
The instructions on the voting machine are *bilingual;* they are in English and Spanish.

**bipartisan** (*adj.*)
bī-'pär-tə-zən

representing two political parties
Congressional committees are *bipartisan;* they include Democratic and Republican members.

**bisect** (*v.*)
'bī-,sekt

divide into two equal parts
A diameter is a line that *bisects* a circle.

**semicircle** (*n.*)
'se-mē-,sər-kəl

half of a circle
At the end of the lesson, students gathered about the teacher in a *semicircle* to ask additional questions.

**semiconscious** (*adj.*)
,se-mē-'kän(t)-shəs

half conscious; not fully conscious
In the morning, as you begin to awaken, you are in a *semiconscious* state.

**semidetached** (*adj.*)
,se-mē-di-'tacht

partly detached; sharing a wall with an adjoining building on one side, but detached on the other
All the houses on the block are attached, except the corner ones, which are *semidetached.*

**semiskilled** (*adj.*)
,se-mē-'skild

partly skilled
Workers in a *semiskilled* job usually do not require a long period of training.

 **EXERCISE 4.4:** *BI-* AND *SEMI-* WORDS

Write the most appropriate word from groups 5 and 6.

1. Everyone will benefit from the warmth of the fireplace if you arrange the chairs around it in a __?__ .

2. The inspections are __?__ ; there is one every six months.

3. A state that has both an assembly and a senate has a __?__ legislature.

4. America's foreign policy is __?__ ; it represents the views of both major political parties.

5. A __?__ house shares a common wall.

## *Review Exercises*

 **REVIEW 1:** LATIN PREFIXES 1–6

For each Latin prefix in column I, write the *letter* of its meaning from column II.

| COLUMN I | COLUMN II |
|---|---|
| 1. ab-, a-, or abs- | *a.* half or partly |
| 2. semi- | *b.* two |
| 3. ante- | *c.* from, away, or off |
| 4. ad- | *d.* after |
| 5. post- | *e.* to, toward, or near |
| 6. bi- | *f.* before |

 **REVIEW 2:** WORD-BUILDING

On your answer paper, write the prefix for column I and the complete word for column III. The answer to question 1 is AD + HERENT = ADHERENT.

| COLUMN I | COLUMN II | COLUMN III |
|---|---|---|
| 1. __?__ <br> *to* | + HERENT <br> *one who sticks* | = __?__ <br> *one who sticks to; follower* |
| 2. __?__ <br> *two* | + LINGUAL <br> *pertaining to a tongue* | = __?__ <br> *speaking two languages* |
| 3. __?__ <br> *after* | + DATED | = __?__ <br> *dated after (the true date)* |
| 4. __?__ <br> *away* | + RASION <br> *scraping* | = __?__ <br> *scraping away (of the skin)* |
| 5. __?__ <br> *before* | + CHAMBER <br> *room* | = __?__ <br> *room before another; waiting room* |

6. __?__ + SKILLED = __?__
   partly                partly skilled

7. __?__ + HORS = __?__
   from    shrinks       shrinks from; loathes; detests

8. __?__ + LATERAL = __?__
   two     pertaining to a side    having two sides

9. __?__ + CIRCLE = __?__
   half                  half circle

10. __?__ + JACENT = __?__
    near    lying        lying near; neighboring

11. __?__ + RUPT = __?__
    off     broken       broken off; sudden; unexpected

12. __?__ + VERSE = __?__
    away    turned       turned away; opposed; unwilling

13. __?__ + PONING = __?__
    after   putting      putting after; deferring; delaying

14. __?__ + EQUATE = __?__
    to      equal        equal to; sufficient; enough

15. __?__ + CAMERAL = __?__
    two     pertaining to    consisting of two chambers
            a chamber

16. __?__ + CENTENNIAL = __?__
    two     hundredth     two-hundredth anniversary
            anniversary

17. __?__ + APTED = __?__
    to      fitted       fitted to; adjusted

18. __?__ + TAINING = __?__
    from    holding      holding oneself from doing
                         something; refraining

19. __?__ + SCRIPT = __?__
    after   written      note added after signature
                         of a letter

20. __?__ + VERT = __?__
    off     turn; ward   ward off; turn away; prevent

**REVIEW 3:** SENTENCE COMPLETION

Write the word from the list below that best fits the context.

| | | |
|---|---|---|
| abdicate | abhor | abrupt |
| abscond | absorbing | adapt |
| addicted | adequate | adjourn |
| advent | adversary | antecedents |
| anteroom | averse | avocation |
| bilingual | bipartisan | postmortem |
| postscript | semidetached | |

1. Ken, who plays golf eight hours a day, claims it is just his __?__, but he is quite obviously __?__ to it.

2. Though it is true that our __?__ were hunters, many of us __?__ the practice.

3. In the __?__ to her letter, Lucille indicated that she would not be __?__ to a phone call from her former friend.

4. Surprisingly enough, the __?__ committee reached agreement quickly and was able to __?__ in less than an hour.

5. Used to rural life, the family could not __?__ to their __?__ city home, where noises from their neighbor penetrated the common wall.

6. The book Alice was reading was so __?__ that she did not notice the __?__ of the storm.

7. In the coroner's __?__, the detective waited patiently for the results of the __?__ on the murder victim.

8. The game came to a(n) __?__ halt when a stranger dashed onto the court and __?__ed with the only basketball we had.

9. Believing his health was no longer __?__ for him to rule, the ailing monarch decided to __?__ his throne.

10. __?__ American officers who knew the language of our __?__ helped to negotiate the truce.

 **REVIEW 4:** SYNONYMS

Avoid repetition by replacing the boldfaced word or expression with a **synonym** from the following words.

| | | |
|---|---|---|
| abnormal | absolve(d) | adjoin(s) |
| adversary | adverse | avert |
| bicentennial | bilateral | bisect |
| semiconscious | | |

1. Two of the suspects were found guilty, and one was **declared free of guilt**.

2. **Cut** this six-foot board **in two** to give us two three-foot lengths.

3. It would be **unusual** if traffic were light at 5 P.M. because that is usually a busy hour.

4. Often, for the first minute or two after I awake, I am only **half awake**.

5. Was the accident unpreventable, or could you have done something to **prevent** it?

6. The weather yesterday was **unfavorable** for sailing, but today it is supposed to be favorable.

7. Who else is opposing you in the election? Is Olga your only **opponent**?

8. Both sides have joined in a **two-sided** effort to improve working conditions.

9. The post office is next to the railroad station, and the hardware store **is next to** the bakery.

10. The United States celebrated its one-hundredth anniversary as a nation in 1876 and its **two-hundredth anniversary** in 1976.

**REVIEW 5:** ANTONYMS

Write the word from the list below that is most nearly the **opposite** of the boldfaced word or words.

| | | |
|---|---|---|
| abhor | abrupt | adequate |
| adherent | adjacent | adversary |
| adverse | antecedents | avocation |
| postgraduate | | |

1. We __?__ villains but **admire** heroes and heroines.

2. Many a nation that was our __?__ in World War II is now our **ally**.

3. General Benedict Arnold was a loyal and courageous __?__ of the Revolutionary cause until 1780, when he turned **renegade**.

4. Though we were promised __?__ school funding, the money voted by the legislature is **insufficient**.

5. There was no parking space in the field __?__ to the building; we had to park in a **distant** lot.

6. The __?__ comments of the judges outweighed their **favorable** ones.

7. As __?__ of future generations, we must protect the resources of this planet. Otherwise, our **descendants** may not forgive us.

8. Growth in childhood is **gradual**; there are usually no __?__ changes.

9. The grades students earn in their __?__ courses are usually better than those they achieved in their **undergraduate** work.

10. From the knowledge Sarah has about gardening, one might think it is her **profession**, but it is just her __?__.

 **REVIEW 6:** CONCISE WRITING

Express the thought of each sentence below in **no more than four words**.

1. Wasn't Antony the one who stood in opposition to Brutus?

2. Skating is what she enjoys doing when she is not at work in her regular occupation.

3. The legislature that France has is made up of two houses.

4. What is the reason that made them depart in secret?

5. We met with circumstances that were not favorable to our interests.

**REVIEW 7:** SYNONYM SUMMARY

Each line, when completed, should have three words similar in meaning. Write the *complete* words.

1. n (2) ghboring    n (2) rby           (2) jacent

2. int (1) r (1) sting    (2) grossing       (2) sorbing

3. l (2) the         (2) test            abh (1) r

4. an (1) estors     foreb (2) rs        (4) cedents

5. f (1) t           su (1) t            (2) apt

6. host (1) le       (2) favorable       (2) verse

7. follow (2)        supp (2) ter        adh (1) r (1) nt

8. (2) expected      sudd (2)            (2) rupt

9. appr (2) ch       arriv (1) l         (2) vent

10. (2) nounce       resi (1) n          abdi (4)

11. d (1) f (1) r    r (1) cess          adj (2) rn

12. (1) scape        fl (2)              (2) scond

13. unus (2) l       (2) regular         (2) normal

14. b (1) rd (1) r   (1) but             (2) join

15. (2) topsy        anal (1) sis        post (3) tem

16. habit (1) ated   (2) voted           (2) dicted

17. prec (1) d (1)   (3) date            ante (4)

18. enou (2)         suffi (2) ent       (3) quate

19. opp (1) n (1) nt (2) tagonist        (2) versary

20. ex (1) nerate    exc (1) lp (1) te   (2) solve

**REVIEW 8:** ANALOGIES

Which lettered pair of words—*a, b, c, d,* or *e*—most nearly expresses the same relationship as the capitalized pair?

1. AVERSE : OPPOSE
   - *a.* devious : elucidate
   - *b.* convinced : doubt
   - *c.* cordial : alienate
   - *d.* frank : disclose
   - *e.* original : imitate

2. POSTSCRIPT : LETTER
   - *a.* postmark : envelope
   - *b.* headline : article
   - *c.* caboose : train
   - *d.* rain : rainbow
   - *e.* bookmark : place

3. UNPLIABLE : ADAPT
   - *a.* law-abiding : trespass
   - *b.* rational : think
   - *c.* literate : write
   - *d.* docile : heed
   - *e.* perceptive : foresee

   *Hint:* An **unpliable** person does not **adapt**.

4. ADHERENT : LOYALTY
   - *a.* beggar : resources
   - *b.* perjurer : credibility
   - *c.* fugitive : pursuit
   - *d.* bigot : tolerance
   - *e.* prodigy : talent

5. BILINGUAL : LANGUAGE
   - *a.* versatile : skill
   - *b.* outspoken : tongue
   - *c.* nimble : agility
   - *d.* observant : vision
   - *e.* ambidextrous : hand

6. ABSOLVE : GUILT
   - *a.* implicate : suspicion
   - *b.* enlighten : ignorance
   - *c.* incarcerate : penitentiary
   - *d.* upgrade : rank
   - *e.* illuminate : light

7. ADVERSARY : ALLY
   - *a.* fan : addict
   - *b.* spy : informer
   - *c.* radical : conservative
   - *d.* poltroon : craven
   - *e.* monarch : despot

8. SEMIANNUAL : YEARLY
   - *a.* half : whole
   - *b.* fragment : piece
   - *c.* month : year
   - *d.* core : exterior
   - *e.* crescent : moon

9. ABRASION : SKIN
   - *a.* fertility : soil
   - *b.* drought : precipitation
   - *c.* erosion : stone
   - *d.* propulsion : wind
   - *e.* conflagration : fire

10. ABSCOND : DEPART
    - *a.* state : proclaim
    - *b.* grant : withhold
    - *c.* conceal : reveal
    - *d.* conspire : agree
    - *e.* declare : announce

 **REVIEW 9:** COMPOSITION

Answer in a sentence or two.

1. Would you rather be paid on a bimonthly or semimonthly basis? Give reasons for your choice.

2. Do you think it is abnormal for people to abhor their adversaries? Why or why not?

3. Why might a doctor at a postmortem take note of any unusual abrasions?

4. Would most people be adverse to riding with a semiconscious driver? Why?

5. Tell how one of your antecedents adapted to life in the United States.

# LATIN PREFIXES 7–12

## *Pretest 2*

Write the *letter* of the best answer.

1. To take part in a school's *intramural* program, you must __?__.

   (A) be on the school team   (B) have approval for competing with students of other schools   (C) be a student at the school

2. A *countermanded* order should __?__.

   (A) be ignored   (B) receive preference   (C) be obeyed

3. When there is an *exclusive* showing of a film at a theater, __?__.

   (A) no other theater in town has it   (B) all seats are reserved
   (C) children unaccompanied by adults are excluded

4. People who *inhibit* their curiosity usually __?__.

   (A) open packages as soon as received   (B) mind their own
   business   (C) have little patience

5. The chairperson said Phil's suggestion was *extraneous,* but I thought it was __?__.

   (A) original   (B) relevant   (C) off the topic

6. A friend who *intercedes* for you __?__.

   (A) takes the blame for you   (B) takes your place
   (C) pleads for you

   **THE ANSWERS ARE**
   **1.** C   **2.** A   **3.** A   **4.** B   **5.** B   **6.** C

The following pages will acquaint you with additional words formed with the six Latin prefixes involved in the pretest: *ex-, in-, extra-, intra-, contra-,* and *inter-.*

## 7. E-, EX-: "out," "from," "away"
## 8. IN-, IM-: "in," "into," "on," "against," "over"

| WORD | MEANING AND TYPICAL USE |
|---|---|
| **emigrate** (*v.*)<br>'e-mə-ˌgrāt | move out of a country or region to settle in another<br>At thirteen, Maria Callas *emigrated* from the United States. |
| **immigrate** (*v.*)<br>'i-mə-ˌgrāt | move into a foreign country or region as a permanent resident<br>At thirteen, Maria Callas *immigrated* to Greece. |
| **eminent** (*adj.*)<br>'e-mə-nənt | standing or jutting out; conspicuous; famous; distinguished; noteworthy<br>Maria Callas became an *eminent* opera singer. |
| **imminent** (*adj.*)<br>'i-mə-nənt | hanging over one's head; threatening; about to occur; impending<br>At the first flash of lightning, the beach crowd scurried for shelter from the *imminent* storm. |
| **enervate** (*v.*)<br>'e-nər-ˌvāt | (literally, "take out the nerves or strength") lessen the strength of; enfeeble; weaken<br>I was so *enervated* by the broiling sun that I had to sit down. |
| **erosion** (*n.*)<br>i-'rō-zhən | gradual wearing away; deterioration; depletion<br>Running water is one of the principal causes of soil *erosion*. |
| **evoke** (*v.*)<br>i-'vōk | bring out; call forth; elicit; produce<br>The suggestion to lengthen the school year has *evoked* considerable opposition. |

**invoke** (*v.*)
in-'vōk

call on for help or protection; appeal to for support
Refusing to answer the question, the witness *invoked* the Fifth Amendment, which protects persons from being compelled to testify against themselves.

**excise** (*v.*)
ek-'sīz

cut out; remove by cutting out
With a penknife, he peeled the apple and *excised* the wormy part.

**incise** (*v.*)
in-'sīz

cut into; carve; engrave
The letters on the cornerstone had been *incised* with a power drill.

**exclusive** (*adj.*)
iks-'klü-siv

1. shutting out, or tending to shut out, others
An *exclusive* club does not readily accept newcomers.

2. not shared with others; single; sole
Before the game, each team had *exclusive* use of the field for a ten- minute practice period.

**inclusive** (*adj.*)
in-'klü-siv

1. (literally, "shutting in") including the limits (dates, numbers, etc.) mentioned
The film will be shown from August 22 to 24, *inclusive,* for a total of three days.

2. broad in scope; comprehensive
An unabridged dictionary is much more *inclusive* than an ordinary desk dictionary.

**exhibit** (*v.*)
ig-'zi-bət

(literally, "hold out") show; display
The museum is now *exhibiting* the art of the Inuit people of northern Canada.

**inhibit** (*v.*)
in-'hi-bət

(literally, "hold in") hold in check; restrain; repress
Many could not *inhibit* their tears; they cried openly.

**expel** (*v.*)
ik-'spel

drive out; force out; compel to leave; banish; eject
The student who was *expelled* from the university because of poor grades applied for readmission the following term.

**impel** (*v.*)
im-'pel

drive on; force; compel
We do not know what *impelled* the secretary to resign.

**implicate** (*v.*)
'im-plə-,kāt

(literally, "fold in or involve") show to be part of or connected with; involve; entangle
One of the accused persons confessed and *implicated* two others in the crime.

**impugn** (*v.*)
im-'pyün

(literally, "fight against") call in question; assail by words or arguments; attack as false; contradict; attack; malign
The treasurer should not have been offended when asked for a financial report. No one was *impugning* his honesty.

**incarcerate** (*v.*)
in-'kär-sə-,rāt

put in prison; imprison; confine
After their escape and recapture, the convicts were *incarcerated* in a more secure prison.

**inscribe** (*v.*)
in-'skrīb

(literally, "write on") write, engrave, or print to create a lasting record; imprint; autograph
The name of the winner will be *inscribed* on the medal.

**insurgent** (*n.*)
in-'sər-jənt

one who rises in revolt against established authority; rebel; mutineer
The ruler promised to pardon any *insurgents* who would lay down their arms.

**insurgent** (*adj.*)

rebellious; insubordinate; mutinous
General Washington led the *insurgent* forces in the Revolutionary War.

 **EXERCISE 4.5:** *E-, EX-, IN-,* AND *IM-* WORDS

Write the most appropriate word from groups 7 and 8.

1. This afternoon the swimming team has __?__ use of the pool. No one else will be admitted.

2. No one can __?__ the settler's claim to the property, since he holds the deed to the land.

3. Over the centuries, the Colorado River has carved its bed out of solid rock by the process of __?__.

4. A lack of opportunity compelled thousands to __?__ from their native land.

5. Proposals to increase taxes usually __?__ strong resistance.

6. The famine-stricken nation is expected to __?__ the help of its more fortunate neighbors.

7. On the front page, I am going to __?__ these words: "To Dad on his fortieth birthday. Love, Ruth."

8. Learning that their arrest was __?__, the insurgent leaders went into hiding.

9. The judge asked the guards to __?__ the spectators who were creating a disturbance.

10. We just had to see what was in the package. We could not __?__ our curiosity.

## 9. EXTRA-: "outside"
## 10. INTRA-: "within"

**extracurricular** (*adj.*)
,ek-strə-kə-'ri-kyə-lər

outside the regular curriculum or course of study
Why don't you join an *extracurricular* activity, such as a club, the school newspaper, or a team?

**extraneous** (*adj.*)
ek-'strā-nē-əs

coming from or existing outside; foreign; not essential; not pertinent; irrelevant
You said you would stick to the topic, but you keep introducing *extraneous* issues.

**extravagant** (*adj.*)
ik-'stra-vi-gənt

1. outside or beyond the bounds of reason; excessive
Reliable manufacturers do not make *extravagant* claims for their products.

2. spending lavishly; wasteful
In a few months, the *extravagant* heir spent the fortune of a lifetime.

**intramural** (*adj.*)
,in-trə-'myür-əl

within the walls or boundaries (of a school, college, etc.); confined to members (of a school, college, etc.)

At most schools, the students participating in *intramural* athletics vastly outnumber the students involved in interscholastic sports.

**intraparty** (*adj.*)
,in-trə-'pär-tē

within a party

The Democrats are trying to heal *intraparty* strife so as to present a united front in the coming election.

**intrastate** (*adj.*)
,in-trə-'stāt

within a state

Commerce between the states is regulated by the Interstate Commerce Commission, but *intrastate* commerce is supervised by the states themselves.

**intravenous** (*adj.*)
,in-trə-'vē-nəs

within or by way of the veins

Patients are nourished by *intravenous* feeding when too ill to take food by mouth.

 **EXERCISE 4.6:** *EXTRA-* AND *INTRA-* WORDS

Write the most appropriate word from groups 9 and 10.

1. Your claim that you would win by a landslide was certainly __?__, as you were nearly defeated.

2. An air conditioner cools a room and helps to shut out __?__ noises.

3. The theft must be regarded as an __?__ matter, unless the stolen goods have been transported across state lines.

4. Some educators want to concentrate on __?__ athletics and do away with interscholastic competition.

5. Though fencing is not in the curriculum, it is offered as an __?__ activity.

## 11. CONTRA-, CONTRO-, COUNTER-: "against," "contrary"

**con** (*adv.*)
'kän

(short for *contra*) against; on the negative side
I abstained from casting my ballot because I could not decide whether to vote *pro* or *con*.

**con** (*n.*)

(used mainly in the plural) opposing argument; reason against
Before taking an important step, carefully study the *pros* and *cons* of the matter.

**contraband** (*n.*)
'kän-trə-,band

merchandise imported or exported contrary to law; smuggled goods
Customs officials examined the luggage of the suspected smuggler but found no *contraband*.

**contravene** (*v.*)
,kän-trə-'vēn

go or act contrary to; violate; disregard; infringe
By invading the neutral nation, the dictator *contravened* an earlier pledge to guarantee its independence.

**controversy** (*n.*)
'kän-trə-,vər-sē

(literally, "a turning against") dispute; debate; quarrel
Our *controversy* with Great Britain over the Oregon Territory nearly led to war.

**counter** (*adv.*)
'kaůn-tər

(followed by *to*) contrary; in the opposite direction
The student's plan to drop out of school runs *counter* to his parents' wishes.

**countermand** (*v.*)
'kaůn-tər-,mand

cancel (an order) by issuing a contrary order; revoke
The health commissioner ordered the plant to close, but a judge *countermanded* the order.

**incontrovertible** (*adj.*)
,in-kän-trə-'vər-tə-bəl

not able to be "turned against" or disputed; unquestionable; certain; indisputable
The suspect's fingerprints on the safe were considered *incontrovertible* evidence of participation in the robbery.

## EXERCISE 4.7: *CONTRA-, CONTRO-,* AND *COUNTER-* WORDS

Write the most appropriate word from group 11.

1. Until we became embroiled in __?__, Peggy and I were the best of friends.
2. A birth certificate is __?__ proof of age.
3. Vessels carrying __?__ are subject to seizure.
4. A superior officer has the power to __?__ the orders of a subordinate.
5. I cannot support you in an activity that you undertook __?__ to my advice.

## 12. *INTER-: "between"*

| | |
|---|---|
| **intercede** (*v.*)<br>‚in-tər-'sēd | (literally, "go between") interfere to reconcile differences; mediate; plead in another's behalf; intervene<br>    I would have lost my place on line if you hadn't *interceded* for me. |
| **intercept** (*v.*)<br>‚in-tər-'sept | (literally, "catch between") stop or seize on the way from one place to another; interrupt; catch<br>    We gained possession of the ball when Russ *intercepted* a forward pass. |
| **interlinear** (*adj.*)<br>‚in-tər-'li-nē-ər | inserted between lines already printed or written<br>    It is difficult to make *interlinear* notes if the space between the lines is very small. |
| **interlude** (*n.*)<br>'in-tər-‚lüd | anything filling the time between two events; interval; break; intermission<br>    Between World War I and II, there was a twenty-one-year *interlude* of peace. |
| **intermediary** (*n.*)<br>‚in-tər-'mē-dē-‚er-ē | go-between; mediator<br>    For his role as *intermediary* in helping to end the Russo-Japanese War, Theodore Roosevelt won the Nobel Peace Prize. |

**intermission** (*n.*)          pause between periods of activity; interval;
,in-tər-'mi-shən          interruption
          During the *intermission* between the first and
second acts, you will have a chance to purchase
refreshments.

**intersect** (*v.*)          (literally, "cut between") cut by passing through
,in-tər-'sekt          or across; divide; cross
          Broadway *intersects* Seventh Avenue at Times
Square.

**interurban** (*adj.*)          between cities or towns
,in-tər-'ər-bən          The only way to get to the next town is by
automobile or taxi; there is no *interurban* bus.

**intervene** (*v.*)          1. come between
,in-tər-'vēn          The summer vacation *intervenes* between the
close of one school year and the beginning of the
next.

          2. come in to settle a quarrel; intercede; mediate
          Let the opponents settle the dispute by
themselves; don't *intervene*.

 **EXERCISE 4.8:** *INTER-* WORDS

Write the most appropriate word from group 12.

1. A conspicuous warning signal must be posted wherever railroad
   tracks __?__ a highway.
2. Though asked repeatedly to be an __?__ in the labor dispute, the
   mayor so far has refused to intercede.
3. Radio stations sometimes offer a brief __?__ of music between the
   end of one program and the start of another.
4. A special task force is trying to __?__ the invaders.
5. Construction funds have been voted for a four-lane __?__ highway
   linking the three cities.

## *Review Exercises*

 **REVIEW 10:** LATIN PREFIXES 7–12

For each Latin prefix in column I, write the *letter* of its meaning from column II.

COLUMN I

1. *intra-*
2. *inter-*
3. *extra-*
4. *e-, ex-*
5. *contra-, contro-, counter-*
6. *in-, im-*

COLUMN II

*a.* out, from, away
*b.* against, contrary
*c.* in, into, on, against, over
*d.* within
*e.* between
*f.* outside

 **REVIEW 11:** WORD-BUILDING

Write the prefix for column I and the complete word for column III.

| COLUMN I | | COLUMN II | | COLUMN III |
|---|---|---|---|---|
| 1. _?_ *between* | + | VENE *come* | = | _?_ *come between* |
| 2. _?_ *in* | + | HIBIT *hold* | = | _?_ *hold in; restrain* |
| 3. _?_ *away* | + | ROSION *wearing* | = | _?_ *gradual wearing away* |
| 4. _?_ *against* | + | VERSY *turning* | = | _?_ *a turning against; dispute* |
| 5. _?_ *against* | + | SURGENT *rising* | = | _?_ *rising against; rebellious* |
| 6. _?_ *within* | + | VENOUS *pertaining to the veins* | = | _?_ *within the veins* |

**7.** _?_ + LINEAR = _?_
*between* *pertaining to lines* *inserted between the lines*

**8.** _?_ + CURRICULAR = _?_
*outside* *pertaining to the* *outside the curriculum*
*curriculum*

**9.** _?_ + MIGRATE = _?_
*into* *move* *move into a foreign country*

**10.** _?_ + CISE = _?_
*out* *cut* *cut out*

**11.** _?_ + MURAL = _?_
*within* *pertaining to walls* *within the walls or boundaries*

**12.** _?_ + MAND = _?_
*against* *command* *cancel by issuing a contrary order*

**13.** _?_ + URBAN = _?_
*between* *pertaining to cities* *between cities or towns*

**14.** _?_ + CISE = _?_
*into* *cut* *cut into; engrave*

**15.** _?_ + VAGANT = _?_
*outside* *wandering* *outside the bounds of reason;*
*excessive*

**16.** _?_ + BAND = _?_
*against* *ban; decree* *goods imported contrary to law*

**17.** _?_ + PEL = _?_
*on* *drive* *drive on; force*

**18.** _?_ + HIBIT = _?_
*out* *hold* *hold out; show; display*

**19.** _?_ + CEDE = _?_
*between* *go* *go between to reconcile*
*differences; mediate*

**20.** _?_ + MINENT = _?_
*out* *projecting* *projecting out; distinguished*

**REVIEW 12:** SENTENCE COMPLETION

Write the word from the list below that best fits the context.

| | | |
|---|---|---|
| contraband | controversy | countermand |
| eminent | evoke | excise |
| exclusive | exhibit | extravagant |
| immigrate | imminent | impel |
| incarcerate | incontrovertible | inscribe |
| insurgent | intercept | intermission |
| intervene | intravenous | |

1. Acting on a tip from an informer, customs agents were able to ⏑？ a shipment of ⏑？.

2. The heir's spending has been so ⏑？ that his financial ruin is ⏑？.

3. When details of the proposed six-lane highway through the center of town are disclosed, they will surely ⏑？ considerable ⏑？.

4. Few had ever heard of Lynn until the Philadelphia Museum of Art ⏑？ ed her work and transformed her into a(n) ⏑？ painter.

5. The thief would have been ⏑？ d for ten years if a higher court had not ⏑？ ed the sentence.

6. If the civil strife in that country continues much longer, it may ⏑？ many more of its inhabitants to ⏑？ to America.

7. The suit charges that the company has been unfairly ⏑？ in its hiring practices, and it asks the court to ⏑？.

8. After the tumor was ⏑？ d, the patient required ⏑？ feeding for three days.

9. During the ten-minute ⏑？, several admirers approached the playwright and asked him to ⏑？ their programs.

10. The dictator's claim that the rebellion has failed is contradicted by ⏑？ evidence that the ⏑？ s are gaining the upper hand.

 **REVIEW 13:** SYNONYMS

Avoid repetition by replacing the boldfaced word or expression with a **synonym**.

| | | |
|---|---|---|
| contravene(s) | extracurricular | extraneous |
| extravagant | implicate(d) | impugn(ed) |
| intercede | intermediary | intersect |
| invoke | | |

1. Not only did they call his ability into question, but they also **questioned** his character.
2. The law protects everyone. Even criminals **call upon** the Constitution **for protection**.
3. Sports are not a part of the curriculum; they are **outside the curriculum**.
4. Let us stick to the topic. We will get nowhere if we keep introducing matters that are **outside the topic of our discussion**.
5. The point where two roads **cross** is a dangerous crossing.
6. The accused falsely **involved** others who had no involvement whatsoever with the plot.
7. We have little regard for anyone who **disregards** regulations that he or she wants others to observe.
8. How can you ask us to be reasonable when you yourself are making demands that are so **beyond the bounds of reason**?
9. Please do not **interfere**; we do not want any interference.
10. Communication between the two adversaries is being conducted through a(n) **go-between**.

**REVIEW 14:** ANTONYMS

Write the word from the list below that is most nearly the **opposite** of the boldfaced word or words.

| | | |
|---|---|---|
| con | enervate | erosion |
| expel | extracurricular | extravagant |
| inhibit | interlinear | intraparty |
| intrastate | | |

1. The tiresome shopping trip had __?__d my sister, but a short nap and a shower **reinvigorated** her.

2. Traffic usually moves faster on **interstate** highways than on __?__ roads.

3. After the severe beach __?__ caused by the storm, the town promised speedy **restoration** of the shoreline.

4. You made so many __?__ corrections that it was hard to read what you had written **on the lines.**

5. Why did he __?__ his resentment for so long before deciding to **express** it?

6. The club voted to __?__ a member for nonpayment of dues and to **admit** two new applicants.

7. Do they realize that they may have to be **frugal** later if they are __?__ now?

8. So far you have told us the **pros** of your plan, but how about the __?__ s?

9. If the Independents continue their self-destructive __?__ sniping, they will be ill-equipped for the **interparty** contests that lie ahead.

10. Anyone who excels both in **curricular** work and __?__ activities is indeed an exceptional person.

 **REVIEW 15:** CONCISE WRITING

Express the thought of each sentence below in **no more than four words.**

1. Who are the ones who have risen in revolt against established authority?

2. You made claims that are beyond the bounds of reason.

3. Shouldn't those who commit the crime of burglary be put behind prison bars?

4. Schools encourage sports activities that involve participation by their own students.

5. Rains are a cause of the gradual wearing away of the soil.

 **REVIEW 16:** SYNONYM SUMMARY

Each line, when completed, should have three words similar in meaning. Write the *complete* words.

1. f (1) rce               comp (1) l            imp (2)

2. interv (1) l            (5) lude              inter (2) ssion

3. disting (2) shed        not (1) worthy        (1) minent

4. can (1) el              rev (1) ke            counter (2) nd

5. elic (1) t              prod (1) ce           (1) voke

6. q (2) rrel              (3) pute              contro (2) rsy

7. thr (2) tening          (2) pending           (2) minent

8. (2) prison              (3) fine              incar (2) rate

9. interf (1) r (1)        (5) vene              inter (2) de

10. compreh (2) sive       br (2) d              (2) clusive

11. restr (2) n            (2) press             (2) hibit

12. inv (1) lve            (2) tangle            (2) plicate

13. unsh (1) red           s (1) le              (2) clusive

14. weak (2)               (2) feeble            (1) nervate

15. cont (2) dict          mal (1) gn            imp (1) gn

16. v (1) olate            (3) regard            (3) travene

17. impr (1) nt            (2) grave             (2) scribe

18. (2) essential          irrel (1) v (1) nt    extran (1) ous

19. deter (2) ration       depl (1) tion         (1) r (1) sion

20. ej (1) ct              b (1) n (1) sh         (2) pel

**REVIEW 17:** ANALOGIES

Which lettered pair of words—*a, b, c, d,* or *e*—most nearly expresses the same relationship as the capitalized pair?

1. IMMINENT : ANXIETY
   - *a.* reasonable : controversy
   - *b.* uncomplicated : confusion
   - *c.* abrupt : surprise
   - *d.* objective : indignation
   - *e.* commonplace: attention

   *Hint:* Something that is **imminent** causes **anxiety**.

2. INHIBIT : REPRESS
   - *a.* grasp : release
   - *b.* withhold : grant
   - *c.* oblige : refuse
   - *d.* conceal : display
   - *e.* withstand : resist

3. INCONTROVERTIBLE : DISPUTE
   - *a.* unimportant : ignore
   - *b.* unique : replace
   - *c.* accessible : approach
   - *d.* vulnerable : injure
   - *e.* excusable : forgive

4. INTERMEDIARY : UNBIASED
   - *a.* interpreter : bilingual
   - *b.* despot : glorified
   - *c.* umpire : partisan
   - *d.* infant : unsupervised
   - *e.* ignoramus : heeded

5. CLIQUE : EXCLUSIVE
   - *a.* benefactor : uncharitable
   - *b.* mob : docile
   - *c.* accomplice : irreproachable
   - *d.* recluse : sociable
   - *e.* conspiracy : clandestine

6. EMINENT : NOTE
   - *a.* corrupt : trust
   - *b.* admirable : contempt
   - *c.* indolent : promotion
   - *d.* culpable : blame
   - *e.* helpless : ridicule

**7.** ENERVATE : FEEBLE

    *a.* misinform : knowledgeable    *b.* pacify : tractable

    *c.* intimidate : intrepid    *d.* accommodate : hostile

    *e.* convince : uncertain

**8.** EXTRANEOUS : PERTINENT

    *a.* outdated : fashionable    *b.* rigid : inflexible

    *c.* foreign : alien    *d.* enigmatic : mysterious

    *e.* improbable : unlikely

**9.** INTERMISSION : PAUSE

    *a.* curtain : window    *b.* commission : service

    *c.* parsley : herb    *d.* truce : combat

    *e.* recess : energy

**10.** MINUTE : INTERLUDE

    *a.* seed : plant    *b.* whale : mammal

    *c.* skyscraper : edifice    *d.* tanker : vessel

    *e.* pittance : amount

 **REVIEW 18:** COMPOSITION

Answer in a sentence or two.

**1.** Why might a king incarcerate insurgent soldiers?

**2.** Are eminent citizens likely to be members of an exclusive club? Explain.

**3.** Give an example of government inhibiting the movement of contraband.

**4.** Why might a leader's extravagant spending cause a controversy during hard economic times?

**5.** Describe a time you were impelled to argue against a rule that ran counter to your interests.

# LATIN PREFIXES 13–18

## *Pretest 3*

Write the *letter* of the best answer.

1. Inhabitants of a *secluded* dwelling have few __?__.

   (A) windows   (B) expenses   (C) neighbors

2. *Malice* cannot exist between __?__.

   (A) old rivals   (B) true friends   (C) close relatives

3. An *illegible* mark cannot be __?__.

   (A) raised   (B) erased   (C) read

4. The opposite of a *benediction* is a __?__.

   (A) curse   (B) contradiction   (C) blessing

5. A *dispassionate* witness is likely to be __?__.

   (A) prejudiced   (B) calm   (C) easily upset

6. *Deciduous* trees __?__.

   (A) shed their leaves   (B) resist disease   (C) are green all year

> **THE ANSWERS ARE**
> 1. C   2. B   3. C   4. A   5. B   6. A

The following pages will introduce you to many more words formed with the six Latin prefixes involved in the pretest: *in-, bene-, mal-, de-, dis-,* and *se-.*

## 13. IN-, IL-, IM-, IR-: "not," "un"

| WORD | MEANING AND TYPICAL USE |
|---|---|
| **illegible** *(adj.)*<br>ˌi(l)-ˈle-jə-bəl | not legible; impossible or hard to read; undecipherable<br>I could read most of the signatures, but a few were *illegible.* |
| **illiterate** *(adj.)*<br>ˌi(l)-ˈli-tə-rət | not literate; unable to read or write; uneducated<br>The new nation undertook to teach its *illiterate* citizens to read and write. |
| **illogical** *(adj.)*<br>ˌi(l)-ˈlä-ji-kəl | not logical; not observing the rules of logic (correct reasoning); irrational; fallacious<br>It is *illogical* to vote for a candidate whom you have no faith in. |
| **immaculate** *(adj.)*<br>i-ˈma-kyə-lət | not spotted; absolutely clean; stainless<br>Before dinner, the tablecloth was *immaculate.* |
| **immature** *(adj.)*<br>ˌi-mə-ˈtür | not mature; not fully grown or developed; young; childish<br>Seniors often consider sophomores too *immature.* |
| **impunity** *(n.)*<br>im-ˈpyü-nə-tē | state of being not punished; freedom from punishment, harm, loss, etc.; immunity<br>As a result of stricter enforcement, speeders are no longer able to break the law with *impunity.* |
| **inaccessible** *(adj.)*<br>ˌi-nik-ˈse-sə-bəl | not accessible; unreachable; hard to get to; unapproachable<br>For most of the year, the Inuit settlements in northern Quebec are *inaccessible,* except by air. |
| **incessant** *(adj.)*<br>(ˌ)in-ˈse-sᵊnt | not ceasing; continuing without interruption; interminable; ceaseless<br>It is almost impossible to cross the street during the rush hour because of the *incessant* flow of traffic. |

**inflexible** *(adj.)*
(,)in-'flek-sə-bəl

not flexible; not easily bent; firm; unyielding
No compromise is possible when both sides remain *inflexible.*

**ingratitude** *(n.)*
in-'gra-tə-,tüd

state of being not grateful; ungratefulness; lack of gratitude
Valerie refuses to let me see her notes, though I have always lent her mine. What *ingratitude!*

**inhospitable** *(adj.)*
,in-(,)hä-'spi-tə-bəl

not hospitable; not showing kindness to guests and strangers; unfriendly
When the visitors come to our school, we should make them feel at home; otherwise they will think we are *inhospitable.*

**insoluble** *(adj.)*
(,)in-'säl-yə-bəl

1. not soluble; incapable of being solved; unsolvable; irresolvable
Scientists are finding solutions to many problems that formerly seemed *insoluble.*

2. not capable of being dissolved
Salt dissolves in water, but sand is *insoluble.*

**irreconcilable** *(adj.)*
i-,re-kən-'sī-lə-bəl

not reconcilable; not able to be brought into friendly accord or compromise; incompatible
After Romeo and Juliet died, their families, who had been *irreconcilable* enemies, became friends.

**irrelevant** *(adj.)*
i-'re-lə-vənt

not relevant; inapplicable; off the topic; extraneous
Stick to the topic; don't make *irrelevant* remarks.

**irrevocable** *(adj.)*
i-'re-və-kə-bəl

not revocable; incapable of being recalled or revoked; unalterable; irreversible
As an umpire's decision is *irrevocable,* it is useless to argue over a call.

 **EXERCISE 4.9:** *IN-, IL-, IM-,* AND *IR-* WORDS

Write the most appropriate word from group 13.

1. Half frozen, the traveler knocked at a strange door, hoping the inhabitants would not be so __?__ as to turn him away from their fire.

2. Prior to their arrest, the gang had committed a number of thefts with __?__.

3. The detective finally succeeded in clearing up the seemingly __?__ mystery by tracking down every clue.

4. On some of the very old tombstones in Boston's Granary Burying Ground, the inscriptions are almost __?__.

5. Before the bridge was built, the island had been __?__ from the mainland, except by ferry.

## 14. BENE-: "good," "well"
## 15. MAL-, MALE-: "evil," "ill," "bad," "badly"

| | |
|---|---|
| **benediction** (*n.*) <br> ˌbe-nə-'dik-shən | (literally, "good saying") blessing; good wishes; approbation <br>      Robinson Crusoe ran off to sea against his parents' wishes and without their *benediction*. |
| **malediction** (*n.*) <br> ˌma-lə-'dik-shən | (literally, "evil saying") curse <br>      With her dying breath, Queen Dido pronounced a *malediction* on Aeneas and all his descendants. |
| **benefactor** (*n.*) <br> 'be-nə-ˌfak-tər | (literally, "one who does good") person who gives kindly aid, money, or a similar benefit <br>      The museum could not have been built without the gift of ten million dollars by a wealthy *benefactor*. |
| **malefactor** (*n.*) <br> 'ma-lə-ˌfak-tər | (literally, "one who does evil") offender; evildoer; criminal <br>      Shortly after the crime, the *malefactor* was apprehended and brought to trial. |
| **beneficial** (*adj.*) <br> ˌbe-nə-'fi-shəl | productive of good; helpful; advantageous <br>      Rest is usually *beneficial* to a person suffering from a bad cold. |

**beneficiary** (*n.*)
,be-nə-'fi-shē-,er-ē

person receiving some good, advantage, or benefit
The sick and the needy will be the *beneficiaries* of your gift to the community fund.

**benevolent** (*adj.*)
bə-'ne-və-lənt

(literally, "wishing well") disposed to promote the welfare of others; kind; charitable
*Benevolent* employers have a sincere concern for the welfare of their employees.

**malevolent** (*adj.*)
mə-'le-və-lənt

(literally, "wishing ill") showing ill will; spiteful; malicious; vicious
In Robert Louis Stevenson's novel Kɪᴅɴᴀᴘᴘᴇᴅ, David Balfour visits a *malevolent* uncle who tries to kill him.

**maladjusted** (*adj.*)
,ma-lə-'jəs-təd

badly adjusted; out of harmony with one's environment
Having grown up in a quiet small town, Jesse was now a *maladjusted* city dweller who complained about noise and crowds.

**malice** (*n.*)
'ma-ləs

ill will; intention or desire to harm another; enmity; malevolence
My tire did not have a leak; someone had deflated it out of *malice*.

**malnutrition** (*n.*)
,mal-nü-'tri-shən

bad or faulty nutrition; poor nourishment
The lack of fresh fruit and vegetables in a person's diet may cause *malnutrition*.

**maltreat** (*v.*)
,mal-'trēt

treat badly or roughly; mistreat; abuse
Jen felt *maltreated* when the teacher scolded her for something that was not her fault.

 **EXERCISE 4.10:** *BENE-, MAL-,* AND *MALE-* WORDS

Write the most appropriate word from groups 14 and 15.

1. Polar bears are at home in cold climates, but their thick fur would leave them __?__ in a warmer environment.
2. The hero of Charles Dickens' novel *Great Expectations* received considerable financial aid from an unknown __?__.

3. Mrs. Adams will inherit a fortune, since she is named as the exclusive __?__ in her wealthy aunt's will.

4. Paula couldn't understand why anyone should bear her so much __?__ as to tear her notebook to bits.

5. Philip Nolan, in Edward Everett Hale's short story "The Man Without a Country," is punished for uttering a __?__ on the United States.

## 16.  DE-: "down," "down from," "opposite of"

| | |
|---|---|
| **decadent** (*adj.*)<br>'de-kə-dənt | (literally, "falling down") deteriorating; growing worse; declining<br>    The *decadent* rooming house was once a flourishing hotel. |
| **deciduous** (*adj.*)<br>di-'si-jə-wəs | having leaves that fall off at the end of the growing season; shedding leaves<br>    Maple, elm, birch, and other *deciduous* trees lose their leaves in the fall. |
| **demented** (*adj.*)<br>di-'men-təd | out of (down from) one's mind; mad; insane; deranged<br>    Whoever did this must have been *demented*; no sane person would have acted in such a way. |
| **demolish** (*v.*)<br>di-'mä-lish | pull or tear down; destroy; raze; wreck<br>    A wrecking crew is *demolishing* the old building. |
| **demote** (*v.*)<br>di-'mōt | move down in grade or rank; degrade; downgrade<br>    For being absent without leave, the corporal was *demoted* to private. |
| **dependent** (*adj.*)<br>di-'pen-dənt | (literally, "hanging down from") unable to exist without the support of another<br>    Children are *dependent* on their parents until they are able to earn their own living. |

**depreciate** (*v.*)
di-'prē-shē-,āt

1. go down in price or value
   New automobiles *depreciate* rapidly, but antiques tend to go up in value.

2. speak slightingly of; belittle; disparage
   The store manager would feel you are *depreciating* him if you refer to him as the "head clerk."

**despise** (*v.*)
di-'spīz

look down on; scorn; feel contempt for; abhor; disdain
   Benedict Arnold was *despised* by his fellow Americans for betraying his country.

**deviate** (*v.*)
'dē-vē-,āt

turn aside, or down (from a route or rule); stray; wander; digress
   Dr. Parker does not see a patient without an appointment, except in an emergency, and she does not *deviate* from this policy.

**devour** (*v.*)
di-'vaú(-ər)

(literally, "gulp down") eat greedily; eat like an animal
   Wendy must have been starved; she *devoured* her food.

 **EXERCISE 4.11:** *DE-* WORDS

Write the most appropriate word from group 16.

1. The bus driver cannot take you to your door because he is not permitted to __?__ from his route.

2. Streets lined with __?__ trees are strewn with fallen leaves each autumn.

3. The patient's speech was not rational but like that of a __?__ person.

4. Retired people like to have an income of their own so as not to be __?__ on others.

5. By A.D. 400, the Romans were well past the peak of their glory and had become a __?__ people.

# 17.  DIS-: "opposite of," "differently," "apart," "away"

**discontent** (*adj.*)
‚dis-kən-'tent

(usually followed by *with*) opposite of "content"; dissatisfied; discontented; disgruntled
Dan was *discontent* with the mark on his Spanish exam; he had expected at least 10 points more.

**discredit** (*v.*)
(‚)dis-'kre-dət

disbelieve; refuse to trust
The parents *discredited* the child's story, since he was in the habit of telling falsehoods.

**discrepancy** (*n.*)
dis-'kre-pən-sē

disagreement; difference; inconsistency; variation
The first witness said the incident had occurred at 10:00 A.M., but the second witness insisted the time was 10:45. This *discrepancy* puzzled the police.

**disintegrate** (*v.*)
di-'sin-tə-‚grāt

do the opposite of "integrate" (make into a whole); break into bits; crumble; decay
The driveway needs to be resurfaced; it is beginning to *disintegrate*.

**dispassionate** (*adj.*)
‚dis-'pa-shə-nət

opposite of "passionate" (showing strong feeling); calm; composed; impartial
For a *dispassionate* account of how the fight started, ask a neutral observer, not a participant.

**disrepair** (*n.*)
dis-ri-'par

opposite of good condition or repair; bad condition
The new owner did not take proper care of the building, and it soon fell into *disrepair*.

**dissent** (*v.*)
di-'sent

feel differently; differ in opinion; disagree
When the matter was put to a vote, 29 agreed and 4 *dissented*.

**dissident** (*adj.*)
'di-sə-dənt

(literally, "sitting apart") not agreeing; dissenting; nonconformist
The compromise was welcomed by all the strikers except a small *dissident* group who felt that the raises were too small.

**distract** (*v.*)
di-'strakt

draw away, or divert the attention of; confuse; bewilder

When the bus is in motion, passengers should do nothing to *distract* the driver.

---

 **EXERCISE 4.12:** *DIS-* WORDS

Write the most appropriate word from group 17.

1. The leader conferred with several __?__ members of his party in an attempt to win them over to his views.

2. Add your marks for the different parts of the test to see if they equal your total mark. If there is a __?__, notify the teacher.

3. The negligent owner allowed her equipment to fall into __?__.

4. I had no reason to __?__ the information, since it came from a reliable source.

5. Turn off the television set while you are trying to concentrate, or it will __?__ your attention.

## 18. SE-: "apart"

**secede** (*v.*)
si-'sēd

(literally, "go apart") withdraw from an organization or federation

When Lincoln was elected President in 1860, South Carolina *seceded* from the Union.

**secession** (*n.*)
si-'se-shən

(literally, "a going apart") withdrawal from an organization or federation

South Carolina's *secession* was followed by that of ten other states and led to the formation of the Confederacy.

**seclude** (*v.*)
si-'klüd

keep apart from others; place in solitude; isolate; sequester

Monica was so upset over losing her job that she *secluded* herself and refused to see anyone.

| | |
|---|---|
| **secure** (*adj.*)<br>si-'kyúr | 1. apart, or free, from care, fear, or worry; confident; assured<br>Are you worried about passing, or do you feel *secure*?<br><br>2. safe against loss, attack, or danger<br>Guests who want their valuables to be *secure* are urged to deposit them in the hotel vault. |
| **sedition** (*n.*)<br>si-'di-shən | going apart from, or against, an established government; action, speech, or writing to overthrow the government; insurrection; treason<br>The signers of the Declaration of Independence, if captured by the enemy, would probably have been tried for *sedition*. |
| **segregate** (*v.*)<br>'se-gri-ˌgāt | (literally, "set apart from the herd") separate from the main body; isolate<br>During the swim period, the nonswimmers are *segregated* from the rest of our group to receive special instruction. |

 ## EXERCISE 4.13: *SE-* WORDS

Write the most appropriate word from group 18.

1. The law forbids public institutions to __?__ people by race, sex, or religion.
2. In a dictatorship, anyone who criticizes the head of state may be charged with __?__.
3. Three of the teams have threatened to __?__ from the league unless at least two umpires are assigned to each game.
4. As the storm approached, coastal residents were evacuated to more __?__ quarters in the interior.
5. Some prefer to study for a test with friends; others like to __?__ themselves with their books.

## *Review Exercises*

 **REVIEW 19:** LATIN PREFIXES 13–18

For each Latin prefix in column I, write the *letter* of its correct meaning from column II.

| COLUMN I | COLUMN II |
|---|---|
| 1. mal-, male- | *a.* opposite of, differently, apart, away |
| 2. se- | *b.* not, un |
| 3. bene- | *c.* down, down from, opposite of |
| 4. dis- | *d.* apart |
| 5. de- | *e.* good, well |
| 6. in-, il-, im-, ir- | *f.* evil, ill, bad, badly |

 **REVIEW 20:** WORD-BUILDING

Write the prefix for column I and the complete word for column III.

| COLUMN I | COLUMN II | COLUMN III |
|---|---|---|
| 1. _?_ <br> *ill* | + VOLENT <br> *wishing* | = _?_ <br> *wishing ill; spiteful* |
| 2. _?_ <br> *not* | + LITERATE <br> *able to read and write* | = _?_ <br> *unable to read and write* |
| 3. _?_ <br> *down* | + VOUR <br> *gulp* | = _?_ <br> *eat greedily* |
| 4. _?_ <br> *apart* | + CURE <br> *care* | = _?_ <br> *apart (free) from care* |
| 5. _?_ <br> *not* | + SOLUBLE <br> *capable of being solved* | = _?_ <br> *incapable of being solved* |

6. _?_     + SPISE     = _?_
   down          look           look down on; scorn

7. _?_     + DICTION     = _?_
   good          saying          blessing

8. _?_     + LEGIBLE     = _?_
   not          able to read          not able to be read

9. _?_     + INTEGRATE     = _?_
   opposite of      make into a whole     break into bits

10. _?_     + FACTOR     = _?_
   evil          one who does        evildoer

11. _?_     + MACULATE     = _?_
   not          spotted          unspotted; absolutely clean

12. _?_     + CREDIT     = _?_
   opposite of      believe          do opposite of believe; refuse
                                          to trust

13. _?_     + MOTE     = _?_
   down          move          move down in rank

14. _?_     + PUNITY     = _?_
   not          punishment        freedom from punishment

15. _?_     + SENT     = _?_
   differently      feel          feel differently; disagree

16. _?_     + NUTRITION     = _?_
   bad          nourishment       poor nourishment

17. _?_     + RELEVANT     = _?_
   not          applicable        not applicable; extraneous

18. _?_     + CEDE     = _?_
   apart          go          go apart; withdraw from
                                          an organization

19. _?_     + CADENT     = _?_
   down          falling          falling down; deteriorating

20. _?_     + MATURE     = _?_
   not          fully grown        not fully grown

**REVIEW 21:** SENTENCE COMPLETION

Write the word from the list below that best fits the context.

| | | |
|---|---|---|
| benefactor | demented | demote |
| depreciate | discontent | discredit |
| disrepair | dissident | distract |
| illiterate | illogical | incessant |
| ingratitude | inhospitable | insoluble |
| malice | malnutrition | secede |
| seclude | secure | |

1. Worried that the daily events of the city would __?__ her from her work, the novelist __?__d herself in a mountain cabin.

2. The Southern states __?__d from the Union because they were __?__ with the policies of the federal government.

3. The aunt never gets a visit from the nephews and nieces whom she put through college. Such __?__ to a(n) __?__ is indeed shocking.

4. When he said, "Madam, this is not a meal to ask a man to," Samuel Johnson __?__d the food his hostess had served. He considered her __?__.

5. By her __?__ stress on the importance of reading, the superintendent hopes to ensure that no one in her district will remain __?__.

6. The colonel has been a model officer. I can only guess that his superior was acting out of __?__ when he tried to __?__ him.

7. Those detectives who termed the case "__?__" did not adhere strictly to the principles of rational thinking. Their approach was __?__.

8. The children felt perfectly __?__ in a tree house that was in such __?__ that its collapse was clearly imminent.

9. The survivor had scarcely slept or eaten for several days. His seemingly __?__ state of mind was the result of fatigue and __?__.

10. A group of __?__ stockholders tried to __?__ the company president by calling attention to his huge annual salary.

## REVIEW 22: SYNONYMS

Avoid repetition by replacing the boldfaced word or expression with a **synonym** from the following words.

| | | |
|---|---|---|
| dependent | demolish(ing) | despise |
| deviate | discrepancy | dissent(ed) |
| immaculate | immature | inaccessible |
| inflexible | | |

1. You deserve a medal for cleanliness; your room is **absolutely clean**.

2. They won't yield an inch. How can we reach a compromise if they are so **unyielding**?

3. We **feel contempt for** the vandals who did this contemptible thing.

4. Almost everyone agreed. I was one of the very few who **disagreed**.

5. You're acting like a child. Stop being **childish**.

6. The crash site is very **hard to get to**, but helicopters may be able to get there.

7. Now, they are **unable to exist without support from others**, but someday they will be able to support themselves.

8. The account of the first eyewitness differs slightly from that of the second. Did you notice the **difference**?

9. One destructive child kept **destroying** what the others were trying to build.

10. Did the plane strictly adhere to its course, or did it **go off course** at any time?

**REVIEW 23:** ANTONYMS

Write the word from the list below that is most nearly the **opposite** of the boldfaced word or words.

| | | |
|---|---|---|
| beneficial | decadent | deciduous |
| dispassionate | illegible | irrelevant |
| maladjusted | malediction | malevolent |
| maltreat | | |

1. It is hard to believe that this __?__ place was once a **flourishing** mining town.
2. Most of the shrubs here are **evergreen**; only the azaleas are __?__.
3. A **biased** observer may be unable to give a(n) __?__ account of what happened.
4. The medication is not entirely __?__; it has some **detrimental** side effects.
5. Some who are now **in harmony with their environment** might become __?__ if they were to find themselves in other surroundings.
6. Prisoners of war are to be **humanely treated**; they must not be __?__ed.
7. We tried to stay **on the topic**; little was said that was __?__.
8. Did you get a **readable** copy? Mine is __?__.
9. They came for a **blessing** but were sent off with a(n) __?__.
10. Relatives could not understand how someone so **benevolent** to strangers could have been __?__ to his own family.

 **REVIEW 24:** CONCISE WRITING

Express the thought of each sentence below in **no more than four words**.

1. The question that Terry is asking has nothing to do with the topic that we are discussing.
2. Maple trees lose their leaves at the end of the growing season.
3. The postcard that came in the mail from Bill is impossible to read.
4. Some did not tell the truth and were able to get away with it.
5. The destination that they are heading for seems hard to get to.

**REVIEW 25:** SYNONYM SUMMARY

Each line, when completed, should have three words similar in meaning. Write the *complete* words.

1. cr (1) m (1) nal      ev (1) ldoer      m (1) l (1) factor

2. diff (1) r (1) nce      inconsisten (1) y      (3) crepancy

3. charit (1) ble      k (1) nd      (4) volent

4. sc (1) rn      (2) hor      (2) spise

5. tr (2) son      ins (2) rection      (2) dition

6. (2) sane      (2) ranged      (2) mented

7. cr (1) mble      (2) cay      dis (2) tegrate

8. enm (1) ty      mal (1) volence      (3) ice

9. w (1) nder      d (1) gress      dev (2) te

10. (2) reversible      (2) alterable      irre (2) cable

11. advantag (2) us      help (3)      benefi (2) al

12. sep (1) rate      is (1) late      se (2) egate

13. inapplic (1) ble      extran (1) ous      irr (1) l (1) v (1) nt

14. (2) terminable      cease (4)      inces (2) nt

15. (2) rational      fallac (2) us      (2) logical

16. disp (1) r (1) ge      (2) little      (2) preciate

17. (3) fident      ass (1) red      sec (1) re

18. dis (2) tisfied      disgr (1) ntled      (3) content

19. r (1) ze      d (1) stroy      (2) molish

20. i (2) late      se (2) ester      (2) clude

**REVIEW 26:** ANALOGIES

Which lettered pair of words—*a, b, c, d,* or *e*—most nearly expresses the same relationship as the capitalized pair?

1. IRREVOCABLE : ALTER
    *a.* unique : match
    *b.* feasible : do
    *c.* disputable : question
    *d.* inconsequential : defer
    *e.* tractable : manage

2. BENEFACTOR : MALICE
    *a.* perpetrator : offense
    *b.* tutor : instruction
    *c.* fledgling : experience
    *d.* curator : museum
    *e.* beneficiary : assistance

3. IMPUNITY : PUNISHMENT
    *a.* merit : reward
    *b.* frailty : injury
    *c.* insecurity : anxiety
    *d.* infallibility : error
    *e.* susceptibility : disease

4. SWINDLER : MALEFACTOR
    *a.* reader : subscriber
    *b.* infant : dependent
    *c.* consumer : manufacturer
    *d.* columnist : publisher
    *e.* physician : pediatrician

5. GLUTTONOUS : DEVOUR
    *a.* lavish : conserve
    *b.* withdrawn : socialize
    *c.* dissident : agree
    *d.* avaricious : hoard
    *e.* determined : waver

6. DISPASSIONATE : PARTIALITY
    *a.* merciless : cruelty
    *b.* indecisive : hesitation
    *c.* maltreated : resentment
    *d.* indifferent : interest
    *e.* malevolent : spite

7. MALNUTRITION : HEALTH

   *a.* scandal : reputation          *b.* exercise : appetite

   *c.* misinformation : inconvenience  *d.* commendation : promotion

   *e.* enlightenment : knowledge

8. IRRATIONAL : LOGIC

   *a.* loyal : allegiance            *b.* facetious : laughter

   *c.* corrupt : ethics              *d.* sturdy : stamina

   *e.* contentious : controversy

9. INCESSANT : INTERMITTENT

   *a.* slovenly : untidy           *b.* dormant : sluggish

   *c.* robust : strong             *d.* meek : acquiescent

   *e.* permanent : transient

10. IMMACULATE : SPOT

   *a.* airtight : weakness        *b.* imperfect : flaw

   *c.* noxious : harm            *d.* priceless : worth

   *e.* versatile : use

 **REVIEW 27:** COMPOSITION

Answer in a sentence or two.

1. Would you rather be shipwrecked on a desert island with a benefactor or a malefactor?

2. Does it make sense to demolish all buildings in disrepair? Why or why not?

3. Why might the leaders of a country claim a dissident group was irrelevant?

4. Should a government treat acts of sedition with impunity? Explain.

5. Would you be surprised if a benevolent organization treated you inhospitably? Why or why not?

# LATIN PREFIXES 19–24

Write the *letter* of the best answer.

**1.** A *protracted* illness is not __?__.

(A) curable   (B) contagious   (C) brief

**2.** The term *circumlocution* in the margin of your composition paper indicates you have __?__.

(A) used too many words to express an idea   (B) wandered off the topic   (C) used a slang expression

**3.** Thoughts that *obsess* you __?__ your mind.

(A) bypass   (B) trouble   (C) relax

**4.** Those who work in *collusion* are seeking to __?__.

(A) escape noise   (B) assist others   (C) commit fraud

**5.** A snowfall in Virginia in __?__ is *premature.*

(A) December   (B) September   (C) March

**6.** If you make a *pertinent* comment, you are __?__.

(A) being rude   (B) delaying the discussion   (C) advancing the discussion

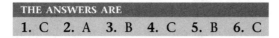

THE ANSWERS ARE

**1.** C   **2.** A   **3.** B   **4.** C   **5.** B   **6.** C

The following pages will introduce several additional words formed with the prefixes involved in the pretest: *circum-, con-, ob-, per-, pre-,* and *pro-.*

# 19.  CIRCUM-: "around," "round"

| WORD | MEANING AND TYPICAL USE |
|---|---|
| **circumference** (*n.*)<br>sər-'kəm-fə-rəns | distance around a circle or rounded body; perimeter<br>The *circumference* of the earth is greatest at the equator and diminishes as we go toward the North or South Pole. |
| **circumlocution** (*n.*)<br>‚sər-kəm-lō-'kyü-shən | roundabout way of speaking; use of excessive number of words to express an idea; verbiage; tautology<br>The *circumlocution* "the game ended with a score that was not in our favor" should be replaced by "we lost the game." |
| **circumnavigate** (*v.*)<br>‚sər-kəm-'na-və-‚gāt | sail around<br>Ferdinand Magellan's expedition was the first to *circumnavigate* the globe. |
| **circumscribe** (*v.*)<br>'sər-kᵊm-‚skrīb | 1. draw a line around<br>On the composition I got back, the teacher had *circumscribed* a misspelled word to call it to my attention.<br><br>2. limit; restrict<br>The patient was placed on a very *circumscribed* diet; there are very few foods she is permitted to eat. |
| **circumspect** (*adj.*)<br>'sər-kᵊm-‚spekt | looking around and paying attention to all possible consequences before acting; cautious; prudent<br>Don't jump to a conclusion before considering all the facts. Be *circumspect*. |
| **circumvent** (*v.*)<br>‚sər-kᵊm-'vent | go around; get the better of; frustrate; skirt; bypass<br>To *circumvent* local sales taxes, shoppers buy in neighboring communities that do not have such taxes. |

**EXERCISE 4.14:** *CIRCUM-* WORDS

Write the most appropriate word from group 19.

1. A physician may decide to __?__ the physical activities and diet of a heart-disease patient.
2. Obey the regulations; don't try to __?__ them.
3. If you had been __?__ you would have tested the used camera before buying it.
4. The __?__ of the earth at the equator is nearly 25,000 miles.
5. The rowers had expected to __?__ the island in a couple of hours, but by evening they were less than halfway around.

## 20. CON-, CO-, COL-, COR-: "together," "with"

**coalesce** (*v.*)
ˌkō-ə-ˈles
grow together; unite into one; join; combine
   During the Revolutionary War, the thirteen colonies *coalesced* into one nation.

**coherent** (*adj.*)
kō-ˈhir-ənt
sticking together; logically connected; consistent; logical
   In *coherent* writing, every sentence is connected in thought to the previous sentence.

**collaborate** (*v.*)
kə-ˈla-bə-ˌrāt
work together with another or others, especially as a coauthor
   George and Helen Papashvily *collaborated* on ANYTHING CAN HAPPEN and several other books.

**collusion** (*n.*)
kə-ˈlü-zhən
(literally, "playing together") secret agreement for a fraudulent purpose; conspiracy; plot
   The federal agency claimed the price increases were due to *collusion* among the producers.

**concord** (*n.*)
ˈkän-ˌkord
state of being together in heart or mind; agreement; harmony
   Neighbors cannot live in *concord* if their children keep fighting with one another.

**congenital** (*adj.*)
kən-'je-nə-t'l

(literally, "born with") existing at birth; inborn; innate
    Helen Keller's deafness and blindness were not *congenital* defects; she was normal at birth.

**convene** (*v.*)
kən-'vēn

come together in a body; meet; assemble
    The House and the Senate will *convene* at noon to hear an address by the President.

**correspond** (*v.*)
‚kȯr-ə-'spänd

1. (literally, "answer together") agree; be in harmony; match; tally
    Helene's account of how the argument started does not *correspond* with Sam's version.

2. communicate by exchange of letters
    Bill and I *correspond* regularly.

### EXERCISE 4.15: *CON-, CO-, COL-,* AND *COR-* WORDS

Write the most appropriate word from group 20.

1. Though elected in November of even-numbered years, the new Congress does not __?__ until the following January.

2. If your seat number does not __?__ to your ticket number, the usher may ask you to move.

3. When Billy Budd, the peacemaker, was aboard, there was perfect __?__ among the sailors.

4. Do you want to __?__ with me, or do you prefer to work alone?

5. Just above St. Louis, the Missouri and Mississippi rivers __?__ into a single waterway.

## 21. OB-: "against," "in the way," "over"

**obliterate** (*v.*)
ə-'bli-tə-‚rāt

(literally, "cover over letters")
erase; blot out; destroy; remove all traces of
    Today's rain has completely *obliterated* yesterday's snow; not a trace remains.

**obsess** (*v.*)
əb-'ses

(literally, "sit over") trouble the mind of; haunt; preoccupy

Ian is *obsessed* with the idea of becoming a professional ballplayer.

**obstacle** (*n.*)
'äb-sti-kəl

something standing in the way; hindrance; obstruction; impediment

If Albert were to visit Rome, the language would be no *obstacle*; he knows Italian.

**obstruct** (*v.*)
əb-'strəkt

be in the way of; hinder; impede; block

The disabled vehicles *obstructed* traffic until removed by a tow truck.

**obtrude** (*v.*)
əb-'trüd

(literally, "thrust against") thrust forward without being asked; intrude; impose

It is unwise for outsiders to *obtrude* their opinions into a family quarrel.

**obviate** (*v.*)
'äb-vē-ˌāt

(literally, "get in the way of") meet and dispose of; make unnecessary; forestall; avert

By removing her hat, the woman in front *obviated* the need for me to change my seat.

 **EXERCISE 4.16:** *OB-* WORDS

Write the most appropriate word from group 21.

1. A dropout will discover that the lack of a high school diploma is a serious __?__ to employment.

2. The pickets sat on the front steps in an attempt to __?__ the entrance.

3. To __?__ waiting on line at the box office, order your tickets by mail.

4. Though Harry is a very careful driver, the possibility of his having a serious accident continues to __?__ his parents.

5. Claire tried to forget the incident, but she couldn't __?__ it from her mind.

# 22. PER-: "through," "to the end," "thoroughly"

**perennial** (*adj.*)
pə-'re-nē-əl

continuing through the years; enduring; unceasing
> Authors have come and gone, but Shakespeare has remained a *perennial* favorite.

**perennial** (*n.*)

plant that lives through the years
> *Perennials* like the azalea and forsythia bloom year after year.

**perforate** (*v.*)
'pər-fə-,rāt

(literally, "bore through") make a hole or holes through; pierce; puncture
> The tack I stepped on went through the sole of my shoe, but luckily did not *perforate* my skin.

**permeate** (*v.*)
'pər-mē-,āt

pass through; penetrate; spread through; pervade
> The aroma of freshly brewed coffee *permeated* the cafeteria.

**perplex** (*v.*)
pər-'pleks

confuse thoroughly; puzzle; bewilder
> I need help with the fourth problem; it *perplexes* me.

**persist** (*v.*)
pər-'sist

(literally, "stand to the end")
1. continue in spite of opposition; refuse to stop; persevere
> Dr. Brown warned Janet of the consequences if she *persisted* in smoking despite his warnings.

2. continue to exist; last; endure
> The rain was supposed to end in the morning, but it *persisted* through the afternoon and evening.

**pertinent** (*adj.*)
'pər-t'n-ənt

(literally, "reaching through to") connected with the matter under consideration; to the point; related; relevant
> Stick to the point; don't give information that is not *pertinent.*

**perturb** (*v.*)
pər-'tərb

disturb thoroughly or considerably; make uneasy; agitate; upset

Sandra's folks were *perturbed* when they learned she had failed two subjects.

 **EXERCISE 4.17:** *PER-* WORDS

Write the most appropriate word from group 22.

1. The claim of wage earners that they are being overtaxed is by no means new; it has been their __?__ complaint.

2. Why do you __?__ in asking to see my notes when I have told you I don't have any?

3. Train conductors use hole punchers to __?__ passenger tickets.

4. We thought the news would upset Jane, but it didn't seem to __?__ her.

5. Road signs that __?__ residents of this community are even more confusing to out-of-town visitors.

## 23. PRE-: "before," "beforehand," "fore-"

**precede** (*v.*)
pri-'sēd

go before; come before

Did your complaint follow or *precede* Jane's?

**preclude** (*v.*)
pri-'klüd

put a barrier before; impede; prevent; make impossible

A prior engagement *precludes* my coming to your party.

**precocious** (*adj.*)
pri-'kō-shəs

(literally, "cooked or ripened before its time")
showing mature characteristics at an early age

If Nancy's three-year-old sister can read, she must be a *precocious* child.

**preconceive** (*v.*)
‚prē-kən-'sēv

form an opinion of beforehand, without adequate evidence

The dislike I had *preconceived* for the book disappeared when I read a few chapters.

**prefabricated** (*adj.*)
prē-'fa-bri-,kā-təd

constructed beforehand
*Prefabricated* homes are quickly erected by putting together large sections previously constructed at a factory.

**preface** (*n.*)
'pre-fəs

foreword; preliminary remarks; author's introduction to a book
The *preface* usually provides information that the reader should know before beginning the book.

**premature** (*adj.*)
,prē-mə-'tyuṙ

before the proper or usual time; early; untimely
Since less than half of the votes have been counted, my opponent's claims of victory are *premature*.

**premeditate** (*v.*)
prē-'me-də-,tāt

consider beforehand
The jury decided that the blow was struck in a moment of panic and had not been *premeditated*.

**presume** (*v.*)
pri-'züm

(literally, "take beforehand") take for granted without proof; assume; suppose
Nineteen of the sailors have been rescued. One is missing and *presumed* dead.

**preview** (*n.*)
'prē-,vyü

view of something before it is shown to the public
Last night Carole and Bob attended a *preview* of a play scheduled to open next Tuesday.

 **EXERCISE 4.18:** *PRE-* WORDS

Write the most appropriate word from group 23.

1. Mozart, who began composing at the age of five, was definitely __?__.

2. The bills they have to pay do not __?__ their making further purchases; they can use their credit.

3. I __?__ the directions to Barbara's house are correct, since she gave them to me herself.

4. A group of distinguished specialists saw a __?__ of the exhibit before it was opened to the public.

5. The report that the President was in town was __?__ because his plane had not yet landed.

# 24. PRO-: "forward," "forth"

**procrastinate** (*v.*)
prə-'kras-tə-nāt

(literally, "move forward to tomorrow") put things off from day to day; delay; dawdle
    Start working on the assignment without delay. It doesn't pay to *procrastinate*.

**proficient** (*adj.*)
prə-'fi-shənt

(literally, "going forward") well advanced in any subject or occupation; skilled; adept; expert
    When I fell behind, the teacher asked one of the more *proficient* students to help me.

**profuse** (*adj.*)
prə-'fyüs

pouring forth freely; exceedingly generous; extravagant; lavish
    Despite a large income, the actor has saved very little because he is a *profuse* spender.

**project** (*v.*)
prə-'jekt

throw or cast forward
    The fireboat's powerful engines *projected* huge streams of water on the blazing pier.

**prominent** (*adj.*)
'prä-mə-nənt

(literally, "jutting forward") standing out; notable; important; conspicuous
    The mayor, the governor, and several other *prominent* citizens attended the preview.

**propel** (*v.*)
prə-'pel

impel forward; drive onward; force ahead; push; thrust
    High winds *propelled* the flames, and they spread rapidly.

**proponent** (*n.*)
prə-'pō-nənt

person who puts forth a proposal or argues in favor of something; advocate; supporter
    At the budget hearing, both *proponents* and opponents of the tax increase will be able to present their views.

**prospect** (*n.*)
'prä-,spekt

thing looked forward to; expectation; vision
To a first-year student, graduation is a distant but pleasant *prospect.*

**prospects** (*n. pl.*)
'prä-,spekts

chances
The *prospects* of our winning are slim.

**protract** (*v.*)
prō-'trakt

(literally, "drag forward") draw out; lengthen; extend; prolong
Our cousins stayed with us only for the day, though we urged them to *protract* their visit.

**protrude** (*v.*)
prō-'trüd

thrust forth; stick out; bulge; jut
Keep your feet under your desk; if they *protrude* into the aisle, someone may trip over them.

**provoke** (*v.*)
prə-'vōk

1. call forth; bring on; cause
Maria's account of her experiences as a babysitter *provoked* much laughter.

2. make angry; annoy; incense; irritate
There would have been no quarrel if Lisa hadn't *provoked* you by calling you a liar.

 **EXERCISE 4.19:** *PRO-* WORDS

Write the most appropriate word from group 24.

1. The __?__ of a sizable raise impelled the new employee to do her best.
2. Your enthusiastic supporters are __?__ in their praise of your merits.
3. George Stephenson was the first to use steam power to __?__ a locomotive.
4. You must not expect an apprentice to be as __?__ as an experienced worker.
5. The proposal to demolish the historic building is sure to __?__ a storm of protest.

## Review Exercises

### REVIEW 28: LATIN PREFIXES 19–24

For each Latin prefix in column I, write the *letter* of its correct meaning from column II.

COLUMN I

1. *per-*
2. *ob-*
3. *circum-*
4. *pro-*
5. *con-, co-, col-, cor-*
6. *pre-*

COLUMN II

*a.* together, with
*b.* through, to the end, thoroughly
*c.* forward, forth
*d.* before, beforehand, fore
*e.* around, round
*f.* against, in the way, over

### REVIEW 29: WORD-BUILDING

Write the prefix for column I and the complete word for column III.

| COLUMN I | COLUMN II | COLUMN III |
|---|---|---|
| 1. __?__ <br> *together* | + HERENT <br> *sticking* | = __?__ <br> *sticking together; logically connected* |
| 2. __?__ <br> *beforehand* | + CONCEIVE <br> *form an opinion* | = __?__ <br> *form an opinion beforehand* |
| 3. __?__ <br> *around* | + NAVIGATE <br> *sail* | = __?__ <br> *sail around* |
| 4. __?__ <br> *forward* | + JECT <br> *throw* | = __?__ <br> *throw or cast forward* |
| 5. __?__ <br> *together* | + LABORATE <br> *work* | = __?__ <br> *work together* |
| 6. __?__ <br> *through* | + MEATE <br> *pass* | = __?__ <br> *pass through; penetrate* |

7. __?__ + STACLE = __?__
   *in the way*    *something standing*    *something standing in the way; obstruction*

8. __?__ + FACE = __?__
   *beforehand*    *something said*    *something said beforehand; foreword*

9. __?__ + VENE = __?__
   *together*    *come*    *come together; assemble*

10. __?__ + FORATE = __?__
    *through*    *bore*    *bore through; pierce*

11. __?__ + TRUDE = __?__
    *against*    *thrust*    *thrust forward without being asked*

12. __?__ + VOKE = __?__
    *forth*    *call*    *call forth; cause*

13. __?__ + LOCUTION = __?__
    *round*    *speaking*    *roundabout way of speaking*

14. __?__ + CLUDE = __?__
    *before*    *put a barrier*    *put a barrier before; prevent*

15. __?__ + RESPOND = __?__
    *together*    *answer*    *match; agree*

16. __?__ + TURB = __?__
    *thoroughly*    *disturb*    *disturb thoroughly; upset*

17. __?__ + CEDE = __?__
    *before*    *go*    *go before; come before*

18. __?__ + PONENT = __?__
    *forth*    *one who puts*    *one who puts forth a proposal*

19. __?__ + FABRICATED = __?__
    *beforehand*    *constructed*    *constructed beforehand*

20. __?__ + SESS = __?__
    *over*    *sit*    *trouble the mind of; haunt*

## REVIEW 30: SENTENCE COMPLETION

Write the word from the list below that best fits the context.

| | | |
|---|---|---|
| circumlocution | circumspect | coalesce |
| collaborate | correspond | obliterate |
| obstruct | perplex | persist |
| preclude | preconceive | prefabricate |
| preface | premature | premeditate |
| presume | preview | prominent |
| prospect | provoke | |

1. The speaker's ineptitude, particularly his fondness for __?__, __?__d some in the audience to leave early.

2. The arrival of spring keeps __?__ing the experts. Sometimes it is late, and sometimes __?__.

3. Many of the people who plan to buy a home have the __?__d notion that __?__d houses are necessarily of low quality.

4. In the __?__ to their book, the authors describe how a chance meeting at a writers' conference led them to __?__.

5. The perpetrator was __?__ enough to __?__ all shreds of incriminating evidence.

6. When the noted reviewer began to get fewer invitations to __?__s, she __?__d it was because of her low ratings of many recent movies.

7. She is determined, nevertheless, to __?__ in writing honest reviews. After all, it was her candor that made her __?__.

8. A longer prison sentence was __?__d when the jury determined that the crime had not been __?__d.

9. So much political support has __?__d around the candidate that the __?__ of his being elected is much stronger.

10. The defense witness's testimony did not at all __?__ with that of the prosecution witness. Was it possibly an attempt to __?__ justice?

 **REVIEW 31:** SYNONYMS

Avoid repetition by replacing the boldfaced word or expression with a
**synonym** from the following words.

| | | |
|---|---|---|
| circumnavigate | circumvent | congenital |
| convene | perturb(ed) | precede |
| procrastinate | proficient | proponent(s) |
| protract | | |

1. We have delayed too long; we must not **delay** any further.

2. Next month the board will **meet** in a new meeting place.

3. When you went sailing, did you **sail around** any of the islands in
   the sound?

4. I don't know who comes after me in the batting order, but I am sure
   that I **come before** you.

5. Drew did not support my proposal at first, but now he is one of its
   chief **supporters.**

6. Prejudice is not **inborn**; no one is born with it.

7. Someone must have said something to upset Amy; she is very
   **upset.**

8. A few wanted to **prolong** the discussion, but the majority refused to
   stay longer.

9. Those who try to **get around** the law may get into trouble.

10. Though Joyce had no computer skills when she was hired, she has
    become a highly **skilled** programmer.

**REVIEW 32:** ANTONYMS

Write the word from the list below that is most nearly the **opposite** of the boldfaced word.

| | | |
|---|---|---|
| circumscribe | congenital | correspond |
| obstacle | persist | pertinent |
| proficient | prominent | proponent |
| protract | | |

1. The poster, unfortunately, was **inconspicuous.** It should have been in a more __?__ place.

2. I was criticized for omitting some __?__ details and including some that were quite **irrelevant**.

3. The scars on my arm were **acquired** through injuries. The birthmarks, of course, are __?__.

4. The patient __?__ed in smoking, though his physician had warned him to **desist**.

5. I am neither an **opponent** nor a(n) __?__ of the proposed changes.

6. The mediators seek to **curtail** the walkout, saying there is little to be gained by __?__ing it.

7. Some graceful and __?__ dancers were once awkward and **inept**.

8. Sometimes, what we perceive as a(n) __?__ turns out to be an **advantage**.

9. The conclusions reached by two independent investigators should have __?__ed, but they **disagreed**.

10. To allow him a greater variety of foods, the patient's strictly __?__d diet has been somewhat **expanded**.

 **REVIEW 33:** CONCISE WRITING

Express the thought of each sentence below in **no more than four words**.

1. Carefully consider all the possible consequences of what you intend to do before you do it.

2. It is obvious that a secret agreement was in existence for fraudulent purposes.

3. Those who are in favor of the proposal please say "aye."

4. The practice of using an excessive number of words to express an idea interferes with communication.

5. Does the question you are asking have anything to do with the matter that we are discussing?

 **REVIEW 34:** SYNONYM SUMMARY

Each line, when completed, should have three words similar in meaning. Write the *complete* words.

| | | |
|---|---|---|
| **1.** p (1) sh | thr (1) st | pr (1) p (1) l |
| **2.** not (1) ble | (3) spicuous | (3) minent |
| **3.** agr (2) ment | h (1) rm (1) ny | c (1) nc (1) rd |
| **4.** p (2) rce | p (1) nct (1) re | p (1) rf (1) rate |
| **5.** comb (1) ne | j (2) n | (2) alesce |
| **6.** h (2) nt | (3) occupy | (2) sess |
| **7.** s (1) ppose | (2) sume | pr (1) s (1) me |
| **8.** l (1) st | (2) dure | pers (1) st |
| **9.** m (1) tch | (1) ally | (3) respond |
| **10.** ann (1) y | ir (2) tate | pr (1) v (1) ke |
| **11.** in (1) orn | (2) nate | (3) genital |
| **12.** ag (1) tate | (2) set | pert (1) rb |
| **13.** l (1) gical | cons (1) stent | co (2) rent |
| **14.** e (1) rly | (2) timely | pre (2) ture |
| **15.** sk (1) rt | b (1) pass | (6) vent |
| **16.** (1) vert | f (1) restall | (2) viate |
| **17.** pen (1) trate | perv (1) de | (3) meate |
| **18.** b (1) lge | j (1) t | (3) trude |
| **19.** end (1) ring | unc (2) sing | per (2) nial |
| **20.** verb (1) age | tautol (1) gy | (6) locution |

**REVIEW 35:** ANALOGIES

Which lettered pair of words—*a, b, c, d,* or *e*—most nearly expresses the same relationship as the capitalized pair?

1. CORRESPOND : LETTERS
   - *a.* obliterate : traces
   - *b.* converse : words
   - *c.* proofread : errors
   - *d.* soundproof : noises
   - *e.* economize : expenses

1. CURTAIL : PROTRACT
   - *a.* attack : impugn
   - *b.* inflate : expand
   - *c.* separate : coalesce
   - *d.* violate : contravene
   - *e.* bicker : wrangle

3. COLLUSION : DEFRAUD
   - *a.* prosecution : exonerate
   - *b.* conservation : deplete
   - *c.* condemnation : laud
   - *d.* revolution : change
   - *e.* recuperation : weaken

4. PREFACE : BOOK
   - *a.* dawn : night
   - *b.* footnote : page
   - *c.* dessert : repast
   - *d.* threshold : door
   - *e.* overture : opera

5. CIRCUMSPECT : CAUTION
   - *a.* objective : facts
   - *b.* tolerant : bigotry
   - *c.* gluttonous : restraint
   - *d.* impulsive : patience
   - *e.* hypocritical : sincerity

6. ADEPT : PROFICIENT
   - *a.* manifest : evident
   - *b.* clandestine : overt
   - *c.* thrifty : wasteful
   - *d.* compatible : uncongenial
   - *e.* domesticated : wild

7. FATIGUE : PROFICIENCY
   - *a.* intimidation : tension
   - *b.* poverty : crime
   - *c.* automation : drudgery
   - *d.* exercise : longevity
   - *e.* repetition : boredom

**8.** PROVOKE : ANGRY

 *a.* impoverish : indigent     *b.* convince : suspicious

 *c.* placate : hostile       *d.* absolve : blameworthy

 *e.* educate : ignorant

**9.** ENIGMA : PERPLEX

 *a.* license : prohibit      *b.* forecast : guarantee

 *c.* rumor : reassure      *d.* relapse : accelerate

 *e.* impediment : obstruct

**10.** PROFUSE : EXTRAVAGANCE

 *a.* frank : evasion       *b.* nonconformist : compliance

 *c.* outgoing : seclusion     *d.* indolent : procrastination

 *e.* uncharitable : benevolence

 **REVIEW 36:** COMPOSITION

Answer in a sentence or two.

 **1.** Why might circumlocutions be an obstacle to communication?

 **2.** Are you perturbed about the prospects of your favorite sports team this year?

 **3.** Would you rather collaborate on a school project with a perplexing student or a precocious student? Explain.

 **4.** Would you be happy if your performance provoked profuse praise? Why or why not?

 **5.** How is obstructing justice similar to circumventing the law?

*Chapter*

# 5

# Enlarging Vocabulary Through Latin Roots

## What is a root?

A *root* is a word or basic element from which other words are derived. For example, *kind* is the root of *unkind, kindest, kindly,* and *unkindness.* As you can see, the *root* is the part of a word that is left after an addition, such as a prefix or a suffix, has been removed.

Sometimes a root has more than one form, as in the words *enjoy, rejoice, joyous,* and *enjoyable.* Here, the root is *joy* or *joi.*

## Why study roots?

Once you know what a particular root means, you have a clue to the meaning of words derived from that root. For example, when you have learned that the root *MAN* means "hand," you are better able to understand—and remember—that *manacles* are *"handcuffs"*; that to *manipulate* is to *"handle"* or "manage skillfully"; and that a *manual* operation is "something done by *hand.*"

## Purpose of this chapter

This chapter aims to enlarge your vocabulary by acquainting you with twenty Latin roots and some English words derived from them. Be sure to memorize the roots; they will help you unlock the meaning of numerous words beyond those discussed in this chapter.

# LATIN ROOTS 1–10

## Pretest 1

Write the *letter* of the best answer.

1. Some people are *gregarious*; others __?__ .

   (A) arrive late   (B) keep to themselves   (C) are ready to help

2. An *enamored* individual is __?__ .

   (A) well rounded   (B) armed   (C) captivated

3. The *literal* meaning of a word is its __?__ .

   (A) original meaning   (B) hidden meaning   (C) meaning in literature

4. A person with an *affinity* for sports is not __?__ them.

   (A) repelled by   (B) absorbed in   (C) talented in

5. Prices in *flux* __?__ .

   (A) keep changing   (B) rise sharply   (C) drop rapidly

6. Don't be __?__ . Give them a *lucid* answer.

   (A) frank   (B) misled   (C) vague

7. There can be no *animus* in a person of __?__ will.

   (A) good   (B) ill   (C) strong

8. There was __?__ , instead of *cohesion*.

   (A) ignorance   (B) disunity   (C) uncertainty

9. Any *unilateral* action is a __?__ undertaking.

   (A) worldwide   (B) cooperative   (C) one-sided

10. A *regenerated* community __?__ .

    (A) shows new life   (B) resists changes   (C) grows steadily worse

THE ANSWERS ARE

**1.** B   **2.** C   **3.** A   **4.** A   **5.** A
**6.** C   **7.** A   **8.** B   **9.** C   **10.** A

In doing the pretest, you would have found it helpful to know the meaning of the roots *greg, amor, litera, fin, flux, luc, anim, hes, lateral,* and *gen.* You will learn how to use these roots in the pages that follow.

## 1. AM, AMOR: "love," "liking," "friendliness"

| WORD | MEANING AND TYPICAL USE |
|------|-------------------------|
| **amateur** (*n.*)<br>'a-mə-(,)tər | (literally, "lover")<br>1. person who follows a particular pursuit as a pastime, rather than as a profession<br>   The performance was staged by a group of *amateurs* who have been studying dramatics as a hobby.<br><br>2. one who performs rather poorly; inexperienced person<br>   When it comes to baking a cake, you are the expert; I'm only an *amateur.* |
| **amiable** (*adj.*)<br>'ā-mē-ə-bəl | likable; good-natured; pleasant and agreeable; obliging<br>   Charlotte is an *amiable* person; everybody likes her. |
| **amicable** (*adj.*)<br>'a-mi-kə-bəl | characterized by friendliness rather than antagonism; friendly; neighborly; not quarrelsome<br>   Let us try to settle our differences in an *amicable* manner. |
| **amity** (*n.*)<br>'a-mə-tē | friendship; goodwill; friendly relations<br>   We must look ahead to the time when the dispute is over and *amity* is restored. |
| **amorous** (*adj.*)<br>'a-mə-rəs | strongly moved by love; loving; inclined to love; enamored<br>   In the famous balcony scene, *amorous* Romeo expresses undying love for Juliet. |

| | |
|---|---|
| **enamored** (*adj.*)<br>i-'na-mərd | (usually followed by *of*) inflamed with love; charmed; captivated<br>Jason became *enamored* of the young woman and asked her to marry him. |

## 2. ANIM: "mind," "will," "spirit"

| | |
|---|---|
| **animosity** (*n.*)<br>ˌa-nə-'mä-sə-tē | ill will (usually leading to active opposition); violent hatred; enmity; antagonism<br>Someday the *animosity* that led to the war will be replaced by amity. |
| **animus** (*n.*)<br>'a-nə-məs | ill will (usually controlled)<br>Though Howard defeated me in the election, I bear no *animus* toward him; we are good friends. |
| **equanimity** (*n.*)<br>ˌē-kwə-'ni-mə-tē | evenness of mind or temper under stress; emotional balance; composure; calmness; equilibrium<br>If you become extremely upset when you lose a game, it is a sign that you lack *equanimity*. |
| **magnanimous** (*adj.*)<br>mag-'na-nə-məs | showing greatness or nobility of mind; chivalrous; forgiving; generous in overlooking injury or insult<br>The first time I was late for practice, Ms. O'Neill excused me with the warning that she would not be so *magnanimous* the next time. |
| **unanimity** (*n.*)<br>ˌyü-nə-'ni-mə-tē | oneness of mind; complete agreement<br>In almost every discussion there is bound to be some disagreement. Don't expect *unanimity*. |
| **unanimous** (*adj.*)<br>yü-'na-nə-məs | of one mind; in complete accord<br>Except for one student, who voted "no," the class was *unanimous* in wanting the party. |

**EXERCISE 5.1:** *AM, AMOR,* AND *ANIM* WORDS

Write the most appropriate word from groups 1 and 2.

1. After his first success as a screen lover, the actor was cast only in __?__ roles.

2. The prospect of financial reward has induced many a(n) __?__ to turn professional.

3. Don't brood over your defeat. Accept it with __?__.

4. Narcissus was too conceited to like anyone else; he was __?__ of himself.

5. The 9–0 verdict shows that the judges were __?__.

## 3. *FIN: "end," "boundary," "limit"*

| | |
|---|---|
| **affinity** (*n.*)<br>ə-'fi-nə-tē | (literally, condition of being "near the boundary" or "a neighbor") kinship; sympathy; liking; attraction<br>    Because they share the same language and ideals, the Americans and the English have an *affinity* for one another. |
| **confine** (*v.*)<br>kən-'fīn | keep within limits; restrict; limit<br>    I will *confine* my remarks to the causes of inflation; the next speaker will discuss its effects. |
| **definitive** (*adj.*)<br>di-'fi-nə-tiv | serving to end an unsettled matter; conclusive; final<br>    The officials accused of bribery confessed when the district attorney presented *definitive* evidence of their guilt. |
| **finale** (*n.*)<br>fə-'na-lē | end or final part of a musical composition, opera, play, etc.; conclusion<br>    The acting was superb from the opening scene to the *finale*. |
| **finis** (*n.*)<br>'fi-nəs | end; conclusion<br>    The word *finis* on the screen indicated that the film had ended. |

# 4. FLU, FLUC, FLUX: "flow"

**fluctuate** (*v.*)
'flǝk-chǝ-,wāt

flow like a wave; move up and down; change often and irregularly; be unsteady
Last week the stock *fluctuated* from a high of 19 to a low of 17.

**fluent** (*adj.*)
'flü-ǝnt

ready with a flow of words; speaking or writing easily; articulate; eloquent
Do you have to grope for words, or are you a *fluent* speaker?

**fluid** (*n.*)
'flü-ǝd

substance that flows
Air, water, molasses, and milk are all *fluids.*

**fluid** (*adj.*)

not rigid; changeable; unstable
During November, the military situation remained *fluid,* with advances and retreats by both sides.

**flux** (*n.*)
'flǝks

continuous flow or changing; unceasing change
When prices are in a state of *flux,* many buyers delay purchases until conditions are more settled.

**influx** (*n.*)
'in-,flǝks

inflow; inpouring; inrush
The discovery of gold in California in 1848 caused a large *influx* of settlers from the East.

 **EXERCISE 5.2:** *FIN, FLU, FLUC,* AND *FLUX* WORDS

Write the most appropriate word from groups 3 and 4.

1. A diplomat who represents us in Russia should be __?__ in Russian.

2. During the late spring, beach resorts ready themselves for the expected __?__ of summer visitors.

3. The entire cast appeared on stage after the __?__ to acknowledge the applause.

4. Unlike a lower court ruling, which may be reversed on appeal, a Supreme Court decision is __?__.

5. There is a(n) __?__ among classmates that is often as strong as loyalty to one's family.

## 5. GEN, GENER, GENIT: "birth," "kind," "class"

**degenerate** (*v.*)
di-'je-nə-,rāt

sink to a lower class or standard; worsen; deteriorate
But for the skill of the presiding officer, the debate would have *degenerated* into an exchange of insults.

**engender** (*v.*)
in-'jen-dər

give birth to; create; generate; produce; cause
Name-calling *engenders* hatred.

**genre** (*n.*)
'zhän-rə

kind; sort; category
The writer achieved distinction in two literary *genres*—the short story and the novel.

**progenitor** (*n.*)
prō-'je-nə-tər

ancestor to whom a group traces its birth; forefather; forebear
The Bible states that Adam and Eve were the *progenitors* of the human race.

**regenerate** (*v.*)
ri-'je-nə-,rāt

cause to be born again; put new life into; reform completely; revive; reinvigorate
The new manager *regenerated* the losing team and made it a strong contender.

## 6. GREG: "gather," "flock"

**aggregate** (*adj.*)
'a-gri-gət

gathered together in one mass; total; collective
The *aggregate* strength of the allies was impressive, though individually some were quite weak.

**aggregation** (*n.*)
,a-gri-'gā-shən

gathering of individuals into a body or group; assemblage
At the airport, the homecoming champions were welcomed by a huge *aggregation* of admirers.

**congregation** (*n.*)
ˌkäŋ-gri-'gā-shən

"flock" or gathering of people for religious worship
　　The minister addressed the *congregation* on the meaning of brotherhood.

**gregarious** (*adj.*)
gri-'gar-ē-əs

inclined to associate with the "flock" or group; fond of being with others; sociable
　　Human beings, as a rule, are *gregarious*; they enjoy being with other people.

**segregation** (*n.*)
ˌse-gri-'gā-shən

separation from the "flock" or main body; setting apart; isolation; separation
　　The warden believes in *segregation* of first offenders from hardened criminals.

## EXERCISE 5.3: *GEN, GENER, GENIT,* AND *GREG* WORDS

Write the most appropriate word from groups 5 and 6.

1. New housing developments, shopping centers, and schools can __?__ decadent neighborhoods.
2. Everyone in the __?__ rose to sing a hymn.
3. Unless healed soon, these animosities are sure to __?__ armed conflict.
4. The box score shows the points scored by each player, as well as the team's __?__ score.
5. When I first came here, I had no friends and kept to myself. I was not too __?__.

# 7. HERE, HES: "stick"

**adhere** (*v.*)
ad-'hir

stick; hold fast; cling; be attached
　　Apply the sticker according to the directions, or it will not *adhere*.

**cohere** (*v.*)
kō-'hir

stick together; hold together firmly
　　I glued together the fragments of the vase, but they did not *cohere*.

**coherence** (*n.*)
kō-ʹhir-ən(t)s

state of sticking together; consistency; logical connection

  If the relationship between the first sentence and what follows is not clear, the paragraph lacks *coherence*.

**cohesion** (*n.*)
kō-ʹhē-zhən

act or state of sticking together; union; unity; bond

  There can be no real *cohesion* in an alliance if the parties have little in common.

**incoherent** (*adj.*)
‚in-kō-ʹhir-ənt

not logically connected; disconnected; unintelligible

  The speech of a person in a rage may be *incoherent*.

**inherent** (*adj.*)
in-ʹhir-ənt

(literally, "sticking in") deeply infixed; intrinsic; essential

  Because of her *inherent* carefulness, I am sure my sister will be a good driver.

## 8. *LATERAL:* "side"

**bilateral** (*adj.*)
bī-ʹla-tə-rəl

involving two sides

  A *bilateral* team of federal and local experts conducted the survey.

**collateral** (*adj.*)
kə-ʹla-tə-rəl

situated at the side; accompanying; parallel; additional; supplementary

  After voting for the road-building program, the legislature took up the *collateral* issue of how to raise the necessary funds.

**equilateral** (*adj.*)
‚ē-kwə-ʹla-tə-rəl

having all sides equal

  If one side of an *equilateral* triangle measures three feet, the other two must also be three feet each.

**lateral** (*adj.*)
ʹla-tə-rəl

of or pertaining to the side

  The building plan shows both a front and a *lateral* view of the proposed structure.

**multilateral** (*adj.*)
,məl-ti-'la-tə-rəl

having many sides
A parent plays a *multilateral* role as a nurse, housekeeper, shopper, cook, teacher, etc.

**quadrilateral** (*n.*)
,kwä-drə-'la-tə-rəl

plane figure having four sides and four angles
A square is a *quadrilateral.*

**unilateral** (*adj.*)
,yü-ni-'la-tə-rəl

one-sided; undertaken by one side only
Don't judge the matter by my opponent's *unilateral* statement, but wait till you have heard the other side.

 **EXERCISE 5.4:** *HERE, HES,* AND *LATERAL* WORDS

Write the most appropriate word from groups 7 and 8.

1. Most city blocks are shaped like a(n) __?__.

2. Are you speaking for all the members of your club or giving only your __?__ views?

3. Some believe that might is right, but I do not __?__ to that doctrine.

4. When we were studying *Johnny Tremain,* our teacher assigned __?__ reading on the Revolutionary War.

5. The politician's __?__ role as champion of justice, defender of the poor, supporter of education, and friend of business attracted many adherents.

# 9. *LITERA: "letter"*

**alliteration** (*n.*)
ə-,li-tə-'rā-shən

repetition of the same letter or consonant at the beginning of neighboring words
Note the *alliteration* in the line "Sing a song of sixpence."

**literacy** (*n.*)
'li-tə-rə-sē

state of being lettered or educated; ability to read and write
Research required a high degree of *literacy.*

**literal** (*adj.*)
'li-tə-rəl

following the letters or exact words of the original; verbatim; word-for-word
> We translate "laissez-faire" as "absence of government interference," but its *literal* meaning is "let do."

**literary** (*adj.*)
'li-tə-,rer-ē

having to do with letters or literature
> Willa Cather is one of the great writers of novels in our *literary* history.

**literate** (*adj.*)
'li-tə-rət

lettered; able to read and write; educated
> The teacher's main goal in working with adults who can neither read nor write is to make them *literate*.

## 10. LUC, LUM: "light"

**elucidate** (*v.*)
i-'lü-sə-,dāt

throw light upon; make clear; explain; clarify
> I asked the teacher to *elucidate* a point that was not clear to me.

**lucid** (*adj.*)
'lü-səd

(literally, "containing light") clear; easy to understand; comprehensible
> To obviate misunderstanding, state the directions in the most *lucid* way possible.

**luminary** (*n.*)
'lü-mə-,ner-ē

one who is a source of light or inspiration to others; famous person; notable; celebrity
> A number of *luminaries,* including a Nobel Prize winner, will be present.

**luminous** (*adj.*)
'lü-mə-nəs

emitting light; bright; shining; brilliant
> With this watch you can tell time in the dark because its hands and dial are *luminous*.

**translucent** (*adj.*)
tran(t)s-'lü-sᵊnt

letting light through
> Lamp shades are *translucent* but not transparent.

**EXERCISE 5.5:** *LITERA, LUC,* AND *LUM* WORDS

Write the most appropriate word from groups 9 and 10.

1. You need not prove that you can read and write. No one doubts your __?__.

2. __?__ paint is used for road signs so that they may be visible to night drivers.

3. Gary tried to __?__ the matter, but he only made us more confused.

4. A host of admirers surrounded the sports __?__ to ask for her autograph.

5. Did you know that the __?__ meaning of Philip is "lover of horses"?

## Review Exercises

 **REVIEW 1:** LATIN ROOTS 1–10

For each Latin root in column I, write the *letter* of its definition from column II.

| COLUMN I | COLUMN II |
|---|---|
| 1. LATERAL | *a.* light |
| 2. FLU, FLUC, FLUX | *b.* letter |
| 3. AM, AMOR | *c.* birth, kind, class |
| 4. GREG | *d.* side |
| 5. HERE, HES | *e.* flow |
| 6. ANIM | *f.* love, liking, friendliness |
| 7. FIN | *g.* gather, flock |
| 8. LUC, LUM | *h.* end, boundary, limit |
| 9. GEN, GENER, GENIT | *i.* stick |
| 10. LITERA | *j.* mind, will, spirit |

 **REVIEW 2:** WORD-BUILDING

Write the *prefix* for column I, the *root* for column II, and the whole word for column III.

| I<br>PREFIX | | II<br>ROOT | | III<br>WORD |
|---|---|---|---|---|
| **1.** (5)<br>through | + | (3)<br>light | = | (8) ENT<br>*letting light through* |
| **2.** (2)<br>down from | + | (5)<br>class | = | (7) ATE<br>*sink to a lower class; deteriorate* |
| **3.** (2)<br>again | + | (5)<br>birth | = | (7) ATE<br>*cause to be born again;*<br>*reform completely* |
| **4.** (2)<br>together | + | (4)<br>stick | = | (6)<br>*hold together firmly* |
| **5.** (2)<br>in | + | (4)<br>flow | = | (6)<br>*inflow; inpouring* |
| **6.** (3)<br>one | + | (7)<br>side | = | (10)<br>*one-sided* |
| **7.** (2)<br>in | + | (4)<br>stick | = | (6) NT<br>*"sticking in"; deeply infixed;*<br>*intrinsic* |
| **8.** (2)<br>apart | + | (4)<br>flock | = | (6) ATION<br>*separation from the flock;*<br>*isolation* |
| **9.** (2)<br>together | + | (3)<br>stick | = | (5) ION<br>*act of sticking together, union* |
| **10.** (2)<br>not | + | (6)<br>letter | = | (8) TE<br>*unlettered; unable to read or write* |

**REVIEW 3:** SENTENCE COMPLETION

Write the word from the list below that best fits the context.

| | | |
|---|---|---|
| adhere | affinity | alliteration |
| amateur | amicable | amorous |
| animosity | cohere | confine |
| congregation | definitive | degenerate |
| elucidate | engender | finale |
| fluent | gregarious | inherent |
| literary | luminary | |

1. A boundary dispute had __?__ed considerable __?__ between the two neighbors who formerly were friends.

2. Dad was once __?__ in French, but his proficiency in that language has __?__d because he has not used it for twenty years.

3. Being a(n) __?__ person, Roy lingered in the auditorium after the __?__ of the opera to chat with friends.

4. When he addresses the __?__, the spiritual leader is usually—but not always—brief; he does not have to __?__ to a time schedule.

5. The __?__ who had been invited to the convention announced that she would __?__ her oral reading to passages from her prize-winning book.

6. Sheldon is a lawyer by profession, but in painting he is just a(n) __?__, though he has a great __?__ for that calling.

7. In considering the suitor's proposal, Portia had to decide whether her feelings for him were truly __?__, or merely __?__.

8. The witness was asked to __?__ a statement she made that did not seem to __?__ with her earlier testimony.

9. In the line, "The furrow followed free," Samuel T. Coleridge uses the __?__ device known as __?__.

10. The advice "Never make a generalization" cannot be regarded as __?__ because it contains a(n) __?__ contradiction: "Never make a generalization" is itself a generalization.

**REVIEW 4:** SYNONYMS

Avoid repetition by replacing the boldfaced word or expression with a **synonym** from the following words.

| | | |
|---|---|---|
| amiable | amity | animus |
| cohesion | fluctuate | literate |
| luminous | magnanimous | unanimity |
| unilateral | | |

1. Many have forgiven and forgotten the suffering that former enemies caused, but others have not been so **forgiving**.
2. I don't like that ill-tempered grouch; he is not a(n) **likable** person.
3. The moon, which has no brightness of its own, is **bright** at night with light that shines on it from the sun.
4. If many members are resisting goals that a majority in their union supports, there is obviously a lack of **unity**.
5. This is just my **one-sided** opinion; it does not reflect the views of all sides to the dispute.
6. A nation that sets a low priority on education is not likely to have the world's most **educated** population.
7. The 11-to-1 vote shows how strongly the club agrees with your motion. If not for that one negative ballot, we would have had **complete agreement**.
8. There was no **friendship** between us when we were rivals. Lately, however, we have become friends.
9. Last month, there was little movement in stock prices. Usually, they **move up and down** quite a bit.
10. Linda is a person of good will; she has no **ill will** toward any one.

 **REVIEW 5:** ANTONYMS

Write the word from the list below that is most nearly the **opposite** of the boldfaced word.

| | | |
|---|---|---|
| amateur | amicable | amity |
| definitive | degenerate | fluid |
| flux | literate | lucid |
| translucent | | |

1. After a long interval of **stability**, we are now in a period of __?__.
2. The early results are encouraging but **inconclusive**; more __?__ proof is needed before the researchers can claim a medical breakthrough.
3. Ours is a cast of talented __?__s, but we are not **professionals**.
4. Immediately after the operation, the patient was on a rigid diet of __?__s, with no **solids** whatsoever.
5. At last, the feud is over; __?__ has replaced **enmity**.
6. No light penetrates the walls because they are made of **opaque** materials; the windowpanes, of course, are __?__.
7. This firm's prospects for recovery have __?__d rather than **improved**.
8. Explain what happened in __?__ English; don't be **vague**.
9. Earlier in the negotiations, the mood of both parties was __?__; now, it has turned **antagonistic**.
10. A bilingual person is __?__ in two languages but **illiterate** in all others.

 **REVIEW 6:** SYNONYM SUMMARY

Each line, when completed, should have three words similar in meaning. Write the *complete* word.

1. chang (2) ble     unst (1) ble     flu (1) d
2. fr (2) ndly     n (2) ghborly     (1) mic (1) ble
3. fin (1) l     concl (1) sive     def (1) n (1) tive
4. w (1) rd-for-w (1) rd     verb (1) t (1) m     l (1) teral
5. cre (1) te     (1) ause     (2) gender
6. sep (1) ration     is (1) lation     (2) gregation
7. disc (2) nected     unintellig (1) ble     in (2) herent
8. (2) traction     l (1) king     (2) finity
9. (1) nion     b (1) nd     co (2) sion
10. accompan (1) ing     para (2) el     c (2) lateral
11. comp (1) sure     equ (1) librium     e (2) animity
12. k (1) nd     cat (1) gory     (2) nre

| 13. ant (1) g (1) nism | (2) mity | an (1) m (1) sity |
| 14. c (1) l (1) brity | not (1) ble | l (1) min (1) ry |
| 15. g (1) n (1) rous | chiv (1) lrous | mag (2) nimous |
| 16. tot (1) l | c (2) lective | (2) gregate |
| 17. (2) flow | inp (2) ring | infl (1) x |
| 18. (2) sential | intr (1) nsic | (2) herent |
| 19. (1) loquent | artic (1) late | fl (1) ent |
| 20. wors (1) n | deter (2) rate | (2) generate |

 ## REVIEW 7: CONCISE WRITING

In no more than fifty words, rewrite the following passage, keeping all its ideas. *Hint:* Reduce each boldfaced expression to a single word. The first sentence has been done to get you started. Go on from there.

### A Rare Person

Bruce can be **pleasant and agreeable** when others are cranky. When they are unforgiving, he is usually **generous in overlooking injury or insult.** And when they get upset, he maintains his **evenness of mind and temper.** He is a rare person whose moods do not **change continually or vary in an irregular way.** Besides, he is **fond of being with others.** In conversation, he is not only **ready with a flow of words,** but logical and **easy to understand.**

### A Rare Person
(concise version)

Bruce can be amiable when others are cranky.

 ## REVIEW 8: ANALOGIES

Which lettered pair of words—*a, b, c, d,* or *e*—most nearly expresses the same relationship as the capitalized pair?

**1.** MALEVOLENT : ANIMUS
    *a.* blameless : guilt
    *b.* circumspect : foresight
    *c.* indigent : resources
    *d.* audacious : manners
    *e.* trustworthy : deception

**2.** SQUARE : QUADRILATERAL
    *a.* hand : digit
    *b.* weapon : missile
    *c.* bulb : socket
    *d.* access : passageway
    *e.* eighth : fraction

**3.** FLUCTUATION : UNCERTAINTY
    *a.* defect : malfunction
    *b.* pain : inflammation
    *c.* delay : fog
    *d.* boredom : repetition
    *e.* malnutrition : health

**4.** GREGARIOUS : COMPANY
    *a.* reserved : communication
    *b.* slovenly : neatness
    *c.* frugal : waste
    *d.* withdrawn : solitude
    *e.* parsimonious : expenditure

**5.** INDIVIDUAL : AGGREGATION
    *a.* particle : dust
    *b.* chord : note
    *c.* head : hair
    *d.* oyster : pearl
    *e.* message : word

**6.** LUCID : COMPREHEND
    *a.* complex : grasp
    *b.* indelible : erase
    *c.* versatile : adapt
    *d.* inequitable : justify
    *e.* decadent : regenerate

**7.** MAGNANIMOUS : PARDON
    *a.* headstrong : acquiesce
    *b.* reasonable : compromise
    *c.* meek : protest
    *d.* insubordinate : obey
    *e.* persistent : quit

**8.** TRANSLUCENT : LIGHT
    *a.* opinionated : ideas
    *b.* exclusive : people
    *c.* airtight : leak
    *d.* porous : liquid
    *e.* conspicuous : attention

 **REVIEW 9:** COMPOSITION

Answer in a sentence or two.

1. Would you probably be magnanimous toward someone you were enamored of? Why?

2. Who are some people you consider to be literary luminaries? Explain your choices.

3. Why was segregation of the races inherently unfair?

4. Do you think a unilateral or a multilateral effort is more likely to bring about the end of a war? Explain.

5. How might an influx of new industries regenerate a city's economy?

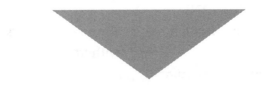

# LATIN ROOTS 11–20

## Pretest 2

Write the *letter* of the best answer.

1. *Video* signals have to do with __?__.

   (A) sounds   (B) pictures   (C) music

2. In a *soliloquy,* you would be __?__.

   (A) doing most of the talking   (B) questioning a group
   (C) talking to yourself

3. A *redundant* expression should be __?__.

   (A) removed   (B) explained   (C) replaced

4. __?__ involves no *manual* operations.

   (A) Dining   (B) Typing   (C) Smiling

5. A *pendant* cannot __?__.

   (A) translate   (B) adorn   (C) dangle

6. Now that my *veracity* has been questioned, I feel deeply __?__.

   (A) honored   (B) insulted   (C) relieved

7. A *scribe* belongs to the __?__ profession.

   (A) teaching   (B) acting   (C) writing

8. We cannot tell whether their interest is *simulated* or __?__.

   (A) real   (B) selfish   (C) pretended

9. The new regulation *imposes* additional __?__ on all.

   (A) responsibilities   (B) privileges   (C) benefits

10. If you are *insolvent,* you cannot __?__.

   (A) vote   (B) pay your debts   (C) think logically

> **THE ANSWERS ARE**
> 1. B   2. C   3. A   4. C   5. A
> 6. B   7. C   8. A   9. A   10. B

Had you known the meaning of the roots *vid, sol, unda, manu, pend, vera, scrib, simul, pos,* and *solv,* you would have had an advantage in the pretest. You will learn about these roots in the following pages.

## 11. MAN, MANU: "hand"

**emancipate** (*v.*)
i-'man(t)-sə-,pāt

(literally, "take from the hand" or power of another) release from bondage; free; liberate

The washing machine has *emancipated* millions of people from a great deal of drudgery.

**manacle** (*n.*)
'ma-ni-kəl

handcuff

The *manacles* were removed from the prisoner's wrists.

**mandate** (*n.*)
'man-,dāt

(literally, something "given into one's hand")
1. authorization to act

The overwhelming vote for the reform slate is regarded as a *mandate* from the people to root out corruption.

2. command; order; injunction

By a close margin, the workers voted to comply with the court's *mandate* against a strike.

**manipulate** (*v.*)
mə-'ni-pyə-‚lāt

1. operate with the hands; handle or manage skillfully; maneuver
In today's lesson I learned how to *manipulate* the steering wheel.

2. manage unethically to serve a fraudulent purpose; falsify; rig
The defeated candidate charged that the election results had been *manipulated*.

**manual** (*n.*)
'man-yə-wəl

small, helpful book capable of being carried in the hand; handbook
Each student has a learner's permit and a copy of the "Driver's *Manual*."

**manual** (*adj.*)

relating to, or done with, the hands
Milking, formerly a *manual* operation, is now done by machine.

**manuscript** (*n.*)
'man-yə-‚skript

document written by hand, or typewritten
The author's *manuscript* is now at the printer.

## 12. PEND, PENS: "hang"

**append** (*v.*)
ə-'pend

(literally, "hang on") attach; add as a supplement
If you hand in your report late, *append* a note explaining the reason for the delay.

**appendix** (*n.*)
ə-'pen-diks

(literally, something "hung on") matter added to the end of a book or document
A school edition of a novel usually has an *appendix* containing explanatory notes.

**impending** (*adj.*)
im-'pen-diŋ

(literally, "overhanging") threatening to occur soon; imminent
At the first flash of lightning, we scurried for shelter from the *impending* storm.

**pendant** (*n.*)
'pen-dənt

hanging ornament
The *pendant* dangling from the chain around her neck looked like a medal, but it was really a timepiece.

**pending** (*adj.*)
'pen-diŋ

(literally, "hanging") waiting to be settled; not yet decided

Has a date been set for the game, or is the matter still *pending*?

   **pending** (*prep.*)

until

Barbara agreed to conduct the meeting, *pending* the election of a presiding officer.

**suspend** (*v.*)
sə-'spend

1. hang by attaching to something

Would you prefer to attach a lamp to the wall or *suspend* one from the ceiling?

2. stop temporarily; hold up; make inoperative for a while

Service will be *suspended* from midnight to 4 A.M. to permit repairs.

**suspense** (*n.*)
sə-'spen(t)s

condition of being left "hanging" or in doubt; mental uncertainty; anxiety; apprehension

If you have seen the marks posted, please tell me whether I passed or failed; don't keep me in *suspense*!

 **EXERCISE 5.6:** *MAN, MANU, PEND,* AND *PENS* WORDS

Write the most appropriate word from groups 11 and 12.

1. Can you operate this gadget? I don't know how to __?__ it.

2. As the enemy approached, the defenders got ready for the __?__ attack.

3. Because of a lengthy labor dispute, the city's daily newspapers had to __?__ publication.

4. Is it possible to __?__ addicts from their bondage to drugs?

5. The retiring manager has agreed to stay on, __?__ the choice of a successor.

## 13. PON, POS: "put"

**depose** (*v.*)
di-'pōz

1. (literally, "put down") put out of office; dethrone
   Did the king abdicate, or was he *deposed*?

2. state under oath; testify; swear
   He *deposed* on the witness stand that he had never taken a bribe.

**impose** (*v.*)
im-'pōz

put on as a burden, duty, tax, etc.; inflict
   Cleaning up after the job is the repair crew's responsibility. Don't let them *impose* it on you.

**postpone** (*v.*)
pōs(t)-'pōn

(literally, "put after") put off; defer; delay
   Our instructor has *postponed* the test until tomorrow to give us an extra day to study.

**superimpose** (*v.*)
,sü-pər-im-'pōz

put on top of or over; attach as an addition
   Today's snowfall *superimposed* a fresh two inches on yesterday's accumulation.

**transpose** (*v.*)
tran(t)s-'pōz

(literally, "put across") change the relative order of; interchange
   There is a misspelled word on your paper, "strenght." Correct it by *transposing* the last two letters.

## 14. SCRIB, SCRIPT: "write"

**conscript** (*v.*)
kən-'skript

enroll (write down) into military service by compulsion; draft
   When there were not enough volunteers for the armed forces, the government had to *conscript* additional men and women.

**inscription** (*n.*)
in-'skrip-shən

something inscribed (written) on a monument, coin, etc.
   The *inscription* on the inside of their wedding bands read, "Nicole and Adam forever."

| | |
|---|---|
| **prescribe** (*v.*)<br>pri-'skrīb | (literally, "write before")<br>1. order; dictate; direct<br>The law *prescribes* that aliens may not vote.<br><br>2. order as a remedy<br>Her physician *prescribed* some pills, a light diet, and plenty of rest. |
| **proscribe** (*v.*)<br>prō-'skrīb | condemn as harmful or illegal; prohibit; forbid<br>The dumping of wastes into the waterways is *proscribed*. |
| **scribe** (*n.*)<br>'skrīb | person who writes; author; journalist<br>Both candidates used professional *scribes* to prepare their campaign speeches. |
| **script** (*n.*)<br>'skript | 1. written text of a play, speech, etc.<br>How much time did the actors have to memorize the *script*?<br><br>2. handwriting; penmanship<br>I knew the note was from Mabel because I recognized her *script*. |
| **subscriber** (*n.*)<br>səb-'skrī-bər | one who writes his or her name at the end of a document, thereby indicating approval; one who regularly receives a magazine, newspaper, etc.<br>The petition to nominate Sue for president of the junior class already has forty-three *subscribers*. |

 **EXERCISE 5.7:** *PON, POS, SCRIB,*
AND *SCRIPT* WORDS

Write the most appropriate word from groups 13 and 14.

1. In his address, the President inserted some remarks that were not in the __?__ previously released to the press.

2. The insurgents aim to __?__ the dictator and establish a republic.

3. According to the __?__ on its cornerstone, this school was erected in 1969.

4. With war impending, the nation hastened to __?__ all able-bodied citizens.

5. You cannot __?__ your decision much longer; the deadline for submitting applications is Monday.

## 15. SIMIL, SIMUL: "similar," "like," "same"

**assimilate** (*v.*)
ə-'si-mə-ˌlāt

1. make similar or like
    The letter "n" in the prefix "in-" is often *assimilated* to the following letter. For example, "in" plus "legible" becomes "illegible."

2. take in and incorporate as one's own; absorb
    A bright student *assimilates* knowledge rapidly.

**dissimilar** (*adj.*)
ˌdi(s)-'si-mə-lər

opposite of *similar*; unlike; different
    These gloves are not a pair; they are quite *dissimilar*.

**similarity** (*n.*)
si-mə-'lar-ə-tē

likeness; resemblance
    The two pills are alike in color and shape, but there the *similarity* ends.

**simile** (*n.*)
'si-mə-(ˌ)lē

comparison of two different things introduced by *like* or *as*
    "What happens to a dream deferred?" asks Langston Hughes in one of his poems. "Does it dry up/Like a raisin in the sun?" Note that the last six words are a *simile*.

**simulate** (*v.*)
'sim-yə-ˌlāt

give the appearance of; feign; imitate
    Nancy was the star of the show; she *simulated* the bewildered mother very effectively.

**simultaneous** (*adj.*)
ˌsī-məl-'tā-nē-əs

existing or happening at the same time; contemporary; concurrent
    The flash of an explosion comes to us before the sound, though the two are really *simultaneous*.

# 16. SOL, SOLI: "alone," "lonely, "single"

**desolate** (*v.*)
'de-sə-ˌlāt

(literally, "make lonely or deprive of inhabitants"); lay waste; ravage; devastate
A large section of the neighborhood was *desolated* by the disastrous fire.

**desolate** (*adj.*)
'de-sə-lət

left alone; deserted; forlorn; abandoned; forsaken
At 5:30 A.M. the normally crowded intersection looks *desolate*.

**sole** (*adj.*)
'sōl

one and only; single; lone
Franklin D. Roosevelt was the *sole* candidate to be elected President for a fourth term.

**soliloquy** (*n.*)
sə-'li-lə-kwē

speech made to oneself when alone
What an actor says in a *soliloquy* is heard by no one except the audience.

**solitary** (*adj.*)
'sä-lə-ˌter-ē

opposite of *accompanied*; being or living alone; without companions
A hermit leads a *solitary* existence.

**solitude** (*n.*)
'sä-lə-ˌtüd

condition of being alone; loneliness; seclusion
Though I like company, there are times when I prefer *solitude*.

**solo** (*n.*)
'sō-lō

musical composition (or anything) performed by a single person
Instead of singing a *solo*, Brenda would prefer to join with me in a duet.

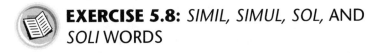

## EXERCISE 5.8: *SIMIL, SIMUL, SOL,* AND *SOLI* WORDS

Write the most appropriate word from groups 15 and 16.

1. Did you know you were using a(n) _?_ when you said I was as sly as a fox?

2. After the chorus sang the first number, Stanley played a violin _?_.

3. The closing of the huge factory did not __?__ the area, as few of the workers moved away.

4. Don't compare Jane with Peggy; the two are entirely __?__.

5. If you speak too rapidly, your audience may be unable to __?__ what you are saying.

## 17. SOLV, SOLU, SOLUT: "loosen"

**absolute** (*adj.*)
'ab-sə-,lüt

1. completely free ("loosened") of constitutional or other restraint; autocratic; despotic
   A democratic ruler is restricted by a constitution, a legislature, and courts, but a dictator has *absolute* power.

2. utter; outright; unquestionable
   The sudden rainstorm turned our picnic into an *absolute* mess.

**dissolution** (*n.*)
,di-sə-'lü-shən

act of "loosening" or breaking up into component parts; disintegration; ruin; destruction
   When President Lincoln took office, the Union faced imminent *dissolution*.

**dissolve** (*v.*)
di-'zälv

(literally, "loosen apart")
1. break up; disintegrate; disband
   Since the members lack mutual interests, the group will probably *dissolve*.

2. cause to disappear; end
   After our quarrel, Grace and I *dissolved* our friendship.

**resolution** (*n.*)
,re-zə-'lü-shən

(literally, "act of unloosening") solving; solution; answer
   The *resolution* of our air and water pollution problems will be difficult and costly.

**resolve** (*v.*)
ri-'zälv

(literally, "unloosen") break up; solve; explain; unravel
   A witness provided the clue that *resolved* the mystery.

| | |
|---|---|
| **soluble** (*adj.*)<br>'säl-yə-bəl | (literally, "able to be loosened")<br>1. capable of being dissolved or made into a liquid<br>Sugar is *soluble* in water.<br><br>2. solvable<br>Someone would have found the answer by now if the problem were *soluble*. |
| **solvent** (*n.*)<br>'säl-vənt | substance, usually liquid, able to dissolve ("loosen") another substance, known as the "solute"<br>In a saltwater solution, the water is the *solvent* and the salt is the solute. |
| **solvent** (*adj.*) | able to pay all one's debts<br>The examiners found the bank *solvent,* much to the relief of its depositors. |

## 18. UND, UNDA: "wave," "flow"

| | |
|---|---|
| **abound** (*v.*)<br>ə-'baůnd | (literally, "rise in waves" or "overflow")<br>1. (used with *in* or *with)* be well supplied; teem<br>Our nation *abounds* in (or with) opportunities for well-educated young men and women.<br><br>2. be plentiful; be present in great quantity<br>Fish *abound* in the waters off Newfoundland. |
| **abundant** (*adj.*)<br>ə-'bən-dənt | (literally, "rising in waves") more than sufficient; plentiful<br>Before Christmas, the stores have *abundant* supplies of merchandise. |
| **inundate** (*v.*)<br>'i-nən-,dāt | flood; overflow; deluge; overwhelm<br>On Election Night, the victor's offices were *inundated* by congratulatory messages. |
| **redound** (*v.*)<br>ri-'daůnd | flow back as a result; contribute<br>The success of so many of its graduates *redounds* to the credit of the school. |

| | |
|---|---|
| **redundant** (*adj.*)<br>ri-'dən-dənt | (literally, "flowing back") exceeding what is necessary; superfluous; surplus; opposite of *concise*<br>    Remove the last word of the following sentence because it is *redundant*: "My report is longer than Bob's report." |

## EXERCISE 5.9: *SOLV, SOLU, SOLUT, UND,* AND *UNDA* WORDS

Write the most appropriate word from groups 17 and 18.

1. Mutual suspicion and jealousy led to the eventual __?__ of the alliance.
2. The blue whale, once __?__ in Antarctic waters, is becoming more and more scarce.
3. The firm is in no danger of bankruptcy; it is completely __?__.
4. Several offshore areas __?__ in oil.
5. Either of the signers can __?__ the agreement by giving thirty days' written notice to the other.

## 19. *VER, VERA, VERI: "true," "truth"*

| | |
|---|---|
| **aver** (*v.*)<br>ə-'vər | state to be true; affirm confidently; assert; depose; opposite of *deny*<br>    Two eyewitnesses *averred* they had seen the defendant at the scene. |
| **veracity** (*n.*)<br>və-'ra-sə-tē | truthfulness<br>    Since he has lied to us in the past, he should not wonder that we doubt his *veracity*. |
| **verdict** (*n.*)<br>'vər-‚dikt | (literally, something "truly said") decision of a jury; opinion; judgment<br>    A hung jury is one that has been unable to reach a *verdict*. |
| **verify** (*v.*)<br>'ver-ə-‚fī | prove to be true; confirm; substantiate; corroborate<br>    So far, the charges have been neither disproved nor *verified*. |

**veritable** (*adj.*)
'ver-ə-tə-bəl

true; actual; genuine; real; authentic
As the pretended heirs of Peter Wilks were disposing of his fortune, the *veritable* heirs arrived.

**verity** (*n.*)
'ver-ə-tē

truth (of things); something true; true statement
That smoking is injurious to health is a scientifically established *verity*.

## 20. VID, VIS: "see," "look," "sight"

**envision** (*v.*)
in-'vi-zhən

foresee; envisage; have a mental picture of (something not yet a reality)
Mr. Brown *envisions* for Marcia a bright career as a fashion designer.

**improvise** (*v.*)
'im-prə-,vīz

(literally, "do something without having prepared or seen it beforehand") compose, recite, or sing on the spur of the moment; invent offhand; extemporize
Did you prepare your jokes before the program or *improvise* them as you went along?

**invisible** (*adj.*)
in-'vi-zə-bəl

not able to be seen; imperceptible; indiscernible
The microscope enables us to see organisms *invisible* to the naked eye.

**revise** (*v.*)
ri-'vīz

look at again to correct errors and make improvements; examine and improve
Before handing in your composition, be sure to *revise* it carefully.

**video** (*adj.*)
'vi-dē-,ō

having to do with the transmission or reception of what is seen
The audio (sound) and *video* signals of a television program can be recorded on magnetic tape.

**videotape** (*v.*)
'vi-dē-ō-,tāp

make a videotape recording of an event or TV program
If we *videotape* the party, we can show it later to those who could not attend.

| | |
|---|---|
| **visibility** (*n.*) | degree of clearness of the atmosphere, with |
| ˌvi-zə-ˈbi-lə-tē | reference to the distance at which objects can be |
| | clearly seen |
| |     With the fog rolling in and *visibility* |
| | approaching zero, it was virtually impossible for |
| | planes to land. |

| | |
|---|---|
| **visual** (*adj.*) | having to do with sight |
| ˈvi-zhə-wəl |     Radar tells us of an approaching object long |
| | before *visual* contact is possible. |

**EXERCISE 5.10:** *VER, VERA, VERI, VID,*
AND *VIS* WORDS

Write the most appropriate word from groups 19 and 20.

1. I am not much of a student, but Norma is a(n) __?__ scholar.
2. Since words alone may fail to convey an idea, teachers often use __?__ aids, such as pictures, charts, and films.
3. La Guardia Airport reports low clouds and reduced __?__.
4. Since the speaker was not prepared, he had to __?__ his talk.
5. You may believe this statement; it comes from a person of unquestionable __?__.

## *Review Exercises*

**REVIEW 10:** WORD-BUILDING

Write the *prefix* for column I, the *root* for column II, and the whole word for column III.

| I<br>PREFIX | | II<br>ROOT | III<br>WORD |
|---|---|---|---|
| **1.** (3)<br>*apart* | + | (4)<br>*loosen* | = (7) ED<br>*separated into parts* |
| **2.** (2)<br>*not* | + | (3)<br>*seen* | = (5) IBLE<br>*not able to be seen* |

**3.** (2)  + (3)  = (5) ED
  *on*  *put*  *put on as a burden; inflicted*

**4.** (3)  + (4)  = (8) ION
  *apart*  *loosen*  *act of breaking up; disintegration*

**5.** (2)  + (3)  = (2) D (4) NT
  *back*  *flow*  *exceeding what is necessary;*
  *superfluous*

**6.** (3)  + (5)  = (8) ED
  *before*  *write*  *ordered as a remedy*

**7.** (2)  + (3)  = (5) ING
  *again*  *look*  *looking at again to correct*

**8.** (2)  + (4)  = (6) TE
  *over*  *flow*  *overflow; overwhelm*

**9.** (3)  + (5)  = (8) ER
  *under*  *write*  *one who writes his or her name*
  *at the end of a document*

**10.** (2)  + (3)  = (5) ED
  *down*  *put*  *put out of office; dethroned*

 **REVIEW 11:** LATIN ROOTS 11–20

For each Latin root in column I, write the *letter* of its definition from column II.

| COLUMN I | COLUMN II |
|---|---|
| **1.** SOL, SOLI | *a.* hang |
| **2.** MAN, MANU | *b.* see, look, sight |
| **3.** PEND, PENS | *c.* put |
| **4.** SOLV, SOLU, SOLUT | *d.* write |
| **5.** UND, UNDA | *e.* alone, lonely, single |
| **6.** VER, VERA, VERI | *f.* similar, like, same |
| **7.** SCRIB, SCRIPT | *g.* wave, flow |
| **8.** VID, VIS | *h.* hand |
| **9.** SIMIL, SIMUL | *i.* true, truth |
| **10.** PON, POS | *j.* loosen |

**REVIEW 12:** SENTENCE COMPLETION

Write the word from the list below that best fits the context.

| | | |
|---|---|---|
| abound | appendix | desolate |
| dissimilar | manipulate | manual |
| manuscript | pending | redundant |
| resolution | resolve | revise |
| simulate | simile | sole |
| soliloquy | solitude | veracity |
| verdict | video | |

1. Since the __?__ on my TV has gone out for the third time this week, I am afraid there may be no early __?__ of the problem. The only thing
I see is "snow."

2. By closing her door, Jane was able to get the __?__ she needed to complete the __?__ of her term paper.

3. The owner's __?__ explains how to __?__ the controls on the air conditioner.

4. Gulliver, the __?__ survivor of a shipwreck, landed on an apparently __?__ coast, since there were no signs of other humans or dwellings.

5. One thing I had to do when I __?__d my paper was to eliminate all __?__ words and phrases.

6. Homer's *Iliad* __?__s in vivid __?__s. Here is a sample: "Achilles ran toward Hector as a hawk swoops for a trembling dove."

7. The __?__ to the annual report informs stockholders about __?__ lawsuits against the company.

8. The suspect's handwriting and the writing on the ransom note proved to be __?__. That was a blow to the detectives trying to __?__ the case.

9. Othello thinks Iago is his true friend. However, in a(n) __?__ later in the play, Iago reveals that his friendship for Othello is __?__d.

10. The jury's "not guilty" __?__ shows that they must have had confidence in the __?__ of the defense witness's testimony.

**REVIEW 13:** SYNONYMS

Avoid repetition by replacing the boldfaced word or expression with a
**synonym** from the following words.

| | | |
|---|---|---|
| absolute | abundant | emancipate |
| impending | postpone(d) | similarity |
| simultaneous | solvent | suspend(ed) |
| verify | | |

1. In many respects, the partners do not resemble each other, but
   there is a striking **resemblance** in their voices.

2. Play will be **temporarily stopped** until it stops raining.

3. Her guilt is beyond question; there is **unquestionable** proof that
   she evaded the law.

4. Shouldn't we leave sooner? A storm is **threatening to occur soon.**

5. Since the two programs were **on at the same time**, I turned on one
   and videotaped the other.

6. Though the company is indebted to many suppliers, it is still **able
   to pay its debts.**

7. In late summer, there is plenty of fresh corn; the markets get
   **plentiful** supplies of it daily.

8. Several independent researchers are trying to **confirm** the scientist's
   claims. As yet, there is no confirmation.

9. The trial has already been **deferred** twice; now, the defendant is
   again requesting a deferment.

10. The revolution gave the people freedom from tyranny, but it did
    not **free** them from poverty.

## REVIEW 14: ANTONYMS

Write the word from the list below that is most nearly the **opposite** of the boldfaced word or words.

| | | |
|---|---|---|
| append | aver | depose |
| impose | inundate | manual |
| pending | proscribe | simultaneous |
| soluble | | |

1. Before the clearance sale, the old price tickets were **detached** from the garments, and new ones were __?__ed.
2. Now that there is a promising clue, the case thought to be **beyond resolution** may indeed be __?__.
3. The legislature voted to **remove** nuisance taxes that it had previously __?__d on business.
4. Two witnesses __?__ that the suspect tried to intimidate them, but he continues to **deny** that charge.
5. Engineers are working to **drain** the tunnel __?__d by last night's heavy rainstorm.
6. Most drivers prefer an **automatic** transmission rather than a(n) __?__ one because it allows them to shift gears without using their hands.
7. I can usually answer the telephone and the doorbell if they ring **at different times**, but not if they are __?__.
8. Few who had seen the monarch **enthroned** were present when he was __?__d.
9. Is the matter already **decided**, or is it still __?__?
10. Most of the dumping that used to be **permitted** is now __?__d.

## REVIEW 15: CONCISE WRITING

Using no more than sixty words, rewrite the following passage, keeping all its ideas. The first sentence has been rewritten to get you started. Go on from there.

### Broker vs. Clients

In one of the cases waiting to be settled, two clients are accusing a broker of managing their investments in a manner that is not ethical. They say that he has made huge profits, while they are now not able to pay their debts. The broker insists that he has never acted in a way that is fraudulent. When he was asked if he wanted to look back over his testimony to correct misstatements or make additions, he said "no." The decision of the jury is expected to be out in a short time.

**Broker vs. Clients**
(concise version)

In a pending case, two clients are accusing a broker of manipulating their funds.

 ### REVIEW 16: SYNONYM SUMMARY

Each line, when completed, should have three words similar in meaning. Write the *complete* words.

| | | |
|---|---|---|
| **1.** att (1) ch | (1) dd | app (1) nd |
| **2.** disint (1) grate | d (1) sband | d (2) solve |
| **3.** auth (1) r | journ (1) list | scr (1) be |
| **4.** lib (1) rate | (1) ree | eman (1) ipate |
| **5.** dev (1) state | r (1) vage | (2) solate |
| **6.** gen (1) ine | (2) thentic | v (1) r (1) table |
| **7.** fl (2) d | over (1) helm | in (2) date |
| **8.** c (1) mm (1) nd | (2) thorization | m (1) nd (1) te |
| **9.** d (1) rect | d (1) ctate | p (2) scr (1) be |
| **10.** utt (1) r | (3) right | abs (1) l (1) te |
| **11.** h (1) nd (1) riting | pen (3) ship | (2) ript |
| **12.** test (1) fy | (1) wear | (2) pose |
| **13.** s (1) l (1) tion | ans (1) er | res (1) l (1) tion |
| **14.** proh (1) b (1) t | (3) bid | pr (1) scribe |
| **15.** im (1) tate | f (2) gn | s (1) m (1) late |
| **16.** lon (1) l (1) ness | s (1) cl (1) sion | sol (1) t (1) de |

17. anx (2) ty          appre (3) sion          (3) pense

18. abs (1) rb          inc (1) rp (1) rate          as (2) milate

19. conf (1) rm          substant (2) te          v (1) r (1) fy

20. c (1) nc (1) rr (1) nt          (3) temporary          s (1) multan (2) us

 **REVIEW 17:** ANALOGIES

Which lettered pair of words—*a, b, c, d,* or *e*—most nearly expresses the same relationship as the capitalized pair?

**1.** ACTOR : SCRIPT
  *a.* physician : prescription      *b.* composer : score
  *c.* navigator : course      *d.* author : manuscript
  *e.* dramatist : play

**2.** GREGARIOUS : SOLITUDE
  *a.* economical : conservation      *b.* contentious : argument
  *c.* autocratic : power      *d.* conservative : change
  *e.* independent : freedom

**3.** EMANCIPATE : BONDAGE
  *a.* indict : accusation      *b.* promote : rank
  *c.* enlighten : ignorance      *d.* commission : task
  *e.* laud : commendation

**4.** APPEND : DETACH
  *a.* prohibit : ban      *b.* frustrate : circumvent
  *c.* debilitate : weaken      *d.* heed : mind
  *e.* curtail : protract

**5.** ENIGMA : RESOLVE
  *a.* ball : roll      *b.* smoke : rise
  *c.* perfection : achieve      *d.* rumor : spread
  *e.* fish : swim

**6.** INSOLVENT : CURRENCY

 *a.* magnanimous : generosity  *b.* amiable : cordiality

 *c.* undaunted : courage   *d.* arrogant : pride

 *e.* solitary : company

**7.** POSTPONEMENT : DEFERRAL

 *a.* scarcity : abundance   *b.* exploit : feat

 *c.* redundancy : conciseness  *d.* calamity : boon

 *e.* impasse : resolution

**8.** PERJURER : VERACITY

 *a.* bulldog : tenacity    *b.* celebrity : renown

 *c.* jack-of-all-trades : versatility *d.* upstart : resources

 *e.* monopolist : competition

**9.** EARRING : PENDANT

 *a.* water : solvent    *b.* ornament : ring

 *c.* moisture : sponge   *d.* vegetable : asparagus

 *e.* animal : deer

**10.** IMPROVISE : EXTEMPORANEOUS

 *a.* obey : insubordinate   *b.* lurk : conspicuous

 *c.* conspire : clandestine  *d.* rage : rational

 *e.* sneeze : voluntary

 **REVIEW 18:** COMPOSITION

Answer in a sentence or two.

**1.** Why is revising a manuscript for redundant words a useful thing to do?

**2.** Why does the resolution of a story usually end the suspense?

**3.** Is a magazine with many subscribers likely to be dissolved? Why?

**4.** Would tourists abound in a desolated region? Explain.

**5.** Why is veracity an important trait for a scribe?

# 6

# Enlarging Vocabulary Through Greek Word Elements

## Why study Greek word elements?

English contains a substantial and growing number of words derived from Greek. Some of these words are general words in everyday use, e.g., *authentic, chronological, economical, homogeneous,* etc. Others are used in specialized fields. Certainly you have heard terms like *antibiotic, orthopedic,* and *pediatrician* in the field of medicine; *astronaut, protoplasm,* and *thermonuclear* in science; and *autonomous, demagogue,* and *protocol* in government.

These important words, and others like them in this chapter, are constructed from Greek word elements. Once you know what a particular word element means, you have a clue to the meaning of words derived from it. When, for example, you have learned that *PAN* or *PANTO* means "complete" or "all," you are better able to understand—and remember—that a *panacea* is a "remedy for *all* ills," a *panorama* is a "*complete* and unobstructed view in *all* directions," and a *pantomime* is "*all* gestures and signs, i.e., a performance without words."

## Purpose of this chapter

This chapter aims to enlarge your vocabulary by acquainting you with twenty Greek word elements and some English words derived from them. As you study each word group, make it a special point to memorize the meaning of the word element so that you will be able to recognize it in derivatives.

# GREEK WORD ELEMENTS 1–10

## Pretest 1

Write the *letter* of the best answer.

1. In a *plutocracy,* __?__ govern.

   (A) technical experts   (B) the wealthy   (C) the nobles

2. A *pedagogue is* mainly concerned with __?__.

   (A) politics   (B) medicine   (C) teaching

3. *Pandemonium* is a condition of __?__.

   (A) wild disorder   (B) poor nourishment   (C) absolute peace

4. People who lack *autonomy* are __?__.

   (A) unreliable   (B) selfish   (C) not self-ruled

5. You study *orthography* mainly in your __?__ classes.

   (A) English   (B) mathematics   (C) social studies

6. A mistake in __?__ order is a mistake in *chronology.*

   (A) word   (B) alphabetical   (C) time

7. In a *homogeneous* group, the members are of __?__ ability.

   (A) similar   (B) varied   (C) high

8. A *kleptomaniac* is a menace mainly to __?__.

   (A) liberty   (B) property   (C) life

9. The *odometer* on your automobile dashboard measures __?__.

   (A) distance   (B) speed   (C) motor temperature

10. A *demagogue* stirs up the people __?__.

   (A) when they forget their responsibilities   (B) to protect democratic principles   (C) for personal advantage

**THE ANSWERS ARE**

1. B   2. C   3. A   4. C   5. A
6. C   7. A   8. B   9. A   10. C

Each italicized word in the pretest came from a different word element: *plutocracy* from CRACY, meaning "government"; *pedagogue* from PED, meaning "child," etc. You will now study ten such word elements and some words derived from them.

# 1. AUT, AUTO: "self"

| WORD | MEANING AND TYPICAL USE |
|---|---|
| **authentic** (*adj.*)<br>ȯ-'then-tik | (literally, "from the master himself") genuine; real; reliable; trustworthy<br>When you withdraw money, the bank may compare your signature with the one in its files to see if it is *authentic*. |
| **autobiography** (*n.*)<br>ˌȯ-tō-bī-'ä-grə-fē | story of a person's life written by the person himself or herself<br>In her *autobiography* THE STORY OF MY LIFE, Helen Keller tells how unruly she was as a young child. |
| **autocrat** (*n.*)<br>'ȯ-tə-ˌkrat | ruler exercising self-derived, absolute power; despot; dictator<br>The *autocrat* was replaced by a ruler responsible to the people. |
| **autograph** (*n.*)<br>'ȯ-tə-ˌgraf | person's signature written by himself or herself<br>The baseball star wrote his *autograph* for an admirer who came up to him with a pencil and scorecard. |

**automatic** (*adj.*)
,ȯ-tə-'ma-tik

acting by itself; self-regulating
   Some cars require the driver to shift gears manually, while others have an *automatic* transmission.

**automation** (*n.*)
,ȯ-tə-'mā-shən

technique of making a process self-operating by means of built-in electronic controls
   Many workers have lost their jobs as a result of *automation*.

**automaton** (*n.*)
ȯ-'tä-mə-tən

(literally, "self-acting thing") purely mechanical person following a routine; robot
   An autocrat prefers subjects who are *automatons* rather than intelligent human beings.

**autonomous** (*adj.*)
ȯ-'tä-nə-məs

self-governing; independent; sovereign
   The Alumni Association is not under the control of the school. It is a completely *autonomous* group.

**autonomy** (*n.*)
ȯ-'tä-nə-mē

right of self-government; independence; sovereignty
   After World War II, many former colonies were granted *autonomy* and became independent nations.

**autopsy** (*n.*)
'ȯ-,täp-sē

(literally, "a seeing for oneself") medical examination of a dead body to determine the cause of death; postmortem examination
   The cause of the celebrity's sudden death will not be known until the *autopsy* has been performed.

 **EXERCISE 6.1:** *AUT, AUTO* WORDS

Write the most appropriate word from group 1.

1. Some members want to censure the president for ignoring the club's constitution and behaving like an __?__.

2. You are no better than an __?__ if you act mechanically without using your intelligence.

3. The prime minister left her life story to others, for she had neither the time nor the desire to write an __?__.

4. The camera has a built-in __?__ flash, which works whenever there's not enough light.

5. For generations, colonial peoples who asked for __?__ were usually told that they were not ready to govern themselves.

# 2. CRACY: "government"

**aristocracy** (*n.*)
,ar-ə-'stä-krə-sē

1. (literally, "government by the best") government or country governed by a small privileged upper class
    Before 1789, France was an *aristocracy*.

2. ruling class of nobles; nobility; privileged class; gentry
    When the Revolution of 1789 began, many members of the French *aristocracy* fled to other lands.

**autocracy** (*n.*)
ȯ-'tä-krə-sē

government. or country governed by one individual with self-derived, unlimited power
    Germany under Adolf Hitler was an *autocracy*.

**bureaucracy** (*n.*)
byü-'rä-krə-sē

government by bureaus or groups of officials; administration characterized by excessive red tape and routine
    The mayor was criticized for setting up an inefficient *bureaucracy* unresponsive to the needs of the people.

**democracy** (*n.*)
di-'mä-krə-sē

government or country governed by the people; rule by the majority
    The thirteen colonies developed into the first *democracy* in the Western Hemisphere.

**plutocracy** (*n.*)
plü-'tä-krə-sē

government or country governed by the rich
    If only millionaires can afford to run for office, we may soon become a *plutocracy*.

**technocracy** (*n.*)
tek-'nä-krə-sē

government or country governed by technical experts
    In a *technocracy*, the governing class would consist largely of engineers.

The form *crat* at the end of a word means "advocate of a type of government," "member of a class," or, if the word is capitalized, "member of a political party." Examples:

**aristocrat** (*n.*)  
ə-'ris-tə-,krat  

1. advocate of aristocracy  
An *aristocrat* would like to see members of the upper class in control of the government.

2. member of the aristocracy; noble; patrician  
Winston Churchill was born an *aristocrat*; he was the son of Sir Randolph Churchill.

**Democrat** (*n.*)  
'de-mə-,krat  

member of the Democratic Party  
The senator used to be a Republican, but she is now a *Democrat*.

Also: **bureaucrat, plutocrat, technocrat**

 **EXERCISE 6.2:** *CRACY* WORDS

Write the most appropriate word from group 2.

1. It was most unusual for a member of the __?__ to marry someone not belonging to the nobility.
2. If you believe that only the affluent are fit to govern, you must be a(n) __?__.
3. In a(n) __?__, the ruler has absolute and unlimited power.
4. How can you call yourself a(n) __?__ if you do not believe in majority rule?
5. Many are opposed to a(n) __?__ because they do not wish to be ruled by technical experts.

## 3. DEM, DEMO: "people"

**demagogue** (*n.*)  
'de-mə-,gäg  

political leader who stirs up the people for personal advantage; rabble-rouser  
No responsible leader, only a *demagogue*, would make campaign speeches promising to solve all the people's problems.

**democratic** (*adj.*)
de-mə-'kra-tik

based on the principles of democracy, or government by the people
    A nation cannot be considered democratic unless its leaders are chosen by the people in free elections.

**democratize** (*v.*)
di-'mä-krə-,tīz

make democratic
    The adoption of the 19th Amendment, giving women the franchise, greatly *democratized* our nation.

**epidemic** (*adj.*)
,e-pə-'de-mik

(literally, "among the people") affecting many people in an area at the same time; widespread
    Greater federal and state aid is needed in areas where unemployment is *epidemic*.

**epidemic** (*n.*)

outbreak of a rapidly spreading, contagious disease affecting many people at the same time; plague; rash
    The high rate of absenteeism was caused by the flu *epidemic*.

 **EXERCISE 6.3:** *DEM, DEMO* WORDS

Write the most appropriate word from group 3.

1. Millions of people died in the 14th century as the result of a(n) __?__ known as the Black Death.

2. The election was not __?__ because some people voted more than once and others were prevented from voting.

3. An intelligent voter can distinguish the unselfish political leader from the __?__.

4. To __?__ the country, a new constitution was drawn up, giving equal rights to all segments of the population.

5. It is more __?__ for a governor to be chosen by the people than to be appointed by the king.

# 4.  PAN, PANTO: "all," "complete"

**panacea** (*n.*)
ˌpa-nə-'sē-ə

remedy for all ills; cure-all; universal remedy; elixir

The international treaty will reduce tensions, but it will not resolve all conflict. It is no *panacea*.

**Pan-American** (*adj.*)
ˌpa-nə-'mer-ə-kən

of or pertaining to all the countries of North, South, and Central America

The *Pan-American* Highway links all the countries of the Western Hemisphere from Alaska to Chile.

**pandemonium** (*n.*)
ˌpan-də-'mō-nē-əm

(literally, "abode of all the demons," i.e., hell) wild uproar; very noisy din; wild disorder; tumult; racket

The huge crowds in Times Square grew noisier as the old year ticked away, and when midnight struck there was *pandemonium*.

**panoply** (*n.*)
'pa-nə-plē

complete suit of armor; complete covering or equipment; magnificent array

The opposing knights, mounted and in full *panoply*, awaited the signal for the tournament to begin.

**panorama** (*n.*)
ˌpa-nə-'ra-mə

complete, unobstructed view

From the Verrazano-Narrows Bridge, you can get an excellent *panorama* of New York's harbor.

**pantomime** (*n.*)
'pan-tə-ˌmīm

dramatic performance that is all signs and gestures without words

Not until THE GREAT DICTATOR did Charlie Chaplin play a speaking part. All his previous roles were in *pantomime*.

**EXERCISE 6.4:** *PAN, PANTO* WORDS

Write the most appropriate word from group 4.

1. When Karen scored the tie-breaking goal with five seconds left to play, __?__ broke out.
2. Many regard education as the __?__ that will cure all of society's ills.
3. The top of 3605-foot Mt. Snow in Vermont offers a fine __?__ of the Green Mountains.
4. In a __?__, the actors express themselves only by facial expressions, bodily movements, and gestures.
5. The woods in their full __?__ of autumn color are a breathtaking sight.

## 5. *CHRON, CHRONO: "time"*

**anachronism** (*n.*)
ə-'na-krə-ˌni-zəm

error in chronology or time order
The actor playing the Roman gladiator forgot to remove his wristwatch, creating an amusing *anachronism*.

**chronicle** (*n.*)
'krä-ni-kəl

historical account of events in the order of time; history; annals
One of the earliest accounts of King Arthur occurs in a 12th-century *chronicle* of the kings of Britain by Geoffrey of Monmouth.

**chronological** (*adj.*)
ˌkrä-nə-'lä-ji-kəl

arranged in order of time
The magazines in this file are not in *chronological* order. I found the February issue after the October one.

**chronology** (*n.*)
krə-'nä-lə-jē

arrangement of data or events in order of time of occurrence
In the *chronology* of American Presidents, Ulysses S. Grant comes after Andrew Johnson.

**synchronize** (*v.*)
'siŋ-krə-,nīz

cause to agree in time; make simultaneous
The clocks in the library need to be *synchronized*; one is a minute and a half behind the other.

 **EXERCISE 6.5:** *CHRON, CHRONO* WORDS

Write the most appropriate word from group 5.

1. Can you recall the World Series champions of the last five years in the correct _?_?

2. To say that the ancient Greeks watched the siege of Troy on television would be an amusing _?_.

3. The film begins near the climax and then goes back to the hero's childhood, violating the usual _?_ order.

4. The townspeople used to _?_ their timepieces with the clock outside the village bank.

5. The current *World Almanac* gives a(n) _?_ of last year's events.

## 6. MANIA: "madness," "insane impulse," "craze"

**kleptomania** (*n.*)
,klep-tə-'mā-nē-ə

insane impulse to steal
The millionaire arrested for shoplifting was found to be suffering from *kleptomania*.

**mania** (*n.*)
'mā-nē-ə

1. madness; insanity
For a student with an A average to quit school two months before graduation is sheer *mania*.

2. excessive fondness; craze
Though I still read science fiction, I no longer have the *mania* for it that I originally had.

**maniac** (*n.*)
'mā-nē-,ak

raving lunatic; mad or insane person; crackpot
The deranged behavior of the narrator in "The Tell-Tale Heart" leaves little doubt that he is a *maniac*.

| | |
|---|---|
| **maniacal** (*adj.*)<br>mə-'nī-ə-kəl | characterized by madness; insane; raving<br>You protested in such a loud, violent, and *maniacal* manner that onlookers must have thought you had lost your sanity. |
| **pyromania** (*n.*)<br>‚pī-rō-'mā-nē-ə | insane impulse to set fires<br>The person charged with setting the fire had been suspected of *pyromania* on two previous occasions. |

The form *maniac* at the end of a word means "person affected by an insane impulse or craze." Examples: **kleptomaniac, pyromaniac.**

 **EXERCISE 6.6:** *MANIA* WORDS

Write the most appropriate word from group 6.

1. The weird, _?_ shrieks and groans coming from the house might have made one believe that it was inhabited by a raving lunatic.
2. Sharon has a _?_ for chocolates; she will finish a whole box in no time at all if not restrained.
3. Herb can't help taking things belonging to others; he is a _?_.
4. Officials believe the recent series of small fires to be the work of a _?_.
5. The spoiled brat raved like a _?_ when he didn't get his way.

# 7. PED: "child"

| | |
|---|---|
| **encyclopedia** (*n.*)<br>in-‚sī-klə-'pē-dē-ə | (literally, "well-rounded rearing of a child") work offering alphabetically arranged information on various branches of knowledge<br>There are four different *encyclopedias* in the reference section of our school library. |

**orthopedic** (*adj.*)
ˌȯr-thə-ˈpē-dik

(literally, "of the straight child") having to do with *orthopedics*, the science dealing with the correction and prevention of deformities, especially in children
    Patients recovering from broken limbs are treated in the hospital's *orthopedic* ward.

**pedagogue** (*n.*)
ˈpe-də-ˌgäg

(literally, "leader of a child") teacher of children
    The new teacher received a great deal of help from the more experienced *pedagogues*.

**pedagogy** (*n.*)
ˈpe-də-ˌgō-jē

art of teaching
    Dr. Dworkin's lessons are usually excellent. She is a master of *pedagogy*.

**pediatrician** (*n.*)
ˌpē-dē-ə-ˈtri-shən

physician specializing in the treatment of babies and children
    When the baby developed a fever, the parents telephoned the *pediatrician*.

**pediatrics** (*n.*)
ˌpē-dē-ˈa-triks

branch of medicine dealing with the care, development, and diseases of babies and children
    From the number of baby carriages outside the office, you can tell that Dr. Enders specializes in *pediatrics*.

 **EXERCISE 6.7:** *PED* WORDS

Write the most appropriate word from group 7.

1. __?__ deals with diseases that afflict the young.

2. You can now purchase an entire twenty-two-volume __?__ on one CD, saving a considerable amount of space in your home.

3. A teacher's professional training includes courses in __?__.

4. Until the age of six months, the baby was taken to the __?__ every month.

5. A(n) __?__ specialist performed the operation to correct the deformity of the child's spinal column.

## 8. ORTHO: "straight," "correct"

**orthodontist** (*n.*)
,ȯr-thə-'dän-tist

dentist specializing in orthodontics, a branch of dentistry dealing with straightening and adjusting of teeth
    A teenager wearing braces is obviously under the care of an *orthodontist*.

**orthodox** (*adj.*)
'ȯr-thə-,däks

(literally, "correct opinion") generally accepted, especially in religion; conventional; approved; conservative
    There was no religious liberty in the Massachusetts Bay Colony. Roger Williams, for example, was banished because he did not accept *orthodox* Puritan beliefs.

**orthography** (*n.*)
ȯr-'thä-grə-fē

(literally, "correct writing") correct spelling
    American and English *orthography* are very much alike. One difference, however, is in words like "honor" and "labor," which the English spell "honour" and "labour."

**orthopedist** (*n.*)
,ȯr-thə-'pē-dist

physician specializing in the correction and prevention of deformities, especially in children
    A deformity of the spine is a condition that requires the attention of an *orthopedist*.

**unorthodox** (*adj.*)
,ən-'ȯr-thə-,däks

not orthodox; not in accord with accepted, standard, or approved belief or practice; unconventional; heretical
    Vaccination was rejected as *unorthodox* when Dr. Jenner first suggested it.

 **EXERCISE 6.8:** *ORTHO* WORDS

Write the most appropriate word from group 8.

1. It is __?__ to begin a meal with the dessert.
2. Phyllis has won the spelling bee again. She excels in __?__.

**3.** The young patient is under the care of a well-known __?__ for a leg deformity.

**4.** The infant gets up at 4 A.M. We should prefer him to wake at a more __?__ hour, such as 7 A.M.

**5.** Laura's parents have been assured by an __?__ that her teeth can be straightened.

# 9. GEN, GENO, GENEA: "race," "kind," "birth"

**genealogy** (*n.*)
ˌjē-nē-'ä-lə-jē

(literally, "account of a race or family") history of the descent of a person or family from an ancestor; lineage; pedigree
　　Diane can trace her descent from an ancestor who fought in the Mexican War. I know much less about my own *genealogy*.

**genesis** (*n.*)
'je-nə-səs

birth or coming into being of something; origin
　　According to legend, the Trojan War had its *genesis* in a dispute among three Greek goddesses.

**heterogeneous** (*adj.*)
ˌhe-tə-rə-'jē-nē-əs

differing in kind; dissimilar; not uniform; varied
　　Many different racial and cultural groups are to be found in the *heterogeneous* population of a large American city.

**homogeneous** (*adj.*)
ˌhō-mə-'jē-nē-əs

of the same kind; similar; uniform
　　All the dancers in the ballet corps wore the same costume to present a *homogeneous* appearance.

**homogenize** (*v.*)
hō-'mä-jə-ˌnīz

make homogeneous
　　If dairies did not *homogenize* milk, the cream would be concentrated at the top instead of being evenly distributed.

**EXERCISE 6.9:** *GEN, GENO, GENEA* WORDS

Write the appropriate word from group 9.

1. The class consists of intermediate and advanced dancers, as well as a few beginners. It is a _?_ group.

2. A family Bible in which births, marriages, and deaths have been recorded for generations is a source of information about a person's _?_.

3. There are always lumps in the cereal when you cook it. You don't know how to _?_ it.

4. When every house on the block has the same exterior, the result is a _?_ dullness.

5. Democracy is not an American creation; it had its _?_ in ancient Greece.

## 10. METER, METR: *"measure"*

**barometer** (*n.*)
bə-'rä-mə-tər

instrument for measuring atmospheric pressure as an aid in determining probable weather changes
    When the *barometer* indicates a rapid drop in air pressure, it means a storm is coming.

**chronometer** (*n.*)
krə-'nä-mə-tər

instrument for measuring time very accurately
    Unlike ordinary clocks and watches, *chronometers* are little affected by temperature changes or vibration.

**diameter** (*n.*)
dī-'a-mə-tər

(literally, "measure across") straight line passing through the center of a body or figure from one side to the other; length of such a line; thickness; width
    Some giant redwood trees measure up to 30 feet (9.14 meters) in *diameter*.

**meter** (*n.*)
'mē-tər

1. device for measuring
When water *meters* are installed, it will be easy to tell how much water each home is using.

2. unit of measure in the metric system; 39.37 inches
A *meter* is 3.37 inches longer than a yard.

**odometer** (*n.*)
ō-'dä-mə-tər

instrument attached to a vehicle for measuring the distance traversed
All eyes, except the driver's, were fastened on the *odometer* as it moved from 9,999.9 to 10,000 miles.

**photometer** (*n.*)
fō-'tä-mə-tər

instrument for measuring intensity of light
The intensity of a source of light, such as an electric lightbulb, can be measured with a *photometer.*

**speedometer** (*n.*)
spi-'dä-mə-tər

instrument for measuring speed; tachometer
I advised Ann to slow down, as we were in a 30-mile-an-hour zone and her *speedometer* registered more than 40.

**symmetry** (*n.*)
'si-mə-trē

correspondence in measurements, shape, etc., on opposite sides of a dividing line; well-balanced arrangement of parts; harmony; balance
As the planes passed overhead, we were impressed by the perfect *symmetry* of their V-formation.

 **EXERCISE 6.10:** *METER, METR* WORDS

Write the most appropriate word from group 10.

1. Every apple in this package has a(n) __?__ of no less than 2¼ inches.

2. We couldn't tell how fast we were going because the __?__ was out of order.

3. Notice the __?__ of the human body. The right side is the counterpart of the left.

4. You can tell how many miles a car has been driven since its manufacture if you look at its __?__.

5. In the 100-__?__ dash, the course is more than 100 yards long.

# Review Exercises

 **REVIEW 1:** GREEK WORD ELEMENTS 1–10

For each Greek word element in column I, write the *letter* of its correct meaning from column II.

| COLUMN I | COLUMN II |
|----------|-----------|
| 1. ORTHO | *a.* child |
| 2. MANIAC | *b.* all; complete |
| 3. GEN, GENO, GENEA | *c.* madness; insane impulse; craze |
| 4. CHRON, CHRONO | *d.* straight; correct |
| 5. CRAT | *e.* government |
| 6. AUT, AUTO | *f.* race; kind; birth |
| 7. METER, METR | *g.* people |
| 8. PAN, PANTO | *h.* advocate of a type of government |
| 9. MANIA | *i.* measure |
| 10. CRACY | *j.* self |
| 11. PED | *k.* time |
| 12. DEM, DEMO | *l.* person affected by an insane impulse |

 **REVIEW 2:** WORD-BUILDING

Write the word defined below. The number in parentheses indicates how many letters must be added to the word part given.

| DEFINITION | WORD |
|------------|------|
| 1. arranged in order of time | (6) LOGICAL |
| 2. technique of making a process self-operating | (4) MATION |
| 3. instrument for measuring atmospheric pressure | BARO (5) |
| 4. remedy for all ills | (3) ACEA |
| 5. differing in kind | HETERO (3) EOUS |
| 6. person affected by an insane impulse to set fires | PYRO (6) |
| 7. government by small privileged upper class | ARISTO (5) |

8. dentist specializing in straightening teeth        (5) DONTIST
9. teacher of children                                (3) AGOGUE
10. self-governing                                    (4) NOMOUS
11. correspondence in shape, size,
    measurements, etc.                                SYM (4) Y
12. complete equipment                                (3) OPLY
13. contrary to approved or conservative practice     UN (5) DOX
14. physician specializing in treatment of children   (3) IATRICIAN
15. member of wealthy ruling class                    PLUTO (4)
16. of the same kind                                  HOMO (3) EOUS
17. affecting many people in an area at the
    same time                                         EPI (3) IC
18. characterized by madness                          (5) CAL
19. cause to agree in time                            SYN (5) IZE
20. government by the people                          (4) CRACY

 ## **REVIEW 3:** SENTENCE COMPLETION

Write the word from the list below that best fits the context.

| | | |
|---|---|---|
| anachronism | aristocracy | authentic |
| autobiography | autocrat | autograph |
| chronological | democracy | encyclopedia |
| genesis | heterogeneous | homogeneous |
| maniacal | panacea | pandemonium |
| pedagogue | pedagogy | pyromaniac |
| synchronize | unorthodox | |

1. In his __?__, the famous teacher describes some personal experiences that taught him the art of __?__.

2. When the home team won the championship, __?__ broke out, and thousands of __?__ fans charged the goal posts to knock them down.

3. A handwriting expert was called in to determine whether the __?__ of Babe Ruth on the old baseball was __?__.

4. Hoping to oust the __?__ ruling the country with an iron fist, the conspirators __?__d their watches and moved cautiously toward the palace.

5. The psychiatrist treating the __?__ is trying to discover the __?__ of his urge to set fires.

6. Only if I were a "walking __?__" could I have recited the names of all the kings and queens of England in perfect __?__ order.

7. The __?__ explained to her class that the striking of the clock in *Julius Caesar* is a(n) __?__, since the play is set in ancient Rome.

8. Though the young man had grown up among the __?__, his father had instilled in him the principles of __?__.

9. The __?__ candidate readily admitted to the voters that she had no __?__ for their problems.

10. The athletes participating in the international meet were __?__ in ethnic origin, but __?__ in their quest for glory.

 **REVIEW 4:** SYNONYMS

Avoid repetition by replacing the boldfaced word or expression with a **synonym** from the following words.

| | | |
|---|---|---|
| automatic | automaton | autonomous |
| chronology | diameter | genealogy |
| kleptomania | orthography | pantomime |
| pediatrician(s) | | |

1. The helper was a(n) **purely mechanical person** who mechanically repeated everything that the boss said.

2. Posts with a **thickness** of six inches are much sturdier than those that are only four inches thick.

3. **Physicians who specialize in the treatment of children** see more cases of measles than most other physicians.

4. Once we set the temperature, the heating system is **self-regulating**; we don't have to regulate it.

5. Most colonies governed by a mother country eventually became **self-governing**.

6. Jack would be a better speller if he learned some of the rules of **spelling**.

7. If you say that something happened at an earlier time than it really did, you are making an error in **time sequence**.

8. The defendant claims she took to stealing not because of greed, but because of **an insane impulse to steal.**

9. From history and from conversations with your grandparents and great-grandparents, you may learn a good deal about your **family history.**

10. Not a word was spoken; the performers used **signs and gestures, but no words.**

 **REVIEW 5:** ANTONYMS

Write the word from the list below that is most nearly the **opposite** of the boldfaced word or words.

| | | |
|---|---|---|
| aristocrat | authentic | automatic |
| democratic | genesis | heterogeneous |
| homogeneous | maniac | symmetry |
| unorthodox | | |

1. In the olden days, it was rare for a **commoner** to marry a(n) _?_.

2. The insurgents hope to topple the **authoritarian** regime and replace it with a(n) _?_ government.

3. From its _?_ to its **cessation**, the epidemic took a heavy toll.

4. Is the car equipped with a(n) _?_ transmission, or a **manual** one?

5. It is hard to believe that a **sane person** could suddenly turn into a(n) _?_.

6. Is the class _?_, or does it consist of students of **dissimilar** ability?

7. An occasional **lack of balance** in the marching formations somewhat marred the _?_ of the parade.

8. The documents would have seemed _?_ to most people, but experts knew they were **false.**

9. The establishment favors **conventional** ways of dealing with the crisis and frowns on _?_ approaches.

10. We looked through a(n) _?_ assortment of lamps reduced for final sale, in which no two were **of the same kind.**

**REVIEW 6:** CONCISE WRITING

In no more than eighty words, rewrite the following passage, keeping all its ideas. *Hint:* Reduce each boldfaced expression to a single word.

### The Peloponnesian War: 431–404 B.C.

In 431 B.C., Athens, a small **country governed in accordance with the wishes of the majority of its citizens,** went to war with Sparta, a **nation governed by a small privileged upper class.** Athens would have won if not for two misfortunes. First, it was devastated in 430-428 B.C. by a **rapidly spreading contagious disease** that killed a quarter of its population. Then, because of **political leaders who stirred up the people for their own selfish advantage,** it undertook reckless offensives on which it squandered its finest troops. As a result, Athens lost not only the war, but its **right to govern itself.**

Most of the above facts were recorded by Thucydides in his **historical account of the events, in the order of time,** of the Peloponnesian War.

### The Peloponnesian War: 431–404 B.C.
(concise version)

 **REVIEW 7:** SYNONYM SUMMARY

Each line, when completed, should have three words similar in meaning. Write the *complete* words.

1. dictat (1) r            d (1) spot            (2) tocrat

2. ins (1) ne            r (1) ving            (2) niacal

3. b (1) rth            (1) rigin            genes (2)

4. w (1) dth            th (1) ckness            d (1) ameter

5. tr (1) stworthy            gen (1) ine            aut (2) ntic

6. l (1) natic            cr (1) ckp (1) t            man (2) c

7. ind (1) pend (1) nt            self-gov (2) ning            aut (1) n (1) mous

8. sim (1) l (1) r            un (1) form            homogen (2) us

9. n (1) b (1) lity            g (1) ntry            a (3) tocracy

10. (2) sanity            m (1) dness            (2) nia

11. b (1) lance           harm (1) ny            s (2) metry

12. convent (2) nal       (3) servative          (2) thodox

13. t (1) mult            r (1) cket             (3) demonium

14. (2) story             ann (1) ls             chr (1) n (1) cle

15. ped (1) gree          lin (2) ge             gene (1) logy

16. n (1) ble             patri (2) an           (1) r (1) st (1) crat

17. (2) dependence        sover (2) gnty         aut (1) n (1) my

18. (2) conventional      h (1) retical          (2) ortho (3)

19. plag (2)              r (1) sh               ep (1) d (1) mic

20. (3) similar           v (1) ried             h (1) t (1) r (1) geneous

 **REVIEW 8:** ANALOGIES

Which lettered pair of words—*a, b, c, d,* or *e*—most nearly expresses the same relationship as the capitalized pair?

**1.** DUCHESS : ARISTOCRACY

    *a.* retiree : staff        *b.* student : faculty

    *c.* voter : electorate      *d.* employment : management

    *e.* alien : citizenry

**2.** PANDEMONIUM : HEARING

    *a.* glare : sight         *b.* praise : learning

    *c.* abundance : scarcity    *d.* fog : collision

    *e.* disharmony : agreement

    *Hint:* **pandemonium** makes **hearing** difficult.

**3.** DEMAGOGUE : POLITICS

    *a.* civilian : warfare      *b.* quack : medicine

    *c.* amateur : sports       *d.* clown : circus

    *e.* apprentice : trade

    *Hint:* A **demagogue** is an unscrupulous person in **politics**.

**4.** AUTHENTIC : ACCEPTANCE

    *a.* futile : effort

    *b.* corrupt : contempt

    *c.* incredible : belief

    *d.* insignificant : concern

    *e.* demagogic : trust

**5.** AUTOMATION : PRODUCTIVITY

    *a.* rest : fatigue

    *b.* air conditioning : temperature

    *c.* bickering : amity

    *d.* resentment : achievement

    *e.* refrigeration : shelf life

**6.** SUBJUGATE : AUTONOMY

    *a.* demote : authority

    *b.* initiate : membership

    *c.* vindicate : innocence

    *d.* gag : censorship

    *e.* elevate : prestige

**7.** BIOGRAPHY : CHRONOLOGICAL

    *a.* height : vertical

    *b.* index : alphabetical

    *c.* novel : fictional

    *d.* width : horizontal

    *e.* news story : factual

**8.** ORTHODONTICS : DENTISTRY

    *a.* astronomy : physics

    *b.* orthopedics : fractures

    *c.* biology : zoology

    *d.* pyrotechnics : fireworks

    *e.* pediatrics : childhood

**9.** GENESIS : BEGINNING

    *a.* diagnosis : disease

    *b.* prognosis : recovery

    *c.* crisis : downfall

    *d.* status : promotion

    *e.* metamorphosis : change

 **REVIEW 9:** COMPOSITION

Answer in a sentence or two.

1. Would you prefer to live in an autocracy or a democracy? Explain your choice.

2. How might the outbreak of a deadly and unknown new epidemic cause pandemonium in a city?

3. Would most pediatricians see and cure cases of pyromania on a regular basis? Why or why not?

4. Why does chronology play an important role in most genealogies?

5. Are most pedagogues more interested in automation or orthography? Tell why you think so.

# GREEK WORD ELEMENTS 11–20

## Pretest 2

Write the *letter* of the best answer.

1. If a product is *synthetic,* it was not made by __?__.

   (A) hand   (B) nature   (C) humans

2. A *thermostat* __?__.

   (A) regulates temperature   (B) keeps liquids warm
   (C) provides heat

3. The reference mark __?__ is called an *asterisk.*

   (A) [;]   (B) [']   (C) [*]

4. An *anonymous* poem is __?__.

   (A) by an unknown author   (B) humorous   (C) a nursery rhyme

5. The __?__ in a series of similar things is the *prototype.*

   (A) latest   (B) first   (C) best

6. Usually, a *nemesis* brings __?__.

   (A) defeat   (B) luck   (C) victory

7. A *phenomenon* can be __?__.

(A) a ghost or a shadow only   (B) an extraordinary fact only
(C) any observable fact or event

8. A *dermatologist* is a __?__ specialist.

(A) skin   (B) foot   (C) heart

9. If you have an *antipathy* to a subject, you have a(n) __?__ for it.

(A) enthusiasm   (B) dislike   (C) talent

10. The word __?__ is an *anagram* of "meat."

(A) "meet"   (B) "flesh"   (C) "team"

| THE ANSWERS ARE | | | | |
|---|---|---|---|---|
| 1. B | 2. A | 3. C | 4. A | 5. B |
| 6. A | 7. C | 8. A | 9. B | 10. C |

Each italicized word in the pretest came from a different word element: *synthetic* from THET, meaning "put"; *thermostat* from THERMO, meaning "heat," etc. In the following pages you will learn about ten such word elements and some of their derivatives.

## 11. ANT, ANTI: "against," "opposite"

**antagonist** (*n.*)
an-'ta-gə-,nist

one who is against, or contends with, another in a struggle, fight, or contest; opponent; adversary; foe

Great Britain was our *antagonist* in the War of 1812.

**antibiotic** (*n.*)
,an-tē-,bī-'ä-tik

substance obtained from tiny living organisms that works against harmful bacteria

The *antibiotic* penicillin stops the growth of bacteria that cause pneumonia, tonsillitis, and certain other diseases.

**antibody** (*n.*)
'an-ti-,bä-dē

substance manufactured in the body that works against germs or poisons produced by germs

When the body is invaded by foreign agents, such as bacteria or viruses, the *antibodies* go to work against them.

| | |
|---|---|
| **antidote** (*n.*)<br>'an-ti-,dōt | 1. remedy that acts against the effects of a poison<br>By telephone, the physician prescribed the exact *antidote* to be given immediately to the poison victim.<br><br>2. countermeasure<br>Heavy fines are an *antidote* to illegal parking. |
| **antihistamine** (*n.*)<br>,an-tē-'his-tə-,mən | drug used against certain allergies and cold symptoms<br>The *antihistamine* prescribed for my cold was not too effective. |
| **antipathy** (*n.*)<br>an-'ti-pə-thē | feeling against; distaste; repugnance; dislike; enmity<br>A few of the neighbors have an *antipathy* to dogs, but most are fond of them. |
| **antiseptic** (*n.*)<br>,an-tə-'sep-tik | (literally, "against decaying") substance that prevents infection by checking the growth of microorganisms; germicide<br>The wound was carefully washed; then hydrogen peroxide was applied as an *antiseptic*. |
| **antitoxin** (*n.*)<br>,an-ti-'täk-sən | substance formed in the body as the result of the introduction of a toxin (poison) and capable of acting against that toxin<br>We are injected with diphtheria *antitoxin* produced in horses because the *antitoxin* manufactured by our bodies may not be enough to prevent diphtheria. |
| **antonym** (*n.*)<br>'an-tə-,nim | word meaning the opposite of another word; opposite<br>"Temporary" is the *antonym* of "permanent." |

 **EXERCISE 6.11:** *ANT, ANTI* WORDS

Write the most appropriate word from group 11.

1. An _?_ prescribed by a physician may give temporary relief to some cold and allergy sufferers.

2. Our armed forces must be capable of defending us against any foreign _?_.

3. Streptomycin, an __?__ developed from living microorganisms, is used in the treatment of tuberculosis.

4. The infection would not have developed if an __?__ had been used.

5. I have had an __?__ to ship travel ever since I became seasick on a lake cruise.

# 12. ONYM, ONOMATO: "name," "word"

**acronym** (*n.*)
'a-krə-ˌnim

name formed from the first letter or letters of other words
    The word "radar" is an *acronym* for *RA*dio *D*etecting *A*nd *R*ange.

**anonymous** (*adj.*)
ə-'nä-nə-məs

nameless; unnamed; unidentified
    An *anonymous* American killed in combat in World War I lies in the Tomb of the Unknowns.

**homonym** (*n.*)
'hä-mə-ˌnim

word that sounds like another but differs in meaning
    "Fair" and "fare" are *homonyms.*

**onomatopoeia** (*n.*)
ˌä-nə-ˌma-tə-'pē-ə

use of words whose sound suggests their meaning
    Notice the *onomatopoeia* in these lines by the poet John Dryden: "The double, double, double beat/Of the thundering drum."

**pseudonym** (*n.*)
'sü-dᵊn-ˌim

(literally, "false name") fictitious name used by an author; pen name; alias
    Because of antipathy to female authors in her time, Mary Ann Evans wrote under the *pseudonym* "George Eliot."

**synonym** (*n.*)
'si-nə-ˌnim

word having the same meaning as another word
    "Building" is a *synonym* for "edifice."

**EXERCISE 6.12:** *ONYM, ONOMATO* WORDS

Write the most appropriate word from group 12.

1. "Deer" and "dear" are __?__s.
2. There is no need to use a(n) __?__, unless you wish to conceal your identity.
3. Scuba is a(n) __?__ for "self-contained underwater breathing apparatus."
4. I was embarrassed when the __?__ test paper my teacher spoke about turned out to be mine. I had forgotten to put my name on it.
5. "Hiss," "mumble," and "splash" are good one-word examples of __?__.

## 13. DERM, DERMATO: "skin"

**dermatologist** (*n.*)
dər-mə-'tä-lə-jist

physician specializing in *dermatology,* the science dealing with the skin and its diseases
The patient with the skin disorder is under the care of a *dermatologist.*

**dermis** (*n.*)
'dər-məs

inner layer of the skin
The tiny cells from which hairs grow are located in the *dermis.*

**epidermis** (*n.*)
,e-pə-'dər-məs

outer layer of the skin
Although very thin, the *epidermis* protects the underlying dermis.

**hypodermic** (*adj.*)
,hī-pə-'dər-mik

beneath the skin
A *hypodermic* syringe is used for injecting medication beneath the skin.

**taxidermist** (*n.*)
'tak-sə-,dər-mist

one who practices *taxidermy,* the art of preparing, stuffing, and mounting the skins of animals in lifelike form
The lifelike models of animals that you see in museums are the work of skilled *taxidermists.*

**EXERCISE 6.13:** *DERM, DERMATO* WORDS

Write the most appropriate word from group 13.

1. The __?__ stretched the skin over a plastic cast of the animal's body.
2. Was the antibiotic taken by mouth or administered by __?__ injection?
3. There are numerous tiny openings, or pores, in the __?__, or outer layer of the skin.
4. It took three visits for the __?__ to remove Rita's painful wart in the skin of her left sole.
5. The sweat glands are located in the __?__, or inner layer of the skin.

## 14. NOM, NEM: "management," "distribution," "law"

**agronomy** (*n.*)
ə-'grä-nə-mē

(literally, "land management") branch of agriculture dealing with crop production and soil management; husbandry
    The science of *agronomy* helps farmers obtain larger and better crops.

**astronomical** (*adj.*)
ˌas-trə-'nä-mi-kəl

1. having to do with *astronomy* (literally, "distribution of the stars"); the science of the sun, moon, planets, stars, and other heavenly bodies
    The first *astronomical* observations with a telescope were made by the Italian scientist Galileo.

2. inconceivably large
    It is difficult to conceive of so *astronomical* a sum as a trillion dollars.

**economic** (*adj.*)
ˌe-kə-'nä-mik

having to do with *economics* (literally, "household management"); the social science dealing with production, distribution, and consumption
    The President's chief *economic* adviser expects that production will continue at the same rate for the rest of the year.

| | |
|---|---|
| **economical** (*adj.*)<br>,e-kə-'nä-mi-kəl | managed or managing without waste; thrifty; frugal; sparing<br>    Which is the most *economical* fuel for home heating—gas, electricity, or oil? |
| **gastronome** (*n.*)<br>'gas-trə-,nōm | one who follows the principles of *gastronomy,* the art or science of good eating (literally, "management of the stomach"); lover of good food; epicure; gourmet<br>    Being a *gastronome,* my uncle is well-acquainted with the best restaurants in the city. |
| **nemesis** (*n.*)<br>'ne-mə-səs | (from *Nemesis,* the Greek goddess of vengeance who distributes or deals out what is due)<br>1. person that inflicts just punishment for evil deeds; avenger; scourge<br>    The tyrant Macbeth was invincible in combat until he faced Macduff, who proved to be his *nemesis.*<br><br>2. formidable and usually victorious opponent<br>    We would have ended the season without a defeat if not for our old *nemesis,* Greeley High. |

 **EXERCISE 6.14:** *NOM, NEM* WORDS

Write the most appropriate word from group 14.

1. The villain had engineered several robberies before encountering his _?_ in the person of Sherlock Holmes.
2. Overproduction is a serious _?_ problem.
3. Some museums and art collectors have gone to _?_ expense to acquire famous paintings.
4. Underdeveloped nations are trying to improve the yield and quality of their crops by applying the principles of _?_.
5. The acknowledged _?_ cheerfully aided her dining companions in making their selections from the menu.

## 15. PHAN, PHEN: "show," "appear"

**cellophane** (*n.*)
'se-lə-,fān

cellulose substance that "shows" through or permits seeing through; transparent cellulose substance used as a wrapper
When used as a wrapper, *cellophane* lets the purchaser see the contents of the package.

**diaphanous** (*adj.*)
dī-'a-fə-nəs

of such fine texture as to permit seeing through; sheer; transparent
Pedestrians on the sidewalk could see some of the inside of the restaurant through its *diaphanous* curtains.

**fancy** (*n.*)
'fan-sē

imagination; illusion
We must be able to distinguish between fact and *fancy*.

**fantastic** (*adj.*)
fan-'tas-tik

based on fantasy rather than reason; imaginary; unreal; odd; unbelievable
Robert Fulton's proposal to build a steamboat was at first regarded as *fantastic*.

**fantasy** (*n.*)
'fan-tə-sē

illusory image; play of the mind; imagination; fancy
Selma is not sure whether she saw a face at the window. Perhaps it was only a *fantasy*.

**phantom** (*n.*)
'fan-təm

something that has appearance but no reality; apparition; ghost; specter
The *phantom* of the slain Caesar appeared to Brutus in a dream.

**phenomenal** (*adj.*)
fi-'nä-mə-n°l

extraordinary; remarkable; exceptional; unusual
Bernadine has a *phenomenal* memory; she never forgets a face.

**phenomenon** (*n.*)
fə-'nä-mə-,nän

(literally, "an appearance")
1. any observable fact or event
　We do not see many adults traveling to work on bicycles, but in some foreign cities it is a common *phenomenon.*

2. extraordinary person, event, or thing; wonder; prodigy
　Renowned as a composer and performer while yet in his teens, Mozart was a musical *phenomenon.*

 **EXERCISE 6.15:** *PHAN, PHEN* WORDS

Write the most appropriate word from group 15.

1. Sarah Bernhardt was no ordinary actress; she was a __?__.

2. Though these conclusions may seem __?__, I can show you they are based on reason.

3. If the apples are in a __?__ bag, you can tell how many there are without opening it.

4. Joan was sure someone was behind the door, but no one was there. It was just a __?__.

5. Mrs. Potter thought Christine's performance was __?__, but I found nothing extraordinary or remarkable in it.

## 16. *THERM, THERMO: "heat"*

**diathermy** (*n.*)
'dī-ə-,thər-mē

generation of heat in body tissues through high-frequency electric currents for medical purposes
　*Diathermy* may be used to treat arthritis, bursitis, and other conditions requiring heat treatment.

**thermal** (*adj.*)
'thər-məl

pertaining to heat; hot; warm
　At Lava Hot Springs in Idaho, visitors may bathe in the *thermal* mineral waters.

**thermometer** (*n.*)
thər-'mä-mə-tər

instrument for measuring temperature
At 6 A.M. the *thermometer* registered 32°
Fahrenheit (0° Celsius).

**thermonuclear** (*adj.*)
,thər-mō-'nü-klē-ər

having to do with the fusion (joining together),
at an extraordinarily high temperature,
of the nuclei of atoms (as in the hydrogen bomb)
It is believed that the sun gets its energy from
*thermonuclear* reactions constantly taking place
within it.

**thermostat** (*n.*)
'thər-mə-,stat

automatic device for regulating temperature
You can set the *thermostat* to shut off the heat
when the room reaches a comfortable
temperature.

 **EXERCISE 6.16:** *THERM, THERMO* WORDS

Write the most appropriate word from group 16.

1. The room was cold because the __?__ had been set for only 59°
Fahrenheit (19° Celsius).

2. If you have a __?__ mounted outside your window, you don't need to
go outside to learn what the temperature is.

3. The unbelievably intense heat required to start the __?__ reaction in a
hydrogen bomb is obtained by exploding an atomic bomb.

4. Drugs, hot baths, and __?__ are some of the means used to relieve the
pain of arthritis.

5. Hot Springs, Arkansas, derives its name from its numerous __?__
springs.

## 17. PROT, PROTO: "first"

**protagonist** (*n.*)
prō-'ta-gə-,nist

the leading ("first") character in a play, novel, or
story
Brutus is the *protagonist* in William
Shakespeare's JULIUS CAESAR, and Anthony is the
antagonist.

**protocol** (*n.*)
'prō-tə-,kȯl

1. first draft or record (of discussions, agreements, etc.) from which a treaty is drawn up; preliminary memorandum
    The *protocol* initiated by the representatives of the three nations is expected to lead to a formal treaty.

2. rules of etiquette of the diplomatic corps, military services, etc.
    It is a breach of *protocol* for a subordinate publicly to question the judgment of a superior officer.

**protoplasm** (*n.*)
'prō-tə-,pla-zəm

(literally, "first molded material") fundamental substance of which all living things are composed
    The presence of *protoplasm* distinguishes living from nonliving things.

**prototype** (*n.*)
'prō-tə-,tīp

first or original model of anything; model; pattern
    The crude craft in which the Wright brothers made the first successful flight in 1903 was the *prototype* of the modem airplane.

**protozoan** (*n.*)
,prō-tə-'zō-ən

(literally, "first animal") animal consisting only of a single cell
    The tiny *protozoan* is believed to be the first animal to have appeared on earth.

 ## EXERCISE 6.17: *PROT, PROTO* WORDS

Fill the blank with the appropriate word from group 17.

1. At the opening game of the baseball season in Washington, D.C., the President, according to __?__, is invited to throw out the first ball.

2. The amoeba, a one-celled animal living in ponds and streams, is a typical __?__.

3. Our Constitution has served as the __?__ of similar documents in democratic nations all over the world.

4. The movie star will not accept a minor part; she wants the role of the __?__.

5. Living plants and animals consist of __?__.

## 18. THESIS, THET: "set," "put"

**antithesis** (*n.*)
an-'ti-thə-səs

(literally, "a setting against") direct opposite; contrary; reverse

> I cannot vote for a candidate who stands for the *antithesis* of what I believe.

**epithet** (*n.*)
'e-pə-,thet

(literally, something "placed on" or "added") characterizing word or phrase; descriptive name or title

> Anna Mary Robertson Moses earned the *epithet* "Grandma" because she did not begin to paint until her late seventies.

**hypothesis** (*n.*)
hī-'pä-thə-səs

(literally, "a placing under" or "supposing") supposition or assumption made as a basis for reasoning or research

> When Columbus first presented his *hypothesis* that the earth is round, very few believed it.

**synthesis** (*n.*)
'sin(t)-thə-səs

(literally, "putting together") combination of parts or elements into a whole

> Much of the rubber we use is not a natural product but a *synthesis* of chemicals.

**synthetic** (*adj.*)
sin-'the-tik

(literally, "put together") artificial; factitious; not of natural origin

> Cotton is a natural fiber, but rayon and nylon are *synthetic*.

**thesis** (*n.*)
'thē-səs

(literally, "a setting down")
1. claim put forward; proposition; statement; contention

> Do you agree with Ellen's *thesis* that a student court would be good for our school?

2. essay written by a candidate for an advanced degree

> Candidates for Ph.D. degrees usually must write a *thesis* based on original research.

Note: To form the plural of a word ending in *is*, change the *is* to *es*.
Examples: *antitheses, hypotheses, theses,* etc.

**EXERCISE 6.18:** *THESIS, THET* WORDS

Write the most appropriate word from group 18.

1. __?__ rubber is superior to natural rubber in some respects and inferior in others.

2. Jonathan's jalopy is a(n) __?__ of parts from several old cars.

3. In the *Odyssey,* you will often find the __?__ "wily" before Ulysses' name because he had a reputation for cunning.

4. Anyone who undertakes to write a(n) __?__ must know how to do research.

5. Their leader, timid, complaining, and weak, is the __?__ of what a leader should be.

# 19. *ASTER, ASTR, ASTRO: "star"*

**aster** (*n.*)
'as-tər

plant having small, starlike flowers
Most *asters* bloom in the fall.

**asterisk** (*n.*)
'as-tə-,risk

(literally, "little star") star-shaped mark (*) used to call attention to a footnote, omission, etc.
The *asterisk* after "Reduced to $9.95" refers the shopper to a footnote reading "Small and medium only."

**asteroid** (*n.*)
'as-tə-,róid

1. very small planet resembling a star in appearance
Compared to planet Earth, some *asteroids* are tiny, measuring less than a mile in diameter.

2. starfish
If an *asteroid* loses an arm to an attacker, it can grow back the missing arm.

**astrologer** (*n.*)
ə-'strä-lə-jər

person who practices *astrology,* a study professing to interpret the supposed influence of the moon, sun, and stars on human affairs
An *astrologer* would have people believe that their lives are regulated by the movements of the stars, planets, sun, and moon.

**astronaut** (*n.*)
'as-trə-,nȯt

(literally, "star sailor") traveler in outer space
Yuri Gagarin, the world's first *astronaut,* orbited the earth in an artificial satellite on April 12, 1961.

**astronomer** (*n.*)
ə-'strä-nə-mər

expert in *astronomy,* science of the stars, planets, sun, moon, and other heavenly bodies
Because the stars are so far away, as*tronomers* measure their distance from Earth in "light-years" (one light-year equals about six trillion miles).

**disaster** (*n.*)
di-'zas-tər

(literally, "contrary star") sudden or extraordinary misfortune; calamity; catastrophe
The attack on Pearl Harbor was the worst *disaster* in the history of the U.S. Navy.

 **EXERCISE 6.19:** *ASTER, ASTR, ASTRO* WORDS

Write the most appropriate word from group 19.

1. Some __?__s are regarded as pests because they feed on oysters.
2. __?__s claim that your life is influenced by the position of the stars at the moment of your birth.
3. __?__s undergo a long and difficult period of training that equips them for the challenges of space travel.
4. Nations that continue to spend beyond their means are headed for economic __?__.
5. A(n) __?__ alerts the reader to look for additional information at the foot of the page.

## 20. GRAM, GRAPH: "letter," "writing"

**anagram** (*n.*)
'a-nə-,gram

word or phrase formed from another by transposing the letters
"Moat" is an *anagram* for "atom."

**cartographer** (*n.*)
kär-'tä-grə-fər

(literally, "map writer") person skilled in *cartography,* the science or art of mapmaking
Ancient *cartographers* did not know of the existence of the Western Hemisphere.

**cryptogram** (*n.*)
'krip-tə-,gram

something written in secret code
Military leaders, diplomats, and industrialists use *cryptograms* to relay secret information.

**electrocardiogram** (*n.*)
i-,lek-trō-'kär-dē-ə-,gram

"writing" or tracing made by an *electrocardiograph,* an instrument that records the amount of electricity the heart muscles produce during the heartbeat
After reading Henrietta's *electrocardiogram,* the physician assured her that her heart was working properly.

**epigram** (*n.*)
'e-pə-,gram

(literally, something "written on" or "inscribed") bright or witty thought concisely and cleverly expressed
"The more things a man is ashamed of, the more respectable he is" is one of George Bernard Shaw's *epigrams.*

**graphic** (*adj.*)
'gra-fik

written or told in a clear, lively manner; vivid; picturesque
The reporter's *graphic* description made us feel that we were present
at the scene.

**graphite** (*n.*)
'gra-,fīt

soft black carbon used in lead pencils
"Lead" pencils do not contain lead, but rather a mixture of clay and *graphite.*

**monogram** (*n.*)
'mä-nə-,gram

(literally, "one letter") person's initials interwoven or combined into one design
*My monogram* appears on the front of my warm-up jacket.

**monograph** (*n.*)
'mä-nə-,graf

written account of a single thing or class of things
For her thesis, my sister wrote a *monograph* on the life of an obscure 19th-century composer.

**stenographer** (*n.*)
stə-'nä-grə-fər

person skilled in, or employed to do, *stenography* (literally, "narrow writing") the art of writing in shorthand
A court *stenographer* has to be able to take down more than 250 words a minute.

**typographical** (*adj.*)
,tī-pə-'gra-fi-kəl

pertaining to or occurring in printing or *typography* (literally, "writing with type")

Proofs submitted by the printer should be carefully checked to eliminate *typographical* errors.

 **EXERCISE 6.20:** *GRAM, GRAPH* WORDS

Write the most appropriate word from group 20.

1. Modern __?__s use aerial photography to aid in mapmaking.
2. There is a(n) __?__ account of London in the 1580s in Marchette Chute's *Shakespeare of London.*
3. The patient's physicians cannot be certain that a heart attack has occurred until they have studied his __?__.
4. "Reform" is a(n) __?__ for "former."
5. I knew it was Annabel's handkerchief because her __?__ was on it.

## Review Exercises

 **REVIEW 10:** GREEK WORD ELEMENTS 11–20

For each Greek word element in column I, write the *letter* of its correct meaning from column II. (Exercise continues on next page.)

| COLUMN I | COLUMN II |
|---|---|
| 1. NOM, NEM | *a.* heat |
| 2. ASTER, ASTR, ASTRO | *b.* first |
| 3. THERM, THERMO | *c.* skin |
| 4. ANT, ANTI | *d.* management, distribution, law |
| 5. DERM, DERMATO | *e.* name, word |
| 6. GRAM, GRAPH | *f.* star |
| 7. ONYM, ONOMATO | *g.* show, appear |

8. THESIS, THET           *h.* against, opposite
9. PROT, PROTO            *i.* letter, writing
10. PHAN, PHEN            *j.* set, place, put

 **REVIEW 11:** WORD-BUILDING

Write the word defined below.

| DEFINITION | WORD |
|---|---|
| 1. putting together of parts into a whole | SYN (6) |
| 2. remedy against the effects of a poison | (4) DOTE |
| 3. punishment distributor | (3) ESIS |
| 4. outer layer of the skin | EPI (4) IS |
| 5. skilled writer of shorthand | STENO (5) ER |
| 6. of unnamed origin | AN (4) OUS |
| 7. first draft leading to a treaty | (5) COL |
| 8. feeling against | (4) PATHY |
| 9. expert in the science of the stars | (5) NOMER |
| 10. any observable fact or event | (4) OMENON |
| 11. automatic temperature-regulating device | (6) STAT |
| 12. managing without waste | ECO (3) ICAL |
| 13. first or original model | (5) TYPE |
| 14. small star-resembling planet | (5) OID |
| 15. use of words whose sound suggests their meaning | (7) POEIA |
| 16. something having appearance but no reality | (4) TOM |
| 17. word formed of transposed letters of another | ANA (4) |
| 18. characterizing name added to ("put on") a person | EPI (4) |
| 19. pertaining to heat | (5) AL |
| 20. beneath the skin | HYPO (4) IC |

**REVIEW 12:** SENTENCE COMPLETION

Write the word from the list below that best fits the context.

| | | |
|---|---|---|
| anonymous | antagonist | antidote |
| antipathy | antithesis | asterisk |
| asteroid | astrology | astronomy |
| epigram | gastronome | homonym |
| hypodermic | nemesis | phenomenal |
| protagonist | protocol | pseudonym |
| thesis | typographical | |

1. Henry's _?_ in the finals was the longtime _?_ who had defeated him in all six of their previous matches.

2. Nadine is the _?_ of a(n) _?_; she doesn't go to fancy restaurants, and she will eat any food that is wholesome and nourishing.

3. Pip, the _?_ of *Great Expectations,* has his education financed by a(n) _?_ benefactor who later identifies himself as Abel Magwitch.

4. The _?_ of this article is that dinosaurs became extinct after the earth collided with a(n) _?_.

5. Unfortunately, many people know more about the false science of _?_ than about the true science of _?_.

6. Because the author has a(n) _?_ to being in the public eye, she wrote her best-selling novels under a(n) _?_.

7. The sentence ends with *mens sana in corpore sano.** The _?_ leads to a footnote explaining that the words are a Latin _?_ meaning "a healthy mind in a healthy body."

8. Because of a(n) _?_ error in the phonetic spelling of *wary* in my dictionary, I pronounced it as if it were a(n) _?_ of weary.

9. The patient who had accidentally swallowed the poisonous liquid was given a(n) _?_ injection of the appropriate _?_.

10. Sending an undersecretary to greet the visiting foreign potentate was a breach of _?_, as well as a(n) _?_ diplomatic blunder.

## REVIEW 13: SYNONYMS

Avoid repetition by replacing the boldfaced word or expression with a **synonym** from the following words.

| | | |
|---|---|---|
| antiseptic | astronomical | cryptogram(s) |
| disaster | epithet | graphic |
| hypothesis | phenomenon | prototype |
| synthetic | | |

1. The flowers were artificial. The fruit in the basket was artificial. The whole place had a(n) **artificial** appearance.

2. If no **substance to prevent infection** is applied, the wound may become infected.

3. Our enormous national debt keeps growing larger and larger; it has become **inconceivably large**.

4. Dealers had catastrophic losses in the fall. If sales had not picked up before Christmas, the year would have ended in financial **catastrophe**.

5. What **descriptive title** can better describe America than "the Beautiful"?

6. Their **coded messages** were undecipherable only so long as no one else knew their code.

7. Her **lively** manner of expression makes everything she describes come to life.

8. The return of spring is truly a(n) **extraordinary event**. Unfortunately, some people are so used to it that they rarely think it is extraordinary.

9. Sometimes a movie is so successful that it becomes the **original model** on which a series of later films is modeled.

10. The alchemists assumed that a way could be found to turn base metals into gold, but they were never able to verify their **assumption**.

**REVIEW 14:** ANTONYMS

Write the word from the list below that is most nearly the **opposite** of the boldfaced word or words.

| | | |
|---|---|---|
| anonymous | antagonist | antipathy |
| antonym | economical | fancy |
| homonym | phenomenal | protagonist |
| synthetic | | |

1. When those that we have befriended become intolerable, our **affection** for them may turn to __?__.
2. Since last summer's drought, we have reduced our **extravagant** uses of water and become more __?__.
3. When we read fairy tales, we leave **reality** and enter the realm of __?__.
4. "Authentic" is a **synonym** of "genuine," and "fraudulent" is one of its __?__s.
5. The soles are made of **natural** leather, but the heels are __?__.
6. In last year's play, Sheila was a **minor character**, but in this one she is the __?__.
7. Joan of Arc had an **ordinary** peasant background, but she provided France with __?__ leadership.
8. **Words that do not sound alike** cannot be called __?__s.
9. The donors have asked not to be **named**; they prefer to remain __?__.
10. Many a nation that was once our __?__ in the United Nations is now our **supporter**.

 **REVIEW 15:** CONCISE WRITING

Express the thought of each sentence below in **no more than four words**.

1. What assumption did you make as a basis for reasoning?
2. No one can predict when sudden or extraordinary misfortunes will strike.
3. Is he the one with whom you have been contending?

4. Letters that do not disclose the name of the writer are not worthy of trust.

5. No one who practices the art of good eating devours food.

6. Everyone enjoys witty thoughts that are concisely and cleverly expressed.

7. Gail is taking courses in crop production and soil management.

8. Amebas are animals that consist of only a single cell.

9. People who do not conform to generally accepted patterns of behavior pay no attention to the rules of etiquette.

10. Our bodies manufacture substances that counteract the effects of disease-causing germs and their poisons.

 **REVIEW 16:** SYNONYM SUMMARY

Each line, when completed, should have three words similar in meaning. Write the *complete* words.

1. unbel (2) vable     (2) real         (3) tastic

2. fr (1) g (1) l       sp (1) ring      eco (3) ical

3. (2) ponent          advers (1) ry    (2) tagonist

4. w (1) rm            h (1) t          th (1) rm (1) l

5. rev (1) rse         opp (1) s (1) te (4) thesis

6. v (1) v (1) d       pictur (2) que   gr (1) ph (1) c

7. artifi (2) al       facti (2) ous    syn (2) etic

8. (1) nmity           rep (1) gn (1) nce (2) tipathy

9. s (1) pposition     as (3) ption     (2) pothesis

10. n (1) meless       (2) identified   an (2) ymous

11. w (1) nder         pr (1) d (1) gy  phe (3) enon

12. c (1) l (1) mity    (2) tastrophe    dis (2) ter

13. sh (2) r           transp (1) rent  (2) aphanous

14. m (1) del          patt (1) rn      (2) ototype

15. app (1) r (1) tion  (1) host         ph (1) nt (1) m

**16.** r (1) m (1) dy               c (2) ntermeasure               an (2) dote

**17.** ill (1) sion                 (1) magination                 f (2) cy

**18.** prop (1) s (1) tion          cont (1) ntion                 th (1) s (1) s

**19.** g (2) rmet                   ep (1) c (1) re                gastr (1) n (1) me

**20.** av (1) nger                  sc (2) rge                     n (1) m (1) sis

 **REVIEW 17:** ANALOGIES

Which lettered pair of words—*a, b, c, d,* or *e*—most nearly expresses the same relationship as the capitalized pair?

**1.** ASTEROID : PLANET
- *a.* skyscraper : edifice
- *b.* deluge : shower
- *c.* crowd : gathering
- *d.* microbe : organism
- *e.* age : interval

**2.** FANTASY : FACT
- *a.* significance : meaning
- *b.* warmth : cordiality
- *c.* antipathy : affection
- *d.* celerity : speed
- *e.* equity : justice

**3.** DERMATOLOGY : SKIN
- *a.* chronology : story
- *b.* psychology : mind
- *c.* anthology : volume
- *d.* biology : science
- *e.* apology : blame

**4.** ASTRONOMICAL : LARGE
- *a.* immature : old
- *b.* nominal : significant
- *c.* extraordinary : common
- *d.* priceless : cheap
- *e.* infinitesimal : small

**5.** STEEL : STEAL
- *a.* ribbon : bow
- *b.* here : there
- *c.* friend : foe
- *d.* peace : piece
- *e.* flaw : defect

**6.** SYNTHETIC : ARTIFICIAL

   *a.* restive : restful
                          *b.* healthful : deleterious

   *c.* partial : objective
                          *d.* toxic : antiseptic

   *e.* sagacious : wise

**7.** PROTAGONIST : STORY

   *a.* standard-bearer : cause
              *b.* tenor : opera

   *c.* finalist : tournament
              *d.* professor : faculty

   *e.* soprano : choir

**8.** PHANTOM : EXISTENCE

   *a.* river : source
                          *b.* progenitor : descendant

   *c.* statue : mobility
                      *d.* cryptogram : solution

   *e.* chaos : disorder

**9.** THERMOSTAT : COMFORT

   *a.* alarm : security
                        *b.* pandemonium : harmony

   *c.* digression : direction
                  *d.* defection : unity

   *e.* lamp : electricity

   *Hint:* A **thermostat** provides **comfort**.

**10.** HYPOTHESIS : REASONING

   *a.* unpacking : moving
                      *b.* landing : flying

   *c.* review : learning
                      *d.* rebuttal : debating

   *e.* soil preparation : planting

 **REVIEW 18:** COMPOSITION

Answer in a sentence or two.

**1.** Why would an anonymous poet not have a monogram?

**2.** In which might you find a typographical error—an epithet or a gastronome? Give your reason.

**3.** Why would most people feel antipathy toward their nemesis?

**4.** Would a dermatologist or a protagonist be more likely to offer you antibiotics? Why?

**5.** Is a diaphanous robe likely to provide thermal value?

# 7

# Expanding Vocabulary Through Derivatives

Suppose you have just learned a new word—*literate,* meaning "able to read and write; educated." If you know how to form derivatives, you have in reality learned not one new word but several: *literate, illiterate,* and *semiliterate; literately, illiterately,* and *semiliterately; literacy, illiteracy,* and *semiliteracy,* etc.

This chapter will help you to expand your vocabulary by teaching you how to form and spell important derivatives.

## *What is a derivative?*

A derivative is a word formed by adding a prefix, a suffix, or both, to a word or root.

| PREFIX | | WORD | | DERIVATIVE |
|---|---|---|---|---|
| with | + | hold | = | withhold |
| *(back)* | | | | *(hold back)* |

| PREFIX | | ROOT | | DERIVATIVE |
|---|---|---|---|---|
| in | + | flux | = | influx |
| *(in)* | | *(flow)* | | *(inflow; inpouring)* |

| WORD | | SUFFIX | | DERIVATIVE |
|---|---|---|---|---|
| literate | + | ly | = | literately |
| *(educated)* | | *(manner)* | | *(in an educated manner)* |

|  | ROOT | | SUFFIX | | DERIVATIVE |
|---|---|---|---|---|---|
|  | leg | + | ible | = | legible |
|  | *(read)* | | *(able to be)* | | *(able to be read)* |

| PREFIX | | WORD | | SUFFIX | | DERIVATIVE |
|---|---|---|---|---|---|---|
| semi | + | literate | + | ly | = | semiliterately |
| *(half, partly)* | | | | | | *(in a partly educated manner)* |

| PREFIX | | ROOT | | SUFFIX | | DERIVATIVE |
|---|---|---|---|---|---|---|
| il | + | leg | + | ible | = | illegible |
| *(not)* | | | | | | *(not able to be read)* |

## *Terms used in this chapter*

A derivative may be a noun, an adjective, a verb, or an adverb.

A **noun** is a word naming a person, place, thing, or quality. In the following sentences, all the italicized words are nouns:

1. The enthusiastic *student* very quickly read the partially finished *composition* to the amused *class.*

2. *Knowledge* is *power.*

An **adjective** is a word that modifies (describes) a noun. The following words in sentence 1 are adjectives: *enthusiastic, finished, amused.*

A **verb** is a word that expresses action or a state of being. The verbs in the sentences above are *read* (sentence 1) and *is* (sentence 2).

An **adverb** is a word that modifies a verb, an adjective, or another adverb. In sentence 1 above, *quickly* is an adverb because it modifies the verb "read"; *partially* is an adverb because it modifies the adjective "finished"; and *very* is an adverb because it modifies the adverb "quickly."

**Vowels** are the letters *a, e, i, o,* and *u.*

**Consonants** are all the other letters of the alphabet.

# FORMING DERIVATIVES BY ATTACHING PREFIXES AND SUFFIXES

## 1. Attaching Prefixes

When you add the prefix *mis* to the word *spelled,* does the new word have one *s* or two? For help with problems of this sort, learn the following rule:

**Rule:** Do not add or omit a letter when attaching a prefix to a word. Keep *all* the letters of the prefix and *all* the letters of the word. Examples:

| PREFIX | | WORD | | DERIVATIVE |
|--------|---|---------|---|-------------|
| mis | + | spelled | = | misspelled |
| mis | + | informed | = | misinformed |

 **EXERCISE 7.1**

Write the derivative formed by attaching the prefix to the word.

| I. PREFIX | | II. WORD |
|-----------|---|----------|
| **1.** over | + | ripe |
| **2.** dis | + | integrate |
| **3.** un | + | necessary |
| **4.** anti | + | aircraft |
| **5.** in | + | audible |

| | | |
|---|---|---|
| 6. under | + | rated |
| 7. fore | + | seen |
| 8. extra | + | ordinary |
| 9. un | + | noticed |
| 10. with | + | held |
| 11. e | + | migrate |
| 12. mis | + | spent |
| 13. over | + | estimated |
| 14. dis | + | interred |
| 15. semi | + | circle |
| 16. un | + | nerve |
| 17. pre | + | existence |
| 18. dis | + | solution |
| 19. extra | + | curricular |
| 20. un | + | navigable |
| 21. over | + | run |
| 22. in | + | appropriate |
| 23. semi | + | autonomous |
| 24. dis | + | satisfied |
| 25. un | + | abridged |

# 2. Attaching the Prefix IN

Sometimes, the N in the prefix IN changes to another letter. To learn when this occurs, study the following rule:

**Rule:** Before *l*, IN becomes IL, as in *illegal, illiterate,* etc.
Before *m* or *p*, IN becomes IM, as in *immature, impure,* etc.
Before *r*, IN becomes IR, as in *irrational, irregular,* etc.

 **EXERCISE 7.2**

Write the negative word by attaching *in, il, im,* or *ir* to the word in column II.

| I. NEGATIVE PREFIX | | II. WORD |
|---|---|---|
| 1. _?_ | + | gratitude |
| 2. _?_ | + | patiently |
| 3. _?_ | + | responsible |
| 4. _?_ | + | equitable |
| 5. _?_ | + | moderate |
| 6. _?_ | + | literacy |
| 7. _?_ | + | replaceable |
| 8. _?_ | + | consistently |
| 9. _?_ | + | personal |
| 10. _?_ | + | legible |
| 11. _?_ | + | plausible |
| 12. _?_ | + | articulate |
| 13. _?_ | + | material |
| 14. _?_ | + | reversible |
| 15. _?_ | + | security |
| 16. _?_ | + | liberal |
| 17. _?_ | + | perceptibly |
| 18. _?_ | + | flexible |
| 19. _?_ | + | relevant |
| 20. _?_ | + | moral |

# 3. *Attaching Suffixes*

What happens when you add the suffix *ness* to *stubborn*? Does the new word have one *n* or two? Questions of this sort will never bother you once you have learned this simple rule:

**Rule:** Do not omit, add, or change a letter when attaching a suffix to a word—unless the word ends in *y* or silent *e*. Keep *all* the letters of the word and *all* the letters of the suffix. Examples:

| WORD | | SUFFIX | | DERIVATIVE |
|------|---|--------|---|------------|
| stubborn | + | ness | = | stubbornness |
| conscious | + | ness | = | consciousness |
| punctual | + | ly | = | punctually |
| anonymous | + | ly | = | anonymously |
| disagree | + | able | = | disagreeable |

 **EXERCISE 7.3**

Attach the suffix to the word.

| I. WORD | | II. SUFFIX |
|---------|---|-----------|
| **1.** govern | + | ment |
| **2.** tail | + | less |
| **3.** synonym | + | ous |
| **4.** radio | + | ed |
| **5.** unilateral | + | ly |
| **6.** embarrass | + | ment |
| **7.** sudden | + | ness |
| **8.** room | + | mate |
| **9.** ski | + | er |
| **10.** foresee | + | able |

## 4. Attaching Suffixes to Words Ending in Y

Final *y* can be troublesome. Sometimes it changes to *i*; sometimes it does not change at all. To learn how to deal with final *y*, follow these helpful rules:

**Rule 1:** If the letter before final *y* is a consonant, change the *y* to *i* before attaching a suffix.

| WORD | | SUFFIX | | DERIVATIVE |
|------|---|--------|---|-----------|
| comply | + | ed | = | complied |
| sturdy | + | est | = | sturdiest |
| costly | + | ness | = | costliness |
| ordinary | + | ly | = | ordinarily |

*Exception A:* Except before *ing.*

| | | | | |
|------|---|--------|---|-----------|
| comply | + | ing | = | complying |

*Exception B:* Learn these special exceptions: *dryly, dryness, shyly, shyness, babyish, jellylike.*

**Rule 2:** If the letter before final *y* is a vowel, do *not* change the *y* before attaching a suffix.

| | | | | |
|------|---|--------|---|-----------|
| destroy | + | ed | = | destroyed |
| play | + | ful | = | playful |

*Exceptions:* laid, paid, said, and their compounds (*mislaid, underpaid, unsaid,* etc.); *daily.*

 **EXERCISE 7.4**

Write the derivatives. Watch your spelling.

| I. WORD | | II. SUFFIX |
|---|---|---|
| 1. decay | + | ed |
| 2. fancy | + | ful |
| 3. stealthy | + | ly |
| 4. foolhardy | + | ness |
| 5. magnify | + | ing |
| 6. plucky | + | est |
| 7. defy | + | ance |
| 8. overpay | + | ed |
| 9. accompany | + | ment |
| 10. costly | + | ness |
| 11. ceremony | + | ous |
| 12. deny | + | al |
| 13. momentary | + | ly |
| 14. crafty | + | er |
| 15. display | + | ed |
| 16. bury | + | al |
| 17. shy | + | ly |
| 18. oversupply | + | ing |
| 19. harmony | + | ous |
| 20. disqualify | + | ed |

 **EXERCISE 7.5**

Four words have been omitted from each line except the first. Complete each of the other lines so that it will correspond to the first. Write the words on your answer paper.

| I. ADJECTIVE | II. ADJECTIVE ENDING IN ER | III. ADJECTIVE ENDING IN EST | IV. ADVERB ENDING IN LY | V. NOUN ENDING IN NESS |
|---|---|---|---|---|
| 1. clumsy | clumsier | clumsiest | clumsily | clumsiness |
| 2. ? | noisier | ? | ? | ? |
| 3. ? | ? | sturdiest | ? | ? |
| 4. ? | ? | ? | uneasily | ? |
| 5. ? | ? | ? | ? | greediness |
| 6. flimsy | ? | ? | ? | ? |
| 7. ? | wearier | ? | ? | ? |
| 8. ? | ? | heartiest | ? | ? |
| 9. ? | ? | ? | warily | ? |
| 10. ? | ? | ? | ? | unhappiness |

## 5. Attaching Suffixes to Words Ending in Silent E

When you add a suffix to a word ending in silent *e*, what happens to the *e*? Is it kept or dropped? Here are the rules:

**Rule 1:** Drop silent *e* if the suffix begins with a vowel.

| WORD | | SUFFIX | | DERIVATIVE |
|---|---|---|---|---|
| blame | + | able | = | blamable |
| secure | + | ity | = | security |
| innovate | + | or | = | innovator |

*Exception A:* If the word ends in *ce* or *ge,* and the suffix begins with *a* or *o,* keep the *e.*

| | | | | | |
|---|---|---|---|---|---|
| service | + | able | = | serviceable |
| courage | + | ous | = | courageous |

*Exception B:* Learn these special exceptions: *acreage, mileage, singeing, canoeing, hoeing, shoeing.*

**Rule 2:** Keep silent *e* if the suffix begins with a consonant.

| | | | | | |
|---|---|---|---|---|---|
| hope | + | ful | = | hopeful |
| profuse | + | ly | = | profusely |
| postpone | + | ment | = | postponement |

*Exceptions: argument, awful, duly, truly, wholly, ninth.*

 **EXERCISE 7.6**

Write the derivatives. Watch your spelling.

| I. WORD | | II. SUFFIX |
|---|---|---|
| 1. depreciate | + | ion |
| 2. survive | + | al |
| 3. suspense | + | ful |
| 4. fatigue | + | ing |
| 5. censure | + | able |
| 6. acquiesce | + | ent |
| 7. nine | + | th |
| 8. hostile | + | ity |
| 9. malice | + | ious |
| 10. dawdle | + | er |
| 11. reverse | + | ible |
| 12. immaculate | + | ly |
| 13. spine | + | less |
| 14. outrage | + | ous |

| | | |
|---|---|---|
| 15. demote | + | ion |
| 16. homogenize | + | ed |
| 17. recharge | + | able |
| 18. abate | + | ment |
| 19. emancipate | + | or |
| 20. dispute | + | able |
| 21. whole | + | ly |
| 22. provoke | + | ing |
| 23. argue | + | ment |
| 24. fragile | + | ity |
| 25. replace | + | able |

## 6.  *Attaching the Suffix LY*

**Rule:** To change an adjective into an adverb, add *ly*.

| ADJECTIVE | | SUFFIX | | ADVERB |
|---|---|---|---|---|
| close | + | ly | = | closely |
| firm | + | ly | = | firmly |
| usual | + | ly | = | usually |

*Exception A:* If the adjective ends in *y,* remember to change *y* to *i* before adding *ly*.

| easy | + | ly | = | easily |
|---|---|---|---|---|

*Exception B:* If the adjective ends in *ic,* add *al* plus *ly*.

| tragic | + | al | + | ly | = | tragically |
|---|---|---|---|---|---|---|
| heroic | + | al | + | ly | = | heroically |

However, *public* can be either:

public + ly = publicly or public + al + ly = publically

*Exception C:* If the adjective ends in *le* preceded by a consonant, simply change the *le* to *ly.*

| ADJECTIVE | ADVERB |
|-----------|--------|
| able | ably |
| simple | simply |
| idle | idly |

 **EXERCISE 7.7**

Change the following adjectives into adverbs.

ADJECTIVE

1. overwhelming
2. normal
3. interscholastic
4. mutual
5. ample
6. conspicuous
7. economic
8. outspoken
9. graphic
10. incontrovertible
11. punctual
12. exclusive
13. unwary
14. chronic
15. synthetic
16. intermittent
17. manual
18. heavy
19. infallible
20. frantic

 **EXERCISE 7.8**

For each noun, write an adjective ending in *ic* and an adverb ending in *ally*; for example: **democracy, democratic, democratically.**

1. autocracy
2. stenography
3. antagonist
4. pedagogy
5. economics
6. astronomy
7. diplomacy
8. bureaucracy
9. autobiography
10. symmetry

## 7. Doubling Final Consonants Before Suffixes

Why is the *r* in *defer* doubled (deferred) when *ed* is added, whereas the *r* in *differ* is not (differed)? Why is the *n* in *plan* doubled (planning) before *ing*, whereas the *n* in *burn* is not (burning)?

To clear up these matters, review two rules for doubling final consonants.

**Rule 1:** In a one-syllable word, double the final consonant before a suffix beginning with a vowel.

| WORD | | SUFFIXES | | DERIVATIVES |
|------|---|----------|---|-------------|
| plan | + | ing, er | = | planning, planner |
| stop | + | ed, age | = | stopped, stoppage |
| big | + | er, est | = | bigger, biggest |

*Exception A:* If the final consonant comes right after two vowels, do not double it.

| | | | | |
|---|---|---|---|---|
| fail | + | ed, ing | = | failed, failing |
| stoop | + | ed, ing | = | stooped, stooping |

*Exception B:* If the final consonant comes right after another consonant, do not double it.

| | | | | |
|---|---|---|---|---|
| warm | + | er, est | = | warmer, warmest |
| last | + | ed, ing | = | lasted, lasting |

**Rule 2:** In a word of two or more syllables, double the final consonant only if it is in an *accented* syllable before a suffix beginning with a vowel.

| | | | | |
|---|---|---|---|---|
| deFER' | + | ed, ing, al | = | deferred, deferring, deferral |
| resubMIT' | + | ed, ing | = | resubmitted, resubmitting |

Note carefully that the rule does not apply if the final consonant is in an *unaccented* syllable.

| | | | | |
|---|---|---|---|---|
| DIF'fer | + | ed, ing, ent | = | differed, differing, different |
| BEN'efit | + | ed, ing | = | benefited, benefiting |

*Exception A:* The rule does not apply if the final consonant comes right after two vowels.

| | | | | |
|---|---|---|---|---|
| obTAIN' | + | ed, ing | = | obtained, obtaining |
| conCEAL' | + | ed, ing | = | concealed, concealing |

*Exception B:* The rule does not apply if the final consonant comes right after another consonant.

| | | | | |
|---|---|---|---|---|
| abDUCT' | + | ed, ing, or | = | abducted, abducting, abductor |
| comMEND' | + | ed, ing, able | = | commended, commending, commendable |

*Exception C:* The rule does not apply if the accent shifts back to the first syllable.

| conFER′ | + | ence | = | CON′ference |
| preFER′ | + | ence | = | PREF′erence |
| reFER′ | + | ence | = | REF′erence |

However: exCEL′ + ence = EX′cellence

 **EXERCISE 7.9**

Write the derivatives, paying careful attention to the spelling.

| I. WORD | | II. SUFFIX |
|---|---|---|
| 1. concur | + | ing |
| 2. entail | + | ed |
| 3. abhor | + | ent |
| 4. flat | + | er |
| 5. retract | + | able |
| 6. refer | + | al |
| 7. dispel | + | ed |
| 8. deter | + | ent |
| 9. ungag | + | ed |
| 10. drum | + | er |
| 11. elicit | + | ing |
| 12. imperil | + | ed |
| 13. absorb | + | ent |
| 14. defer | + | ence |
| 15. propel | + | ant |
| 16. inter | + | ing |
| 17. append | + | age |
| 18. covet | + | ous |
| 19. discredit | + | ed |

| | | |
|---|---|---|
| **20.** adapt | + | able |
| **21.** cower | + | ing |
| **22.** disinter | + | ed |
| **23.** pilfer | + | er |
| **24.** slim | + | est |
| **25.** excel | + | ent |

 **EXERCISE 7.10**

For each word at the left, form the three derivatives indicated.

| | | | |
|---|---|---|---|
| **1.** regret | __?__ing | __?__ed | __?__ful |
| **2.** sin | __?__ing | __?__ed | __?__er |
| **3.** control | __?__ing | __?__ed | __?__er |
| **4.** occur | __?__ing | __?__ed | __?__ence |
| **5.** adjourn | __?__ing | __?__ed | __?__ment |
| **6.** flip | __?__ing | __?__ed | __?__ant |
| **7.** transmit | __?__ing | __?__ed | __?__er |
| **8.** profit | __?__ing | __?__ed | __?__able |
| **9.** defer | __?__ing | __?__ed | __?__ment |
| **10.** dissent | __?__ing | __?__ed | __?__er |
| **11.** protract | __?__ing | __?__ed | __?__or |
| **12.** spot | __?__ing | __?__ed | __?__er |
| **13.** commit | __?__ing | __?__ed | __?__ment |
| **14.** excel | __?__ing | __?__ed | __?__ence |
| **15.** recur | __?__ing | __?__ed | __?__ent |

## 8. Troublesome Suffixes

Why should *dispensable* end in *able* but *sensible* in *ible*? Why should *foreigner* end in *er* but *debtor* in *or*? Unhappily, there are no simple rules to guide you in these matters. You will have to learn individually each word with a troublesome suffix and consult the dictionary when in doubt. The following review should prove helpful:

1. Attaching *able* or *ible*. Study the following adjectives:

| ABLE | IBLE |
|------|------|
| amiable | accessible |
| changeable | credible |
| equitable | fallible |
| formidable | flexible |
| hospitable | illegible |
| impregnable | incompatible |
| indomitable | incontrovertible |
| lovable | invincible |
| noticeable | reversible |
| unquenchable | visible |

Note that adjectives ending in *able* become nouns ending in *ability*. On the other hand, adjectives ending in *ible* become nouns ending in *ibility*.

| ADJECTIVE | NOUN | ADJECTIVE | NOUN |
|-----------|------|-----------|------|
| incapable | incapability | audible | audibility |
| pliable | pliability | resistible | resistibility |

2. Attaching suffixes meaning "one who" or "that which": *er, or, ent,* or *ant.* Study these nouns:

| ER | OR | ENT | ANT |
|----|----|----|-----|
| abstainer | aggressor | adherent | assistant |
| abuser | benefactor | antecedent | consultant |
| commuter | bisector | belligerent | contestant |

| | | | |
|---|---|---|---|
| contender | collaborator | correspondent | defendant |
| dispenser | duplicator | current | deodorant |
| retainer | exhibitor | dependent | immigrant |
| typographer | interceptor | insurgent | inhabitant |
| underseller | precursor | opponent | participant |
| withholder | reflector | precedent | pendant |
| wrangler | transgressor | proponent | tenant |

3. Attaching *ant* or *ent*. Study these adjectives:

| ANT | ENT |
|---|---|
| defiant | adjacent |
| discordant | affluent |
| dormant | coherent |
| extravagant | decadent |
| hesitant | fluent |
| ignorant | imminent |
| incessant | latent |
| irrelevant | negligent |
| reliant | permanent |
| vigilant | vehement |

Note that adjectives ending in *ant* become nouns ending in *ance* or *ancy*. On the other hand, adjectives ending in *ent* become nouns ending in *ence* or *ency*.

| ADJECTIVE | NOUN | ADJECTIVE | NOUN |
|---|---|---|---|
| defiant | defiance | coherent | coherence |
| dormant | dormancy | fluent | fluency |
| hesitant | hesitance, hesitancy | permanent | permanence, permanency |

 **EXERCISE 7.11**

Supply the missing letter, and write the complete word.

1. inflex _?_ ble
2. ten _?_ ncy
3. vehem _?_ nce
4. benefact _?_ r
5. self-reli _?_ nce
6. vis _?_ bility
7. dispens _?_ r
8. relev _?_ nce
9. infall _?_ bility
10. unchange _?_ ble

11. collaborat _?_ r
12. impregn _?_ bility
13. reflect _?_ r
14. curr _?_ ncy
15. correspond _?_ nce
16. contend _?_ r
17. imperman _?_ nt
18. irrevers _?_ ble
19. inaccess _?_ bility
20. semidepend _?_ nt

 **EXERCISE 7.12**

For each noun, write the corresponding adjective. (The first adjective is **capable**.)

NOUN

1. capability
2. urgency
3. resistance
4. infallibility
5. subservience
6. compatibility
7. eminence
8. truancy
9. audibility
10. opulence
11. inconstancy
12. malevolence
13. indefatigability

14. observance
15. cogenc
16. adaptability
17. incandescence
18. unavailability
19. compliance
20. transiency

## Review Exercises

 **REVIEW 1**

Two words have been omitted from each line. Complete each line by writing the missing words on your answer paper. (For the first line, the missing words are **transgressor** and **transgression**.)

| I. VERB | II. NOUN ENDING IN ER, OR, ENT, OR ANT | III. NOUN ENDING IN ION, ENCE, OR ANCE |
|---|---|---|
| 1. transgress | ? | ? |
| 2. ? | ? | dependence |
| 3. ? | correspondent | ? |
| 4. consult | ? | ? |
| 5. ? | ? | exhibition |
| 6. ? | observer | ? |
| 7. intercept | ? | ? |
| 8. ? | ? | opposition |
| 9. ? | immigrant | ? |
| 10. collaborate | ? | ? |

 **REVIEW 2**

Two words have been omitted from each line. Complete each line by writing the missing words on your answer paper. (For the first line, the missing words are **happy** and **happily**.)

| I. NOUN | II. ADJECTIVE | III. ADVERB |
|---|---|---|
| 1. happiness | ? | ? |
| 2. ? | courageous | ? |
| 3. ? | ? | amicably |
| 4. immaturity | ? | ? |
| 5. ? | original | ? |
| 6. ? | ? | coherently |
| 7. benevolence | ? | ? |
| 8. ? | harmonious | ? |
| 9. ? | ? | stubbornly |
| 10. proficiency | ? | ? |
| 11. ? | legible | ? |
| 12. ? | ? | unanimously |
| 13. shyness | ? | ? |
| 14. ? | weary | ? |
| 15. ? | ? | insecurely |
| 16. autonomy | ? | ? |
| 17. ? | logical | ? |
| 18. ? | ? | outrageously |
| 19. consistency | ? | ? |
| 20. ? | hostile | ? |

 **REVIEW 3**

Five words have been omitted from each set. (The missing words for the first set are **immature; maturely, immaturely; maturity**, and **immaturity**.) Complete each of the other sets so that it will correspond to the first.

| ADJECTIVE AND OPPOSITE | ADVERB AND OPPOSITE | NOUN AND OPPOSITE |
|---|---|---|
| 1. mature | ? | ? |
| ? | ? | ? |
| 2. impatient | ? | ? |
| ? | ? | ? |
| 3. ? | dependently | ? |
| ? | ? | ? |
| 4. ? | ? | ? |
| ? | incompetently | ? |
| 5. ? | ? | plausibility |
| ? | ? | ? |
| 6. ? | ? | ? |
| ? | ? | irresponsibility |
| 7. legible | ? | ? |
| ? | ? | ? |
| 8. ? | ? | ? |
| inflexible | ? | ? |
| 9. ? | formally | ? |
| ? | ? | |
| 10. ? | ? | ? |
| ? | unimportantly | ? |

*Chapter*

# 8

# Understanding Word Relationships and Word Analogies

## *Word Relationships*

ROBIN : BIRD

What relationship is there between *robin* and *bird*? Obviously, a *robin* is a *bird*. So, too, is a sparrow, a woodpecker, a crow, a gull, a pigeon, a blue jay, etc. *Bird,* clearly, is the large category of which *robin* is one member.

If we call *robin* word A and *bird* word B, we may express the *robin : bird* relationship by saying "A is a member of the B category."

Here are some additional pairs of words with an explanation of the relationship in each pair. As in the above, let us call the first word A and the second B.

MINE : COAL

*Mine* is the source from which we obtain the substance *coal*. To express the *mine : coal* relationship, we may say "A is the source of B."

SPADE : DIGGING

A *spade* is a kind of shovel that is used for *digging*. The relationship here is "A is used for B."

TEMPERATURE : THERMOMETER

*Temperature* is measured by a *thermometer.* The relationship in this pair is "A is measured by B."

MEEK : SUBMIT

Anyone who is *meek* ("yielding without resentment when ordered about") will usually *submit* ("give in"). We may express this relationship as "An A person is likely to B."

To find the relationship between a pair of words, go through the kind of reasoning shown in the preceding paragraphs. When you have determined the relationship, sum it up in a very short sentence using A and B, as in the following examples:

| WORD PAIR | RELATIONSHIP |
|---|---|
| PAUPER : MEANS | A lacks B. |
| FOUNDATION : EDIFICE | A supports B. |
| SECURITY GUARD : THEFT | A guards against B. |
| BLINDFOLD : VISION | A interferes with B. |
| LITERATE : READ | One who is A can B. |
| ILLNESS : ABSENCE | A may cause B. |
| SEIZING : TAKING | A is a sudden, forcible form of B. |
| GREGARIOUS : COMPANY | One who is A likes B. |
| PEBBLE : STONE | A is a small B. |
| PAINTER : EASEL | A uses B. |

# Word Analogy Questions

So far, we have been dealing only with one relationship at a time. A *word analogy question,* however, tests your ability to see that the relationship between one pair of words is the same as the relationship between another pair of words. Here is a typical word analogy question.

*Directions:* Write the *letter* of the pair of words related to each other in the same way that the capitalized words are related to each other.

PREFACE : INDEX ::

(A) tool : drill          (D) appetizer : dessert

(B) departure : trip      (E) water : well

(C) famine : drought

*Solution:* The first step is to find the relationship in the capitalized pair *preface : index.* Since a *preface* comes at the beginning of a book, and an *index* at the end, the relationship here is "A begins that which B ends."

The next step is to analyze the five suggested answers to see which has the same relationship as *preface : index.* Since an *appetizer* comes at the beginning of dinner and a *dessert* at the end, the correct answer is obviously D.

 **EXERCISE 8.1**

Select the lettered pair that best expresses a relationship similar to that expressed in the capitalized pair. Write the *letter* A, B, C, D, or E.

**1.** NEEDLE : STITCH ::

(A) shears : prune        (D) stake : bush

(B) rake : mow            (E) wrench : soak

(C) spade : level

**2.** FATHOM : DEPTH ::

(A) temperature : calorie   (D) dive : surface

(B) search : treasure        (E) base : height

(C) minute : time

**3.** DAM : FLOW ::
   (A) research : information
   (B) laws : justice
   (C) reporters : news
   (D) autocracy : liberty
   (E) education : opportunity

**4.** FOREST : TIMBER ::
   (A) magnet : filings
   (B) art : museum
   (C) quarry : stone
   (D) clay : earth
   (E) zoo : spectators

**5.** NECK : BOTTLE ::
   (A) bonnet : head
   (B) rim : wheel
   (C) roof : cellar
   (D) metal : leather
   (E) chain : link

**6.** TYRO : EXPERIENCE ::
   (A) despot : power
   (B) razor : sharpness
   (C) artisan : skill
   (D) coward : courage
   (E) farewell : welcome

**7.** GRAVEL : PIT ::
   (A) oil : well
   (B) cement : sand
   (C) tunnel : cave
   (D) asphalt : road
   (E) crest : mountain

**8.** FACULTY : TEACHER ::
   (A) congregation : clergy
   (B) crew : captain
   (C) act : play
   (D) choir : singer
   (E) election : candidate

**9.** KITTEN : CAT ::
   (A) ewe : lamb
   (B) tiger : cub
   (C) seedling : flower
   (D) fawn : deer
   (E) napkin : towel

**10.** MICROSCOPE : BIOLOGIST ::
   (A) horoscope : scientist
   (B) medicine : druggist
   (C) lens : photography
   (D) telescope : astronomer
   (E) spectacles : optometry

11. LIEUTENANT : OFFICER ::
    - (A) actor : understudy
    - (B) moon : planet
    - (C) veteran : newcomer
    - (D) sophomore : undergraduate
    - (E) passenger : conductor

12. BIRTH : DECEASE ::
    - (A) takeoff : flight
    - (B) negligence : dismissal
    - (C) opera : finale
    - (D) dawn : sunset
    - (E) competition : defeat

13. FOG : VISION ::
    - (A) superstition : ignorance
    - (B) evidence : testimony
    - (C) malnutrition : growth
    - (D) rain : overflow
    - (E) vigilance : safety

14. PLANT : HARVEST ::
    - (A) factory : equipment
    - (B) launch : decommission
    - (C) sow : irrigate
    - (D) clump : shrub
    - (E) mishap : carelessness

15. COD : FISH ::
    - (A) immunity : disease
    - (B) band : trumpet
    - (C) mutiny : authority
    - (D) penalty : offense
    - (E) pneumonia : illness

## Working Backwards in Completing Analogies

Sometimes you may find it difficult to determine the exact relationship between word A and word B in a given pair. In such cases it is advisable to work backwards from the five choices suggested for the answer. The chances are that one of these choices will lead you to the A : B relationship. Consider the following question:

BANKRUPTCY : PROFIT ::
- (A) population : housing
- (B) fatigue : effort
- (C) congestion : space
- (D) memory : knowledge
- (E) flood : thaw

Suppose you are having trouble finding the relationship between *bankruptcy* and *profit*. Try the back door: find the relationship of each suggested pair and discover which relationship applies also to the capitalized pair. This method is illustrated below.

BANKRUPTCY : PROFIT ::

(A) population : housing. The relationship is "A needs B" (*population needs housing*). But bankruptcy does not need profit; once bankruptcy has occurred, it is too late for profit to be of help. Therefore, choice A is incorrect.

BANKRUPTCY : PROFIT ::

(B) fatigue : effort. The relationship is "A results from too much B" (*fatigue results from too much effort*). Since bankruptcy does not result from too much profit, choice B is incorrect.

BANKRUPTCY : PROFIT ::

(C) congestion : space. The relationship is "A results from a lack of B" (*congestion results from a lack of space*). Bankruptcy results from a lack of profit. Choice C looks correct, but let's test the remaining choices.

BANKRUPTCY : PROFIT ::

(D) memory : knowledge. The relationship is "A stores B" (*memory stores knowledge*). Since bankruptcy does not store profit, choice D is incorrect.

BANKRUPTCY : PROFIT ::

(E) flood : thaw. The relationship is "A may result from B" (*a flood may result from a thaw*). But bankruptcy does not result from profit. Therefore, choice E is incorrect.

*Answer: C*

 **EXERCISE 8.2**

The following questions are more difficult than those in the previous exercise. If you cannot readily find the relationship between word A and word B in the given pair, try the "working backwards" method described above.

1. SOLVENT : PAY ::
   (A) indigent : thrive
   (B) innocent : acquit
   (C) loyal : adhere
   (D) punctual : tardy
   (E) lavish : economize

2. ANTISEPTIC : BACTERIA ::
   (A) soldier : nation
   (B) hair : scalp
   (C) pseudonym : author
   (D) prescription : cure
   (E) education : ignorance

3. INTERMEDIARY : SETTLEMENT ::
   (A) belligerent : peace
   (B) prosecutor : conviction
   (C) adherent : pact
   (D) strife : recess
   (E) rumor : discovery

4. GENEROUS : FORGIVE ::
   (A) pliable : yield
   (B) spineless : resist
   (C) opinionated : change
   (D) conspicuous : hide
   (E) impatient : delay

5. DISTANCE : ODOMETER ::
   (A) weight : scale
   (B) heat : barometer
   (C) quiz : knowledge
   (D) map : compass
   (E) clock : time

6. GUILTLESS : BLAME ::
   (A) unbiased : prejudice
   (B) bankrupt : debt
   (C) sincere : honesty
   (D) apprehensive : worry
   (E) verdict : acquittal

7. AUTOMATON : ORIGINALITY ::
   (A) ambassador : goodwill
   (B) pioneer : foresight
   (C) hothead : equanimity
   (D) guest : hospitality
   (E) benefactor : generosity

8. CONJUNCTION : CLAUSES ::
   (A) barrier : neighbors
   (B) paragraph : phrases
   (C) door : hinges
   (D) bridge : shores
   (E) preposition : nouns

**9.** IRREVOCABLE : ALTER ::
- (A) irreproachable : trust
- (B) available : obtain
- (C) audible : hear
- (D) intelligible : comprehend
- (E) pressing : defer

**10.** SMOG : POLLUTANTS ::
- (A) fog : travel
- (B) wars : destruction
- (C) ambition : diligence
- (D) contagion : disinfectants
- (E) exhaustion : overwork

**11.** MANACLE : MOVEMENT ::
- (A) sailor : crew
- (B) pendant : chain
- (C) gag : speech
- (D) manual : information
- (E) invalid : vigor

**12.** EROSION : WATER ::
- (A) earthquake : destruction
- (B) ocean : wind
- (C) inauguration : presidency
- (D) aging : time
- (E) solid : liquid

**13.** ARISTOCRAT : COUNT ::
- (A) flower : leaf
- (B) senator : voter
- (C) professional : amateur
- (D) civilian : soldier
- (E) insect : ant

**14.** DESPOTIC : DOMINEER ::
- (A) disgruntled : rejoice
- (B) cordial : rebuff
- (C) timorous : withdraw
- (D) aggressive : tremble
- (E) malcontent : cooperate

**15.** HOLD : VESSEL ::
- (A) tail : airplane
- (B) vault : security
- (C) site : edifice
- (D) garage : vehicle
- (E) basement : house

## Alternate-Type Analogy Questions

In the following alternate type of analogy question, you are given the first pair and the first word of the second pair. You are asked to complete the second pair by selecting one of five suggested words.

 **EXERCISE 8.3**

On your answer page, write the *letter* of the word that best completes the analogy.

**1.** *Justice* is to *judge* as *health* is to

   (A) lawyer       (C) physician       (E) jury

   (B) nutrition      (D) disease

**2.** *Dentist* is to *teeth* as *dermatologist* is to

   (A) heart        (C) eyes         (E) lungs

   (B) feet         (D) skin

**3.** *Quart* is to *gallon* as *week* is to

   (A) pint         (C) liquid       (E) measure

   (B) year        (D) month

**4.** *Horse* is to *stable* as *dog* is to

   (A) leash        (C) bone        (E) kennel

   (B) curb        (D) muzzle

**5.** *Pear* is to *potato* as *peach* is to

   (A) carrot      (C) nectarine      (E) tomato

   (B) cucumber    (D) melon

**6.** *Composer* is to *symphony* as *playwright* is to

   (A) essay       (C) novel       (E) copyright

   (B) cast        (D) drama

**7.** *Friction* is to *rubber* as *repetition* is to

   (A) skill        (C) literacy      (E) knowledge

   (B) novelty     (D) memory

**8.** *Pond* is to *lake* as *asteroid* is to

  (A) moon        (C) planet        (E) meteor

  (B) comet       (D) orbit

**9.** *Bear* is to *fur* as *fish* is to

  (A) seaweed     (C) scales       (E) gills

  (B) fins          (D) water

**10.** *Condemn* is to *criticize* as *scald* is to

  (A) praise       (C) freeze       (E) burn

  (B) heat         (D) thaw

**11.** *Pearl* is to *oyster* as *ivory* is to

  (A) piano        (C) tusks        (E) tortoise

  (B) crocodile   (D) elephant

**12.** *Sheep* is to *fold* as *bluefish* is to

  (A) boat        (C) bait         (E) shore

  (B) line         (D) school

**13.** *Drama* is to *intermission* as *conflict* is to

  (A) feud        (C) reconciliation   (E) stage

  (B) truce      (D) intervention

**14.** *War* is to *hawk* as *peace* is to

  (A) eagle       (C) dove        (E) owl

  (B) gull        (D) falcon

**15.** *Ballistics* is to *projectiles* as *genealogy* is to

  (A) exploration   (C) minerals    (E) missiles

  (B) lineage     (D) causes

**16.** *Pistol* is to *holster* as *airliner* is to

  (A) fuselage    (C) runway     (E) landing

  (B) hangar     (D) fuel

**17.** *Frugal* is to *waste* as *infallible* is to

  (A) dread      (C) criticize    (E) err

  (B) save       (D) prosper

**18.** *Toothpaste* is to *tube* as *graphite* is to

    (A) pencil         (C) coal         (E) tar

    (B) lead          (D) cable

**19.** *State* is to *traitor* as *plant* is to

    (A) soil          (C) leaf         (E) moisture

    (B) absorption     (D) pest

**20.** *Spot* is to *immaculate as name* is to

    (A) autonomous     (C) anonymous     (E) illegible

    (B) illiterate       (D) dependent

# Dictionary of Words Taught in This Text

The following pages contain a partial listing of the words presented in this book. The words included are those likely to offer some degree of difficulty. The definitions given have in many cases been condensed.

The numeral following a definition indicates the page on which the word appears. Roman type (e.g., abate, 61) is used when the word appears in the first column on that page. Italic type (e.g., abandon, 35) is used when the word appears in the second column.

Use this dictionary as a tool of reference and review. It is a convenient means of restudying the meanings of words that you may have missed in the exercises. It is also a useful device for a general review before an important vocabulary test. Bear in mind, however, that you will get a fuller understanding of these words from the explanations and exercises of the foregoing chapters.

**abandon:** give up completely   *35*
**abate:** become less; make less   61
**abduct:** carry off by force   169
**abhor:** hate   170, *208*
**abnormal:** unusual   170
**abode:** home   *123*
**abound:** be well supplied; be plentiful   265
**abrasion:** scraping or wearing away of the skin by friction   170
**abroad:** in or to a foreign land or lands   122
**abrupt:** broken off   170
**abscond:** steal off and hide   170
**absolute:** free from control or restriction   264
**absolve:** set free from some duty or responsibility; declare free from guilt or blame   170
**absorbing:** extremely interesting   170
**abstain:** withhold oneself from doing something   170
**abundant:** plentiful   *5,* 265
**abut:** be in contact with   *172*
**accede:** agree   97
**accessible:** easy to approach   *203*
**accommodate:** hold without crowding or inconvenience; do a favor for   52

**accord:** agreement; agree   61, 97

**accumulate:** pile up   84

**acquiesce:** accept, agree, or give implied consent by keeping silent or by not making objections   97, 126

**acquiescent:** disposed to acquiesce   *126*

**acquit:** exonerate; absolve   *14*

**acronym:** name formed from the first letter or letters of other words   302

**adapt:** adjust; make suitable for a different use   172

**adaptable:** capable of changing so as to fit a new or specific use or situation   *126*

**addicted:** given over (to a habit)   172

**adept:** highly skilled or trained   *228*

**adequate:** enough; sufficient   *6,* 172

**adhere:** stick   *52,* 245

**adherent:** faithful supporter   172

**adjacent:** lying near   172

**adjoin:** be next to   172

**adjourn:** close a meeting   13, 172

**adroit:** expert in using the hands   81

**adroitness:** skill in the use of the hands   77

**advantageous:** helpful   *205*

**advent:** approach   172

**adversary:** opponent   172, *300*

**adverse:** unfavorable   173

**advocate:** supporter   *228*

**affinity:** sympathy   242

**affirm:** declare to be true   *266*

**affluence:** abundance of wealth or property   85

**affluent:** very wealthy   83

**aggravate:** make worse   62

**aggregate:** gathered together in one mass   244

**aggregation:** gathering of individuals into a body or group   244

**aggression:** unprovoked attack   32

**aggressor:** person or nation that begins a quarrel   32

**agitate:** disturb   *226*

**agronomy:** branch of agriculture dealing with crop production and soil management   304

**alertness:** watchfulness   *115*

**alias:** assumed name; otherwise called   95, *302*

**alienate:** turn (someone) from affection to dislike or enmity; make hostile or unfriendly   *99*

**allegiance:** loyalty   126

**alleviate:** lessen; relieve   5

**alliteration:** repetition of the same letter or consonant at the beginning of consecutive words   247

**altercation:** noisy, angry dispute   98

**alternative:** choice   71

**altitude:** height; elevation   32

**amass:** pile up   84

**amateur:** person who follows a particular pursuit because he likes it, rather than as a profession; person who performs rather poorly   240

**ambidextrous:** able to use both hands equally well   81

**ambush:** trap in which concealed persons lie in wait to attack by surprise   *95*

**amiable:** lovable   240

**amicable:** characterized by friendliness rather than antagonism   240

**amity:** friendship   240

**amorous:** having to do with love   240

**amplify:** enlarge   *44*

**anachronism:** error in chronology or time order   284

**anagram:** word or phrase formed from another by transposing the letters   312

**ancestry** line of descent   *72*

**animosity:** violent hatred   241

**animus:** ill will   241

**annals:** record of events arranged in yearly sequence   *284*

**annul:** cancel   *54*

**anonymous:** of unnamed or unknown origin   302

**antagonist:** one who is against, or contends with, another in a struggle, fight, or contest; main opponent of the principal character in a play, novel, or story   *172,* 300

**antagonize:** make an enemy of   98

**antecedents:** ancestors   173

**antechamber:** an outer room leading to another usually more important room   *174*

**antedate:** assign a date before the true date; precede   173

**ante meridiem:** before noon   173

**anteroom:** room placed before and forming an entrance to another   174

**antibiotic:** substance obtained from tiny living organisms that works against harmful bacteria   300

**antibody:** substance in the blood or tissues that works against germs or poisons produced by germs   300

**anticipate:** foresee   *52*

**antidote:** remedy that acts against the effects of a poison   301

**antihistamine:** drug used against certain allergies and cold symptoms   301

**antipathy:** dislike   301

**antiseptic:** substance that prevents infection   301

**antithesis:** direct opposite   310

**antitoxin:** substance formed in the body as the result of the introduction of a toxin and capable of acting against that toxin   301

**antonym:** word meaning the opposite of another word   301

**anxiety:** painful uneasiness of mind usually over an anticipated ill   *115, 258*

**apathy:** lack of interest or concern   *153*

**apparition:** ghost   *306*

**append:** attach   258

**appendix:** matter added to the end of a book or document   258

**apprehend:** anticipate with fear; arrest   51

**apprehension:** alarm; uneasiness   51, *259*

**apprehensive:** expecting something unfavorable   51, 85

**apprentice:** person learning an art or trade under a skilled worker   *5, 81*

**apprise:** inform   96

**appropriate:** fitting; proper   15

**aptitude:** talent; bent   81

**archetype:** prototype; original   5

**aristocracy:** government or country governed by a small privileged upper class; ruling class of nobles   280

**aristocrat:** advocate of aristocracy; member of the aristocracy   281

**articulate:** able to speak effectively   *243*

**artisan:** skilled worker   *82*

**aspersion:** discredit   *35*

**assailant:** one who attacks violently with blows or words   *32*

**assemblage:** gathering   *244*

**assent:** agree   97

**assert:** maintain as true   *43, 266*

**assimilate:** make similar; take in and incorporate as one's own   262

**aster:** plant having small starlike flowers   311

**asterisk:** star-shaped mark (\*) used to call attention to a footnote, omission, etc.   311

**asteroid:** very small planet resembling a star in appearance; starfish   311

**astrologer:** person who practices astrology   311

**astrology:** study dealing with the supposed influence of the stars and planets on human affairs   *311*

**astronaut:** outer-space traveler   312

**astronomer:** expert in astronomy   312

**astronomical:** having to do with the science of the sun, moon, planets, stars, and other heavenly bodies; inconceivably large   304

**astronomy:** science of the sun, moon, planets, stars, and other heavenly bodies   *304, 312*

**astute:** shrewd; wise   13

**audacious:** bold; too bold   86

**audacity:** nerve; rashness   86

**authentic:** genuine   *5, 267, 278*

**autobiography:** story of a person's life written by the person   278

**autocracy:** government, or country governed, by one individual with self-derived, unlimited power   280

**autocrat:** ruler exercising self-derived, absolute power   278

**autocratic:** ruling with absolute power and authority   *24, 264*

**autograph:** person's signature   278

**automation:** technique of making a process self-operating by means of built-in electronic controls   279

**automaton:** robot   279

**autonomous:** self-governing   279

**autonomy:** right of self-government   279

**autopsy:** medical examination of a dead body to determine the cause of death   *174, 279*

**avarice:** excessive desire for wealth   83

**avaricious:** greedy   84

**aver:** state to be true   266

**averse:** opposed   171

**avert:** turn away   171, *224*

**avocation:** hobby   *171*

**avowal:** open acknowledgment   96

**ban:** forbid   *15*

**banish:** compel to leave   *187*

**barometer:** instrument for measuring atmospheric pressure as an aid in determining probable weather changes   290

**beguile:** deceive by means of flattery or by a trick or lie   *141*

**belittle:** speak of in a slighting way   *208*

**belligerent:** fond of fighting   *43, 62*

**benediction:** blessing 205
**benefactor:** person who gives kindly aid, money, or a similar benefit 205
**beneficial:** productive of good 205
**beneficiary:** person receiving some good, advantage, or benefit 206
**benevolent:** disposed to promote the welfare of others 206
**beverage:** drink 71
**bewilder:** confuse *210, 225*
**bicameral:** consisting of two chambers or legislative houses 175
**bicentennial:** two-hundredth anniversary 175
**bicker:** quarrel in a petty way *100*
**biennial:** occurring every two years 175
**bilateral:** having two sides 175, 246
**bilingual:** speaking two languages equally well; written in two languages 175
**bimonthly:** occurring every two months 175
**bipartisan:** representing two political parties 176
**bisect:** divide into two equal parts 176
**blunder:** mistake caused by stupidity or carelessness 71, *141*
**brawl:** quarrel noisily *100*
**breach:** violation of a law or duty *124*
**bulwark:** wall-like defensive structure 111
**bureaucracy:** government by bureaus or groups of officials 280
**bureaucrat:** member of a bureaucracy 281

**cache:** hiding place to store something 23
**calamitous:** disastrous 33
**calamity:** great misfortune 33, *312*
**capsize:** overturn 43
**captivated:** charmed *241*
**cartographer:** person skilled in the science or art of mapmaking 312
**catastrophe:** great misfortune *312*
**category:** kind; sort *244*
**cautious:** wary; circumspect *115, 221*
**cede:** relinquish *35*
**celerity:** speed *45*
**cellophane:** transparent cellulose substance 306
**censure:** act of blaming; find fault with 13, *16*
**chasm:** split; division *99*
**check:** hold back *25*

**chivalrous:** generous and high-minded *241*
**chronic:** marked by long duration and frequent recurrence; having a characteristic, habit, disease, etc., for a long time 127
**chronicle:** historical account of events in the order of time 284
**chronological:** arranged in order of time 284
**chronology:** arrangement of data or events in order of time of occurrence *284*
**chronometer:** instrument for measuring time very accurately 290
**chum:** crony; associate *33*
**circumference:** distance around a circle or rounded body 221
**circumlocution:** roundabout way of speaking 221
**circumnavigate:** sail around 221
**circumscribe:** draw a line around; limit 221
**circumspect:** careful to consider all circumstances and possible consequences 221
**circumvent:** go around 221
**citadel:** fortress 111
**civilian:** person not a member of the armed forces, or police, or fire-fighting forces 4
**clandestine:** carried on in secrecy and concealment 95
**cleavage:** split 99
**cleave:** stick 52
**cling:** stick *52, 245*
**coalesce:** grow together 222
**coerce:** force; compel 30
**cogent:** convincing 112
**cogitation:** thought *35*
**cohere:** stick together 245
**coherence:** state of sticking together 246
**coherent:** sticking together 222
**cohesion:** act or state of sticking together 246
**coincide:** agree *4*
**collaborate:** work together 222
**collateral:** situated at the side 246
**collective:** of a group of individuals as a whole *244*
**collusion:** secret agreement for a deceitful purpose 222
**colossal:** huge 108
**combative:** eager to fight *62*
**comestible:** eatable *100*

**commencing:** beginning   *128*

**commend:** praise   23

**commodious:** spacious and comfortable   109

**commute:** travel back and forth daily, as from a home in the suburbs to a job in the city   123

**commuter:** person who travels back and forth daily   123

**compact:** agreement   97

**compatible:** able to exist together harmoniously   97

**compelling:** forceful   97

**compete:** take part in a contest   *43*

**complex:** hard to analyze or solve   *4*

**complicated:** hard to understand   4

**comply:** act in accordance with another's wishes or in obedience to a rule   *98, 126*

**comprehensible:** understandable   *248*

**compulsory:** required by authority   129

**con:** against; opposing argument   191

**conclusive:** final   *242*

**concord:** state of being together in heart or mind   222

**concur:** agree   4

**concurrent:** occurring at the same time   127, *262*

**concurrently:** at the same time   *45*

**condiment:** something added to or served with food to enhance its flavor   100

**confine:** keep within limits   242

**confirm:** state or prove the truth of   4

**confirmation:** proof   4

**confirmed:** habitual   *128*

**conform:** be in agreement or harmony with   98

**congenial:** agreeable; pleasant   *97*

**congenital:** existing at birth   223

**congregate:** come together into a crowd   33

**congregation:** gathering of people for religious worship   245

**conscientious:** having painstaking regard for what is right   *115*

**conscript:** enroll into military service by compulsion   260

**conservative:** tending or disposed to maintain existing views, conditions, or institutions   *288*

**consistency:** harmony   *246*

**consistent:** keeping to the same principles throughout   98, *222*

**consonant:** in agreement   *98*

**conspicuous:** noticeable   62, *186, 228*

**conspiracy:** plot   *222*

**constant:** steady; unchanging   *128*

**contemplate:** consider carefully and for a long time   *54*

**contend:** take part in a contest; argue   43

**content:** satisfied   53

**contentious:** inclined to argue   *24,* 43

**contraband:** merchandise imported or exported contrary to law   191

**contrary:** opposite   *310*

**contravene:** go or act contrary to   191

**controversy:** dispute   71, 191

**convene:** meet in a group for a specific purpose   33, 223

**convention:** treaty; agreement   33

**conventional:** customary   *288*

**cordial:** warm and friendly   33

**cordiality:** friendliness   33

**correspond:** be in harmony   98, 223

**corroborate:** confirm   *266*

**counter:** contrary   191

**countermand:** cancel (an order) by issuing a contrary order   191

**covenant:** agreement   *97*

**covert:** secret   *95*

**covet:** crave, especially something belonging to another   84

**cow:** make afraid   *34, 86*

**cower:** draw back tremblingly   85

**craft:** skill; cunning   62

**craftsperson:** skilled worker   82

**crafty:** clever   *13,* 62

**craven:** cowardly; coward   *62, 86*

**craze:** fad   *285*

**cringe:** shrink in fear   85

**crony:** close companion   33

**crouch:** cower   *85*

**cryptogram:** something written in secret code   313

**culprit:** one guilty of a fault or crime   53

**cunning:** clever   *13, 62*

**cupidity:** greediness   *83*

**cur:** worthless dog   23

**curb:** hold back   *25, 159*

**cure-all:** remedy for all ills   *283*

**currency:** something in circulation as a medium of exchange   62

**custody:** care   71

**dastardly:** cowardly and mean   *62,* 86

**dauntless:** fearless   87

**dawdle:** waste time   *73, 127, 228*

**debate:** discussion or argument carried on between two sides   *71, 191*

**debilitate:** impair the strength of   110

**decadent:** marked by decay or decline 110, 207

**decease:** death 43

**deciduous:** having leaves that fall down at the end of the growing season 207

**declining:** growing worse *110, 207*

**decrepit:** broken down or weakened by old age or use 111

**default:** failure to do something required; fail to pay or appear when due 113

**defer:** yield to another out of respect, authority, or courtesy 126, *172, 260*

**defiance:** refusal to obey authority 124

**definitive:** serving to end an unsettled matter 242

**deft:** skillful *81*

**deftness:** skill *82*

**degenerate:** sink to a lower class or standard 244

**degrade:** downgrade *207*

**delectable:** delicious *101*

**deliberately:** in a carefully thought out manner; slowly 33

**delude:** lead from truth or into error *141*

**deluge:** flood *44, 265*

**demagogue:** political leader who stirs up the people for personal advantage 281

**demented:** out of one's mind 207

**demise:** death 43

**democracy:** government or country governed by the people 280

**Democrat:** member of the Democratic Party 281

**democratic:** based on the principles of government by the people 282

**democratize** make democratic 282

**demolish:** tear down; destroy 14, 207

**demolition** destruction 14

**demote:** move down in grade or rank 207

**denizen:** inhabitant 123

**dependent:** unable to exist without the support of another 207

**depletion:** using up *186*

**depose:** bear witness; put out of office 260, *266*

**depreciate:** go down in price or value; speak slightingly of 208

**deranged:** insane *207*

**dermatologist:** physician specializing in the diseases of the skin 303

**dermatology:** science dealing with the skin and its diseases *303*

**dermis:** inner layer of the skin 303

**desist:** cease to proceed or act *170*

**desolate:** make lonely; left alone 263

**despise:** look down on 208

**despite:** in spite of *159*

**despot:** ruler with absolute power and authority *278*

**despotic:** domineering 24, *264*

**despotism:** tyranny 24

**destitute:** not possessing the necessities of life 83

**deter:** turn aside through fear 62

**deteriorate:** make or become worse *244*

**deteriorating:** becoming worse or of less value *110, 207*

**deterioration:** worsening; wearing away *186*

**detest:** loathe; hate *170*

**devastate:** ravage; lay waste *263*

**deviate:** turn aside or down (from a route or rule) *4,* 208

**devotion)** loyalty *126*

**devour:** eat up greedily 100, 208

**dexterity:** skill in using the hands or mind 82

**dexterous:** skillful with the hands *81*

**diameter:** straight line passing through the center of a body or figure from one side to the other 290

**diathermy:** method of treating disease by generating heat in body tissues by high-frequency electric currents 307

**dictatorial:** domineering *24*

**differentiate:** tell apart *43*

**digress:** turn aside; get off the main subject in speaking or writing 4

**dilapidated:** failing to pieces 111

**diminish:** become less *61*

**diminutive:** below average size 71

**din:** loud noise 43

**disable:** make unable or incapable *111*

**disaster:** sudden or extraordinary misfortune 312

**disband:** break up the organization of *13, 264*

**disbelieve:** refuse to believe *209*

**discipline:** train in obedience 126

**disclose:** make known *96*

**discontent:** dissatisfied 209

**discord:** lack of agreement or harmony 99

**discredit:** refuse to trust 209

**discrepancy:** difference 99, 209

**disdain:** scorn; despise *208*

**disencumber:** free from encumbrances *14*

**disentangle:** straighten out *14*

**disgruntled:** discontented; dissatisfied *209*

**disinclined:** unwilling *171*

**disintegrate:** break into bits 209, *264*

**disparage:** speak slightingly of *208*

**dispassionate:** calm 209

**dispel:** drive away by scattering 71

**dispense with:** do without 33

**disperse:** scatter *71*

**disputatious:** contentious; controversial 24, *71*

**dispute:** argue about 24

**disregard:** pay no attention to *114*

**disrepair:** bad condition 209

**dissension:** discord; conflict; strife 14, *99*

**dissent:** differ in opinion 14, 99, 209

**dissident:** not agreeing 209

**dissimilar:** unlike 262, *289*

**dissolution:** act of breaking up into component parts 264

**dissolve:** break up; cause to disappear 264

**distinguish:** tell apart 43

**distract:** draw away (the mind or attention) 210

**divert:** turn the attention away *210*

**divulge:** make known 44, 96

**docile:** easily taught 126

**domain:** region; sphere of influence *53*

**domicile:** home 123

**domineering:** ruling in an overbearing way *24, 143*

**dormant:** inactive, as if asleep 71, *95*

**dovetail:** to fit together with, so as to form a harmonious whole 98

**dowry:** money, property, etc., that a bride brings to her husband 84

**draft:** enroll into military service *260*

**drought:** long period of dry weather 44

**dubious:** doubtful 34

**duplicate:** copy 63

**dynamic:** forceful 112

**economic:** having to do with the social science dealing with production, distribution, and consumption 304

**economical:** thrifty; frugal *83,* 305

**economics:** the social science dealing with production, distribution, and consumption 304

**economize:** reduce expenses 83

**edible:** fit for human consumption 100

**edifice:** building, especially a large or impressive building 24

**eject:** force out; expel 187

**elaborate:** complex; intricate *4*

**electrocardiogram:** tracing showing the amount of electricity the heart muscles produce during the heartbeat 313

**electrocardiograph:** instrument that records the amount of electricity the heart muscles produce during the heartbeat *313*

**elevation:** height 32

**elicit:** draw forth 96, 186

**eliminate:** get rid of 53

**elucidate:** make clear 248

**emancipate:** set free 257

**embroil:** involve in conflict 99

**emigrate:** move out of a country or region to settle in another 186

**eminence:** a natural elevation 32

**eminent:** standing out 186

**enamored:** inflamed with love 241

**encyclopedia:** work offering alphabetically arranged information on various branches of knowledge 286

**endurance:** ability to withstand strain, suffering, or hardship *64, 87*

**endure:** hold out; last *159, 225*

**enduring:** lasting *128, 225*

**enervate:** lessen the vigor or strength of 111, *153,* 186

**enfeeble:** weaken *111, 186*

**engender:** give birth to 244

**engrave:** cut or carve on a hard surface *187*

**engrossing:** taking up the whole interest of *170*

**enigma:** puzzle 95

**enigmatic:** puzzling 95

**enlighten:** shed the light of truth and knowledge upon 96

**enmity:** hatred *206, 241, 301*

**enrage:** fill with anger *44*

**entail:** involve as a necessary consequence 129

**entomb:** bury 5

**envisage:** have a mental picture of especially in advance of realization *267*

**envision:** foresee 267

**ephemeral:** not lasting; passing soon *16*

**epicure:** person with sensitive or discriminating tastes in food or wine *305*

**epidemic:** affecting many people in an area at the same time; outbreak of a disease affecting many people at the same time 282

**epidermis:** outer layer of the skin   303

**epigram:** bright or witty thought concisely and cleverly expressed   313

**epithet:** characterizing word or phrase   310

**epoch:** age; period   *24*

**equanimity:** evenness of mind or temper   241

**equilateral:** having all sides equal   246

**equilibrium:** emotional balance   *241*

**equitable:** fair to all concerned   14

**era:** historical period   24

**eradicate:** remove by or as if by uprooting   157

**erosion:** gradual wearing away   186

**essence:** most necessary or significant part, aspect, or feature   129

**essential:** necessary   *130, 246*

**estrange:** turn from affection to dislike or enmity   99

**evidence:** show   *96*

**evident:** clear; obvious   *96*

**evoke:** bring out   *96*, 186

**excise:** cut out   187

**exclude:** shut out   *53*

**exclusive:** shutting out, or tending to shut out, others; not shared with others   72, 187

**exclusively:** without sharing with others   72

**exculpate:** free from blame   *170*

**exempt:** released from an obligation to which others are subject   72, *170*

**exemption:** freedom from something which others are subject to   72

**exhibit:** show   187

**exonerate:** free from blame   14, *170*

**expectation:** something expected   *229*

**expel:** drive out; eject   187

**exploit:** heroic act   87

**extemporaneous:** composed or spoken without preparation   14

**extract:** draw forth   *96*

**extraction:** descent   *72*

**extracurricular:** outside the regular curriculum, or course of study   189

**extraneous:** coming from or existing outside   189, *204*

**extravagant:** outside the bounds of reason; spending lavishly   189, *228*

**extremity:** very end   34

**extricate:** free from difficulties   14

**facetious:** given to joking   53

**fallacious:** illogical   *203*

**famish:** starve   44

**fancy:** imagination   306

**fantastic:** based on imagination rather than reason   142, 306

**fantasy:** illusory image   306

**fatigue:** weariness   53

**feat:** deed notable especially for courage   *87*

**feebleness:** weakness; frailty   *111*

**feign:** give an imitation   *262*

**fictitious:** imaginary; false   63

**fidelity:** loyalty   *126*

**finale:** end or final part of a musical composition, opera, play, etc.   242

**financial:** having to do with money matters   84

**finis:** end   242

**fiscal:** having to do with financial matters   *84*

**fleece:** deprive or strip of money or belongings by fraud   84

**fleeting:** passing rapidly   *16*

**flimsy:** lacking strength or solidity   111

**flinch:** draw back involuntarily   *34*

**fluctuate:** flow like a wave   243

**fluent:** ready with a flow of words   243

**fluid:** substance that flows; not rigid   243

**flux:** continuous flow or changing   243

**foe:** enemy   *172, 300*

**forcible:** showing force   112

**forearm:** part of the arm from the wrist to the elbow   139

**forebear:** ancestor   139, *173, 244*

**foreboding:** feeling beforehand of coming trouble   141

**forecast:** predict   34

**forefather:** ancestor   139, *244*

**forefront:** foremost place or part   139

**foregoing:** preceding   139

**foremost:** standing at the front   140

**foreshadow:** indicate beforehand   140

**foresight:** power of seeing beforehand what is likely to happen   140

**forestall:** prevent; avert   *171, 224*

**foreword:** introduction at the beginning of a book   *34, 140, 227*

**forfeit:** lose or have to give up as a penalty for some error, neglect, or fault   15

**forlorn:** deserted   263

**formidable:** exciting fear by reason of strength, size, difficulty, etc.   112

**forsaken:** abandoned; desolate   263

**forte:** strong point   112

**forthcoming:** about to appear   *157*

**fortitude:** courage in facing danger, hardship, or pain   87

**fragile:** easily broken; breakable   5, *111*

**frail:** not very strong   111

**frailty:** weakness   *111*

**frank:** free and forthright in expressing one's feelings and opinions   *142*

**friction:** conflict of ideas between persons or parties of opposing views   99

**frugal:** barely enough; avoiding waste   83, *305*

**frustrate:** bring to nothing   *221*

**furious:** intense; vehement   *112*

**furtive:** stealthy; catlike   *96*

**fusion:** joining together   *308*

**galore:** plentiful   5

**gamut:** entire range of anything from one extreme to another   109

**gastronome:** a lover and expert judge of excellence in food and drink   305

**gastronomy:** art or science of good eating   *305*

**genealogy:** history of the descent of a person or family from an ancestor   289

**generate:** bring into existence   *244*

**genesis:** birth or coming into being   289

**genre:** category   244

**gentry:** upper class   *280*

**genuine:** real; authentic   5, *267, 278*

**glutton:** greedy eater   101

**gluttonous:** greedy in eating   *101*

**gourmet:** expert judge of good food and drink   *305*

**graphic:** written or told in a clear, lifelike manner   313

**graphite:** soft black carbon used in lead pencils   313

**gratuitous:** uncalled for   129

**gregarious:** fond of being with others   245

**guile** deceitful slyness   *62*

**gutless:** cowardly   *62*

**habitual:** according to habit   *128*

**habituated:** accustomed   *172*

**harmony:** agreement   *97, 222,* 291

**haunt:** come to mind frequently   *224*

**heed:** pay attention   115

**heedless** careless   113, *154*

**heterogeneous:** differing in kind   289

**hibernate:** spend the winter   34

**hinder:** hold back; obstruct   *62, 224*

**hindrance:** something that obstructs or impedes   *224*

**hoard:** save and conceal   84

**homogeneous:** of the same kind   289

**homogenize:** make uniform   289

**homonym:** word that sounds like another but differs in meaning   302

**horde:** great crowd   *24*

**hospitable:** kind to guests and strangers   *204*

**host:** person who receives or entertains a guest or guests; large number   34

**hostile:** of or relating to an enemy or enemies; unfriendly   5, *173*

**husbandry:** agriculture   *304*

**hypodermic:** beneath the skin   303

**hypothesis:** supposition or assumption made as a basis for reasoning or research   310

**ignore:** disregard; overlook   114

**illegible:** not able to be read; very hard to read   15, 203

**illiterate:** unable to read and write   203

**illogical:** not observing the rules of correct reasoning   203

**illuminate:** light up   44

**immaculate:** spotless   63, 203

**immature:** not fully grown or developed   203

**immigrate:** move into a foreign country or region as a permanent resident   186

**imminent:** about to happen   128, 186, 259

**immoderate:** too great   *109*

**immunity:** condition of being not susceptible   *72, 203*

**impartial:** fair   14, *209*

**impatient:** not willing to bear delay   5

**impede:** block   *226*

**impediment:** obstruction *224*

**impel:** drive on   188

**impending:** threatening to occur soon   *186,* 258

**imperative:** not to be avoided   129

**imperil:** endanger   *44,* 72

**impetuous:** impulsive   *87*

**implicate:** show to be part of or connected with   188

**impose:** put on as a burden, duty, tax, etc.   *224,* 260

**impoverish:** make very poor   83

**impregnable:** incapable of being taken by assault   112

**impromptu:** without previous thought or preparation   *14*

**improvise:** compose, recite, or sing on the spur of the moment   267

**improvised:** composed, recited, or sung on the spur of the moment   *14*

**impudent:** marked by a bold disregard of others   *86*

**impugn:** call in question   188

**impunity:** freedom from punishment, harm, loss, etc.   *72, 203*

**inaccessible:** not able to be reached   203

**inadvertent:** careless   114

**inadvertently:** not done on purpose   15

**inappropriate:** not fitting   15

**inaudible:** incapable of being heard   44

**inborn:** born in or with one   *223*

**incapacitate:** render incapable or unfit   111

**incarcerate:** put into prison   188

**incense:** make extremely angry   44, *229*

**incessant:** not ceasing   *128, 203*

**incipient:** beginning to show itself   128

**incise:** cut into   188

**inclusive:** including the limits mentioned   187

**incoherent:** unintelligible   246

**incompatible:** not capable of being brought together in harmonious or agreeable relations   *99, 204*

**inconsistency:** lack of agreement or harmony   *99*

**incontrovertible:** not able to be disputed   191

**incumbent:** imposed as a duty   130

**indifference:** lack of interest; dislike   *153*

**indigence:** poverty   83

**indigent:** needy   *83*

**indispensable:** absolutely necessary   130

**indisputable:** unquestionable   *191*

**indomitable:** incapable of being subdued   87

**induct:** lead in   *24*

**inept:** lacking in skill or aptitude   *82*

**inequitable:** unfair   14

**inexhaustible:** plentiful enough not to give out or be used up   *109*

**inextinguishable:** unquenchable   *153*

**infallible:** incapable of error   53

**infinite:** without ends or limits   109

**infinitesimal:** so small as to be almost nothing   109

**infirmity:** weakness   111

**infixed:** implanted   *246*

**inflate:** swell with air or gas   109

**inflexible:** not easily bent   204

**inflict:** cause (something disagreeable) to be borne; impose   *260*

**influx:** inflow   243

**infraction:** breaking (of a law, regulation, etc.)   124

**infrequent:** seldom happening or occurring   128

**infringe:** violate   *191*

**infuriate:** fill with rage   *44*

**ingratitude:** state of being not grateful   204

**inherent:** belonging by nature   246

**inhibit:** hold in check   187

**inhospitable:** not showing kindness to guests and strangers   204

**initial:** beginning; introductory   6

**initiate:** begin; admit into a club by special ceremonies   24

**initiation:** installation as a member   24

**inmate:** person confined in an institution, prison, hospital, etc.   123

**innate:** inborn   *223*

**inordinate:** much too great   109

**inscribe:** write, engrave, or print to create a lasting record   188

**inscription:** something written on a monument, coin, etc.   260

**insignificant:** of little importance   *110*

**insolent:** lacking in respect for rank or position   86

**insoluble:** not capable of being solved; not capable of being dissolved   204

**insubordinate:** not submitting to authority   125, *188*

**insurgent:** one who rises in revolt against established authority; rebellious   125, 188

**insurrection:** uprising against established authority   125, *211*

**integrate:** make into a whole   *209*

**intensify:** make more acute   *62*

**inter:** bury   5

**intercede:** interfere to reconcile differences   *63, 191*

**intercept:** stop or seize on the way from one place to another   192

**interdict:** forbid; prohibit   *15*

**interlinear:** inserted between lines already printed or written   192

**interlude:** anything filling the time between two events   192

**intermediary:** go-between   192

**interminable:** continual; endless   *204*

**intermission:** pause between periods of activity   193

**intermittent:** coming and going at intervals   128

**intersect:** cut by passing through or across   193

**interurban:** between cities or towns   193

**interval:** space of time between events or states   *193*

**intervene:** occur between; come between to help settle a quarrel   63, 193

**intervention:** intercession; interference   63

**intimidate:** frighten   34, 86

**intramural:** within the walls or boundaries   190

**intraparty:** within a party   190

**intrastate:** within a state   190

**intravenous:** within or by way of the veins   190

**intrepid:** fearless and daring   *87*

**intricate:** not simple or easy   4

**intrinsic:** belonging to the essential nature or constitution of a thing   *246*

**intrude:** come or go in without invitation or welcome   *224*

**inundate:** flood   44, 265

**invigorate:** give life and energy to   112

**invincible:** unconquerable   *87, 112*

**invisible:** imperceptible   267

**invoke:** call on for help or protection   187

**involve:** draw in as a participant   *188*

**iota:** very small quantity   109

**irrational:** illogical; fallacious   *203*

**irreconcilable:** unable to be brought into friendly accord or understanding   99, 204

**irrelevant:** off the topic   *189*, 204

**irrevocable:** incapable of being recalled   204

**isolate:** set apart from others   *211*

**isolated:** infrequent   128

**isolation:** the act or condition of being set apart from others; segregation   *245*

**jeopardize:** expose to danger   44, *72*

**jeopardy:** danger   44

**Jolly Roger:** pirates' flag   24

**journalist:** editor of or writer for a periodical   *261*

**jurisdiction:** territory within which authority may be exercised   53

**jut:** stick out; protrude   *229*

**kinship:** sense of oneness   *242*

**kleptomania:** insane impulse to steal   285

**latent:** present but not showing itself   95

**lateral:** of or pertaining to the side   246

**lavish:** too free in giving, using, or spending; given or spent too freely   84, *228*

**lax:** careless   *114*

**legible:** capable of being read   *15*

**lettered:** able to read and write   *248*

**liberate:** set free   *154, 257*

**lineage:** descent   72, *289*

**literacy:** ability to read and write   247

**literal:** following the letters or exact words of the original   248

**literary:** having to do with letters or literature   248

**literate:** able to read and write   248

**litigation:** lawsuit   99

**loathe:** detest; abhor   *170*

**logic:** correct reasoning   *203*

**logical:** observing the rules of correct reasoning   *222*

**loiter:** hang around idly   *127*

**lucid:** clear   248

**lucrative:** profitable   15, 84

**luminary:** famous person   248

**luminous:** shining   248

**lurk:** be hidden   95

**luscious:** delicious   101

**luxurious:** extravagantly elegant and comfortable   85

**magnanimous:** showing greatness or nobility of mind   241

**magnify:** cause to be or look larger   44

**magnitude:** size   109

**major:** greater   72

**maladjusted:** out of harmony with one's environment   206

**maladroit:** clumsy   82

**malcontent:** discontented person   125

**malediction:** curse   205

**malefactor:** evildoer   205

**malevolence:** ill will   206

**malevolent:** showing ill will   206

**malice:** ill will   206

**malign:** speak evil of; slander   *188*

**malnutrition:** poor nourishment   206

**maltreat:** treat badly or roughly   206

**mammoth:** of very great size   *108*

**manacle:** handcuff   257

opulence: wealth  85
opulent: wealthy  *83*
origin: coming into being; genesis  *289*
original: a work created firsthand and from which copies are made; belonging to the beginning  5
originality: freshness; novelty  6
originate: begin  *24*
orthodontics: branch of dentistry dealing with the straightening and adjusting of teeth  *288*
orthodontist: dentist specializing in the straightening and adjusting of teeth  288
orthodox: generally accepted, especially in religion  288
orthography: correct spelling  288
orthopedic: having to do with the correction and prevention of deformities, especially in children  287
orthopedics: the science dealing with the correction and prevention of deformities, especially in children  *287*
orthopedist: physician specializing in the correction and prevention of deformities, especially in children  288
outfox: outwit  *142*
outgrow: grow too large for  142
outlandish: looking or sounding as if it belongs to a foreign land  142
outlast: last longer than  142
outlive: live longer than  *142*
outlook: a looking beyond  142
output: a yield or product  142
outrun: run faster than  142
outspoken: speaking out freely or boldly  142
outweigh: exceed in weight, value, or importance  *144*
outwit: get the better of by being more clever  142
overawe: subdue by awe  *34*
overbearing: domineering over others  143
overburden: place too heavy a load on  143
overconfident: too sure of oneself  143
overdose: too big a dose  143
overestimate: overrate  144
overhasty: too hasty  87
overpower: overcome by superior force  *144*
overshadow: cast a shadow over  144
oversupply: too great a supply  144
overt: open to view  96

overtax: put too great a burden or strain on  *143*
overvalue: set too high a value on  *144*
overwhelm: overpower  144, *265*

palatable: agreeable to the taste  101
panacea: remedy for all ills  283
Pan-American: of or pertaining to all the countries of North, South, and Central America  283
pandemonium: wild uproar  283
panoply: complete suit of armor  283
panorama: complete, unobstructed view  283
pantomime: dramatic performance that is all signs and gestures without words  283
parallel: running alongside  *246*
passionate: showing strong feeling  *209*
patrician: member of the aristocracy  281
pauperize: make very poor; impoverish  *83*
pecuniary: having to do with money  *84*
pedagogue: teacher of children  287
pedagogy art of teaching  287
pediatrician: physician specializing in the treatment of babies and children  287
pediatrics: the branch of medicine dealing with the care, development, and diseases of babies and children  287
pedigree: ancestral line  *289*
pendant: hanging ornament  258
pending: waiting to be settled; until  259
penetrate: pass into or through  *225*
penury: poverty; indigence  *83*
perceive: become aware of through the senses  25
perception: idea; conception  25
perennial: continuing through the years; plant that lives through the years  128, 225
perforate: make a hole or holes through  *45*, 225
peril: exposure to injury, loss, or destruction  *44*
perimeter: the whole outer boundary of a body or area  *221*
periodic: happening repeatedly  *128*
permanent: enduring; perennial  15, *128*
permeate: pass through  225
perplex: confuse thoroughly  225
persevere: keep at something in spite of difficulties or opposition  *225*

**protrude:** thrust forth   229
**province:** proper business or duty   53
**provoke:** call forth; make angry   229
**prudence:** skill and good sense in taking care of oneself or of one's affairs   *140*
**prudent:** shrewd in the management of practical affairs   *221*
**pseudonym:** fictitious name used by an author   302
**punctual:** on time   15
**punctuality:** promptness   15
**puncture:** make a hole with a pointed object   45, *225*
**puny:** slight or inferior in size, power, or importance   110
**pusillanimous:** cowardly   *62*
**pyromania:** insane impulse to set fires   286

**quadrilateral:** plane figure having four sides and four angles   247
**quench:** put out; satisfy   *101*
**questionable:** not certain   34
**quintet:** group of five   63

**rabble-rouser:** one who stirs up the people, especially to hatred or violence   *281*
**ramble:** aimless walk   *25*
**rampart:** broad bank or wall used as a fortification or protective barrier   111
**ransack:** search thoroughly   *45*
**rarity:** something uncommon, infrequent, or rare   6
**rash:** taking too much risk   87, *154*
**ravage:** lay waste   263
**ravenous:** voracious   *101*
**raze:** tear down; destroy   *14, 207*
**rebel:** one who opposes or takes arms against the government or ruler   *125, 188*
**rebuke:** express disapproval of   13, 16
**reckless:** foolishly bold   87, *113*
**recoil:** draw back because of fear   *6*, 34
**reconcilable:** able to be brought into friendly accord   *204*
**reconcile:** cause to be friends again   63, 98
**recurrent:** returning from time to time   *128*
**redound:** flow back as a result   265
**redundant:** exceeding what is necessary   266
**reflect:** think carefully   54

**reflection:** thought; blame   35
**refrain:** hold oneself back   *170*
**regenerate:** cause to be born again   244
**release:** give up   *35, 154*
**relent:** become less harsh, severe, or strict   98
**relevant:** having something to do with the case being considered   *225*
**relinquish:** give up   35, *169*
**remiss:** careless   114
**remunerative:** advantageous; lucrative   15
**renounce:** resign; abdicate   *169*
**renovate:** modernize   *157*
**repress:** hold back   25, *187*
**reprove:** scold   *16*
**repugnance:** deep-rooted dislike   *301*
**reserved:** restrained in speech or action   25
**resist:** oppose   *159*
**resolution:** solving   264
**resolve:** break up   264
**resources:** available means   85
**restrain:** hold back   25, *159, 187*
**restrict:** keep within bounds   *221, 242*
**resume:** begin again   6
**retain:** keep   73
**retentive:** able to retain or remember   73
**reticent:** silent; reserved   *25*
**retract:** draw back   25
**reveal:** make known   96
**reverse:** turn completely about; defeat   54, *310*
**reversible:** wearable with either side out   54
**revise:** look at again to correct errors and make improvements   267
**revocable:** capable of being recalled   *204*
**revoke:** cancel   *54, 191*
**robot:** purely mechanical person   *279*
**robust:** strong and vigorously healthy   112
**roving:** wandering from place to place   *124*
**rummage:** search thoroughly by turning over all the contents   45
**rural:** having to do with the country   64

**sagacious:** wise; shrewd   *13*
**savory:** pleasing to the taste or smell   *101*
**scanty:** barely enough   *83*
**schism:** split; chasm   *99*
**scorn:** hold in contempt   208

**superabundance:** excessive abundance 110

**superfluous:** beyond what is necessary or desirable 54, 130, *266*

**superimpose:** put on top of or over 260

**supplement:** something that makes an addition *259*

**supplementary:** additional *247*

**surmount:** conquer 54

**surplus:** excess *54, 110, 130, 266*

**survive:** live longer than 45, *142*

**suspend:** hang by attaching to something; stop temporarily 259

**suspense:** mental uncertainty 259

**swarm:** great crowd *24*

**swindle:** cheat *84*

**symmetry:** correspondence in measurements, shape, etc., on opposite sides of a dividing line 291

**synchronize:** cause to agree in time 285

**synonym:** word having the same meaning as another word 302

**synthesis:** combination of parts or elements into a whole 310

**synthetic:** artificially made 310

**tachometer:** instrument for measuring speed 291

**tally:** match *223*

**taxidermist:** one who prepares, stuffs, and mounts the skins of animals in lifelike form 303

**taxidermy:** the art of preparing, stuffing, and mounting the skins of animals in lifelike form *303*

**technocracy:** government or country governed by technical experts 280

**teem:** be present in large quantity *265*

**temerity:** nerve; audacity *86*

**tenacious:** holding fast or tending to hold fast *73*, 112

**testify:** state under oath *260*

**thermal:** pertaining to heat 307

**thermonuclear:** having to do with the fusion, at an extraordinarily high temperature, of the nuclei of atoms 308

**thermostat:** automatic device for regulating temperature 308

**thesis:** claim put forward; essay written by a candidate for a college degree 310

**thrifty:** inclined to save *83, 305*

**throng:** great crowd *24, 34*

**timid:** lacking courage or self-confidence *25*, 86

**timorous:** full of fear 25, *86*

**tolerable:** endurable 35

**tolerate:** endure 35

**toxin:** poison *301*

**tractable:** easily controlled, led, or taught 127

**transgress:** go beyond the set limits of 125

**transient:** not lasting; visitor or guest staying for only a short time 16

**transitory:** short-lived 16

**translucent:** letting light through 248

**transpose:** change the relative order of 260

**traverse:** pass across, over, or through 45

**trepidation:** nervous agitation 86

**trespass:** encroach on another's rights, privileges, property, etc. 125

**trustworthy:** worthy of confidence *278*

**tuition:** payment for instruction 26

**typographical:** pertaining to or occurring in printing 243

**typography:** use of type for printing 243

**tyrannical:** domineering *24*

**tyro:** beginner *5, 81*

**unabridged:** not made shorter 153

**unanimity:** complete agreement 241

**unanimous:** in complete accord 241

**unbiased:** not prejudiced in favor of or against *14*, 153

**unblemished:** spotless *63*

**uncommunicative:** not inclined to talk 25

**unconcern:** lack of concern, anxiety, or interest 153

**undeceive:** free from deception or mistaken ideas 153

**underbrush:** shrubs, bushes, etc., growing beneath large trees in a wood 155

**underdeveloped:** insufficiently developed because of a lack of capital and trained personnel for exploiting natural resources 155

**undergraduate:** student in a college or university who has not yet earned his or her first degree 155

**underhand:** marked by secrecy and deception *95*

**underpayment:** insufficient payment 155

**underprivileged:** deprived through social or economic oppression of some of the fundamental rights supposed to belong to all   155

**underscore:** draw a line beneath   155

**undersell:** sell at a lower price than   155

**undersigned:** person or persons who sign at the end of a letter or document   156

**understatement:** restrained statement in mocking contrast to what might be said   156

**understudy:** one who "studies under" and learns the part of a regular performer so as to be his or her substitute if necessary   156

**ungag:** remove a gag from   153

**unilateral:** one-sided   247

**unintelligible:** incomprehensible   *246*

**unity:** act of sticking together; cohesion   *246*

**unmindful:** careless   113

**unnerve:** deprive of nerve or courage   153

**unorthodox:** not in accord with accepted, standard, or approved belief or practice   *288*

**unquenchable:** not capable of being satisfied   153

**unravel:** solve   *264*

**unscramble:** restore to intelligible form   154

**unshackle:** set free from restraint   154

**unsubstantial:** lacking firmness, strength, or substance   *111*

**untimely:** before the proper time   *227*

**unwarranted:** uncalled for   *129*

**unwary:** not alert   154

**unyielding:** firm and determined   *112*

**upcoming:** being in the near future   157

**update:** bring up to date   157

**upgrade:** raise the grade or quality of   157

**upheaval:** violent heaving up   157

**upkeep:** maintenance   157

**uplift:** elevate; raise   157

**upright:** standing up straight on the feet   157

**uproot:** pull up by the roots   157

**upset:** overturn   *43, 153*

**upstart:** person who has suddenly risen to wealth and power, especially if he or she is conceited and unpleasant   158

**upturn:** upward turn toward better conditions   158

**urban:** having to do with cities or towns   54

**usher in:** preface; introduce   *34*

**vacancy:** job opening; unoccupied apartment   6

**vacant:** empty   6

**valiant:** courageous   *87*

**valor:** courage   *87*

**valorous:** courageous   87

**vanguard:** troops moving at the head of an army   *139*

**at variance:** in disagreement   100

**variation:** change in form, position, or condition   *99, 209*

**vehement:** showing strong feeling   112

**velocity:** speed   45

**veracity:** truthfulness   266

**verbiage:** excessive wordiness   *221*

**verdict:** decision of a jury   266

**verification:** proof; confirmation   *4*

**verify:** prove to be true   *4*, 266

**veritable:** true   267

**verity:** truth   267

**versatile:** capable of doing many things well   82

**version:** account from a particular point of view; translation   26

**vicinity:** neighborhood   54

**video:** having to do with the transmission or reception of what is seen   267

**vie:** strive for superiority   *43*

**vigilance:** alert watchfulness to discover and avoid danger   115

**vigilant:** alertly watchful, especially to avoid danger   *115*

**vigor:** active strength or force   *64*, 113

**visibility:** degree of clearness of the atmosphere, with reference to the distance at which objects can be clearly seen   268

**visual:** having to do with sight   268

**vocal:** inclined to express oneself freely   142

**vocation:** occupation   54

**volition:** act of willing or choosing   64

**voracious:** having a huge appetite   101

**wary:** on one's guard against danger, deception, etc.   115

**wayward:** following one's own and usually improper way   *125*

**wily:** cunning; astute   *13*

**wince:** draw back involuntarily   *6, 34*

**withdraw:** take or draw back or away
*25*, 158

**withdrawal:** act of taking back or drawing
out from a place of deposit   159

**withdrawn:** drawn back or removed from
easy approach   *25*, 159

**withhold:** hold back   159

**withholding tax:** sum withheld or
deducted from wages for tax purposes
159

**withstand:** stand up against   159

**witty:** cleverly amusing in speech or
writing   *53*

**wrangle:** quarrel noisily   *98*, 100

# Pronunciation Symbols

The system of indicating pronunciation is used by permission.
From *Merriam-Webster's Collegiate Dictionary,* Tenth Edition,
© 1993 by Merriam-Webster, Incorporated.

| | |
|---|---|
| ə | banana, collide, abut |
| 'ə, ˌə | humdrum, abut |
| ᵊ | immediately preceding \l\, \n\, \m\, \ŋ\, as in battle, mitten, eaten, and sometimes cap and bells \-ᵊm-\, lock and key \-ᵊŋ-\; immediately following \l\, \m\, \r\, as often in French table, prisme, titre |
| ər | operation, further, urger |
| 'ər-<br>'ə-r | as in two different pronunciations of hurry \'hər-ē, 'hə-rē\ |
| a | mat, map, mad, gag, snap, patch |
| ā | day, fade, date, aorta, drape, cape |
| ä | bother, cot, and, with most American speakers, father, cart |
| à | father as pronounced by speakers who do not rhyme it with bother |
| aú | now, loud, out |
| b | baby, rib |
| ch | chin, nature \'nā-chər\ (actually, this sound is \t\ + \sh\) |
| d | did, adder |

| | |
|---|---|
| e | bet, bed, peck |
| 'ē, ͵ē | beat, nosebleed, evenly, **easy** |
| ē | easy, mealy |
| f | fifty, cuff |
| g | go, big, gift |
| h | hat, ahead |
| hw | **wh**ale as pronounced by those who do not have the same pronunciation for both *whale* and *wail* |
| i | tip, banish, active |
| ī | site, side, **buy**, tripe (actually, this sound is \ä\ + \i\, or \à\ + \i\) |
| j | job, gem, edge, join, judge (actually, this sound is \d\ + \zh\) |
| k | kin, cook, ache |
| k̲ | German i**ch**, Bu**ch** |
| l | lily, pool |
| m | murmur, dim, nymph |
| n | no, own |
| ⁿ | indicates that a preceding vowel or diphthong is pronounced with the nasal passages open, as in French *un bon vin blanc* \oeⁿ-bōⁿ-vaⁿ-bläⁿ\ |
| ŋ | sing \'siŋ\, singer \'siŋ-ər\, finger \'fiŋ-gər\, ink \'iŋk\ |
| ō | bone, know, beau |
| ȯ | saw, all, gnaw |
| œ | French b**oeu**f, German H**ö**lle |
| œ̄ | French f**eu**, German H**öh**le |
| ȯi | coin, destroy, sawing |
| p | pepper, lip |
| r | red, car, rarity |
| s | source, less |
| sh | with nothing between, as in **sh**y, mission, machine, special (actually, this is a single sound, not two); with a hyphen between, two sounds as in death's-head \'deths-͵hed\ |
| t | tie, attack |
| th | with nothing between, as in **th**in, ether (actually, this is a single sound, not two); with a hyphen between, two sounds as in knighthood \'nīt-͵hu̇d\ |
| t̲h̲ | **th**en, either, this (actually, this is a single sound, not two) |

| | |
|---|---|
| ü | rule, youth, union \'yün-yən\, few \'fyü\ |
| u̇ | pull, wood, book, curable \'kyu̇r-ə-bəl\ |
| ue | German füllen, hübsch |
| ūē | French rue, German fühlen |
| v | vivid, give |
| w | we, away; in some words having final \(,)ō\ a variant \ə-w\ occurs before vowels, as in \'fäl-ə-wiŋ\, covered by the variant \ə(-w)\ at the entry word |
| y | yard, young, cue \'kyü\, union \'yün-yən\ |
| ʸ | indicates that during the articulation of the sound represented by the preceding character the front of the tongue has substantially the position it has for the articulation of the first sound of *yard*, as in French *digne* \dēnʸ\ |
| yü | youth, union, cue, few, mute |
| yu̇ | curable, fury |
| z | zone, raise |
| zh | with nothing between, as in vision, azure \'azh-ər\ (actually, this is a single sound, not two); with a hyphen between, two sounds as in gazehound \'gāz-,hau̇nd\ |
| \ | slant line used in pairs to mark the beginning and end of a transcription: \'pen\ |
| ' | mark preceding a syllable with primary (strongest) stress: \'pen-mən-,ship\ |
| , | mark preceding a syllable with secondary (next-strongest) stress: \'pen-mən-,ship\ |
| - | mark of syllable division |
| ( ) | indicate that what is symbolized between is present in some utterances but not in others: *factory* \'fak-t(ə)rē\ |